D1109443

# Operations Excellence

**Roland Berger**
Strategy Consultants

# THINK: ACT

*'think: act–Leadership Know-how'* is derived from the academic research and the consulting experience of Roland Berger Strategy Consultants, one of the world's leading strategy consultancies. With 35 offices in 24 countries, the company has successful operations in all major international markets. Roland Berger Strategy Consultants serve global players and innovative companies as well as public institutions and governments. In 2007, our services generated more than €600 million in revenues with 2,000 employees. The strategy consultancy is an independent partnership exclusively owned by about 160 Partners. This series of management books is based on the success of our international business magazine *think: act* that covers all aspects of leadership challenges and is published in Chinese, Russian, English, German and Polish.

HEIDI SYLVESTER

FLORIAN KAISER

# Operations Excellence

## Smart Solutions for Business Success

Edited by

Roland Schwientek

and

Axel Schmidt

First published 2008 by
PALGRAVE MACMILLAN
Houndmills, Basingstoke, Hampshire RG21 6XS and
175 Fifth Avenue, New York, N.Y. 10010
Companies and representatives throughout the world

PALGRAVE MACMILLAN is the global academic imprint of the Palgrave Macmillan division of St. Martin's Press, LLC and of Palgrave Macmillan Ltd. Macmillan® is a registered trademark in the United States, United Kingdom and other countries. Palgrave is a registered trademark in the European Union and other countries.

ISBN-13: 978–0–230–21780–5
ISBN-10: 0–230–21780–X

This book is printed on paper suitable for recycling and made from fully managed and sustained forest sources. Logging, pulping and manufacturing processes are expected to conform to the environmental regulations of the country of origin.

A catalogue record for this book is available from the British Library.

A catalog record for this book is available from the Library of Congress.

10  9  8  7  6  5  4  3  2  1
17  16  15  14  13  12  11  10  09  08

Printed and bound in Great Britain by
Cromwell Press Ltd, Trowbridge, Wiltshire

# CONTENTS

## PART IV: SUPPLY CHAIN MANAGEMENT

# LIST OF FIGURES AND BOXES

**Figures**

## Boxes

**Ralf Augustin** is a Principal in Roland Berger's Stuttgart office. He has a Master's degree in mechanical engineering and business administration from the TU Darmstadt, where he also gained his PhD in industrial engineering. Before joining Roland Berger's Operations Strategy Competence Center in 2003, he was Engagement Manager at McKinsey for five years and Section Head of Corporate Strategy at the Institute for Production Management at the TU Darmstadt. He specializes in comprehensive cost reduction programs, strategic sourcing, and complexity management in the automotive, engineering products, and electronics industries.

**Alexander Belderok** is a Principal in Roland Berger's Amsterdam office. He studies mechanical engineering at Twente University and gained a degree from TSM Business School. Belderok has worked for Unilever and was a Principal at A.T. Kearney for seven years before switching to Roland Berger in 2006. His focus is on operations, marketing and sales, organization and business re-engineering, and complexity management in the consumer goods and retail sector, and the chemicals industry.

**Kai Bethlehem** is Head of Purchasing at Rothenberger Werkzeuge (Tools). He has worked for Roland Berger as a Senior Consultant, at Eurocopter as a Purchasing Manager and at Procter & Gamble in Switzerland and Germany in purchasing. He gained his engineering degree from the TU Darmstadt. He is an expert in strategic supplier management, cost optimization, and process optimization for the airline, automotive, and non-food consumer goods industries.

**Christian Deckert** studied at the Technical University Hamburg-Harburg, where he gained a degree in industrial engineering and economics. Since joining Roland Berger in 2001, Deckert has been involved in working capital and cost management projects. He also focuses on purchasing and production optimization, reorganization and process management.

**Tobias Franke** has worked at Roland Berger's Operations Strategy Competence Center since 1999. In addition to completing a bank traineeship, he gained a joint degree in European Business Administration from the European School of Business in Reutlingen and Middlesex University Business School in London. He specializes in procurement organization and processes, and supplier and commodity management in the airlines, automotive supplier, and utility industries.

**Jochen Gleisberg** is a Partner at Roland Berger. He gained his degree in business from the University of Marburg and University of Gießen. Since joining the company in 1998, Gleisberg has focused on purchasing and engineering, optimizing organizational structures and globalized processes, transformation management, and operations management in the automotive and engineered product/high-tech sectors.

**Volker Heidtmann** gained a master's degree in mechanical engineering and business administration at TU Darmstadt before completing an MBA at the State University of New York at Buffalo and a doctorate degree in business studies from the Philipps-University Marburg. He joined Roland Berger in 1999. His specialization is in production management, organizational development, post-merger integration, and supply chain management. He tends to work in the machinery, automotive, and utilities industries.

**Thomas Hollmann** completed his business degree at the University of Eichstätt-Ingolstadt before joining Roland Berger in 2005. He has worked on complexity and inventory management, pre- and post-merger integration, and logistics optimization projects in the healthcare, building, and engineered products industries.

**Michel Jacob** is a Partner in Roland Berger's Paris office. Prior to joining Roland Berger in 2001, he was at A.T. Kearney for a decade, where he was Vice-President in charge of strategic sourcing. Jacob also gained industry experience working at Saint-Gobain, where he was an R&D and production engineer in Germany and France. He has assisted clients on numerous purchasing optimization and purchasing re-engineering projects. He also specializes in operational efficiency improvement projects. Jacob has conducted projects in process-related industries like chemicals, oil, paper, steel and building materials, manufacturing, as well as service industries. He gained his MSc from the Ecole Centrale, Paris.

**Steffen Kilimann** gained a degree in industrial engineering and management at the Technical University, Berlin, as well as a master's degree at the Ecole Supérieure de Commerce, Toulouse. He also obtained a PhD degree from Technical University, Dresden. Before joining Roland Berger in 2006, he had management positions at Metro MGL Logistik and Metro Cash & Carry. He has extensive experience in the retail/wholesale and consumer goods sectors as well as in the automotive and transport and logistics industries. His focus is on supply chain management, reorganization of logistics and procurement systems, and the benchmarking and optimization of production processes.

**Thomas Kohr** gained degrees at the University of Cooperative Education in Mannheim and at the Leipzig Graduate School of Management. He obtained his MBA degree from the EADA in Barcelona. Kohr joined Roland Berger in 2005. He has worked on project controlling, process re-engineering, innovation management and procurement optimization projects in the electronics, engineering products, automotive, and DIY industries.

**Thomas Kwasniok** is a Partner at Roland Berger with a focus on operations in the process industries. He gained degrees in electrical engineering and operations research as well as his engineering doctorate in design tools for semiconductor circuits at the RWTH Aachen. He was Principal at Management Engineers and Director of Logistics Division at INFORM prior to joining Roland Berger. He has experience in the chemicals, pharmaceuticals, consumer goods, transportation and information technology sectors. His projects involve supply chain management, manufacturing, product structure, purchasing and business process reengineering.

**Ken Mori** is a Partner at Roland Berger's Tokyo office. He gained a degree in civil engineering at the University of Tokyo and his MBA at the University of Chicago. Prior to joining Roland Berger in 2002, Mori worked for the Kajima Corporation where he was Deputy Chief Engineer and was Vice President and Co-Head of the Asian Automotive Practice at A. T. Kearney in Tokyo. He has specialized in the automotive and engineered products industries, where he worked on operations, strategy, M&A, and post merger integration projects.

**Satoshi Nagashima** is a Partner in Roland Berger's Tokyo office. He gained his master's degree and doctorate in engineering in material science at Waseda University, Japan. He has worked for Roland Berger's Tokyo office since 1996. He has specialized in strategy development (corporate, sales and marketing), R&D, logistics planning and branding. Nagashima tends to work on projects in the automotive, electronics, logistics, and pharmaceutical industries.

**Robert Ohmayer** is a Partner at Roland Berger. He joined the company in 1996 after completing a degree in industrial engineering and an MBA at the University of Miami. Previously, he worked at MTU in Germany and for Mack Trucks in the United States. Ohmayer has broad industry experience. He has conducted projects in the automotive and supplier industry as well as the machinery and plant sector, and spent one year working in our South American office. He has also worked on projects in the consumer goods, construction, and logistics industries. His functional focus is on production, purchasing, supply chain management, R&D, and corporate strategy.

**Walter Pfeiffer** is a Partner in Roland Berger's Oils and Chemicals Competence Center. He gained a degree in mechanical engineering and an MBA from the TU Darmstadt. He joined Roland Berger in 2006 after having worked at Arthur D. Little Strategy and Accenture in Germany, Switzerland, Austria and the United States. His focus is on post-merger integration, supply chain/margin optimization, strategy, reorganization, and cost reduction in the downstream oil, petrochemicals, chemicals, and biofuels industries.

**Stefan Pötzl** gained his mechanical engineering degree with a specialization in production technology at the Technical University of Munich and he completed the Bavarian Elite Academy in parallel. He wrote his diploma these on logistics processes and cost while working at MAN Nutzfahrzeuge. Since joining Roland Berger in 2003, he has concentrated on the automotive, engineering/hi-tech and aerospace industries. He has assisted clients throughout Europe on projects dealing with strategy, performance improvement, procurement/cost reduction, R&D, innovation management, product planning, and process optimization.

**Thomas Rinn** is a Partner in Roland Berger's Stuttgart office. He studied business administration at the Eberhard-Karls-Universität in Tübingen and received his MBA from Portland State University. He joined Roland Berger in 1998 after working for many years in industry, both in Germany and in the United States. He has been a member of HTH Haus und

Technik AG's supervisory board since 2006. Purchasing, product development, and supply chain management are his specializations. He has completed projects in many industries including transportation, aviation, defense, logistics services, engineered products and construction and trade. In addition, he supports private equity-owned companies in performance improvement.

**Axel Schmidt** is a Partner at Roland Berger. He joined the strategy consultancy in 1991 and became Global Head of Operations Strategy in 1997. Previously, he worked for Procter & Gamble in Paris and ACL Engine Parts in Australia. He gained his degree in mechanical engineering at the University of Stuttgart. Schmidt has conducted projects in various industries ranging from consumer goods/retail, and pharmaceuticals through to automotive, engineered products, financial, and security services. He advises clients on the following types of project: supply chain and asset optimization, global footprint optimization, distribution and logistics strategy, turn-around programs, and global purchasing and development organization redesign.

**Ingo Schröter** gained his degree in technical business studies at Stuttgart University. Prior to joining Roland Berger's Operations Strategy Competence Center in 2001, he was a consultant at Arthur D. Little. He is an expert for supply chain management and logistics. He has supported clients on international projects on supply chain strategy, organization, business process re-engineering, and cost cutting. He has worked in these and in other functional fields in the process, aerospace and defense, transportation, and retail and consumer goods industries.

**Roland Schwientek** is a Partner in Roland Berger's Munich office. He studied business administration at the Gerhard-Mercator University of Duisburg. He joined Roland Berger in 1997 after working for several years in various functions in the automotive and automotive supplier industry, latterly as a purchasing manager at Bosch Automotive. Procurement/ purchasing, manufacturing footprint, supply chain management, and working capital optimization are some of his focus issues. He drives projects in many different industries under the action title *'Best practice transfer': what can we learn from leaders and leading industries?* Schwientek is author of a number of studies, including *Purchasing Excellence* and *Working Capital Excellence*.

**Gabriel-Assad Singaby** is a manager in Paris with seven years' consulting experience. He gained his MBA at the University of North Carolina and a degree in industrial engineering and operations research from the University of North Carolina and Ecole des Mines de Paris. Singaby's projects involve lean organization implementation, re-engineering, and lean operations improvement programs. He is also a 6-Sigma expert with a Master Black Belt 6-Sigma diploma from GE. He specializes in the automotive, aerospace, transportation, and chemical industries.

**Stephan M. Wagner** is a Professor at WHU–Otto Beisheim School of Management, where he is Director of the Kuehne Center for Logistics Management and holds the Kuehne Foundation Endowed Chair of Logistics Management. He obtained an MBA degree from Washington State University and a PhD and Habilitation degree from the University of St Gallen in Switzerland. Prior to joining the faculty of WHU, he worked as Director of Supply Chain Management for a Swiss-based technology group and as Senior Manager for an international management consulting firm. Wagner's research interests include supply chain strategy, purchasing and supply management, interfirm relationships in industrial marketing channels, innovation in supply chains, and the management of logistics service firms.

**Stephen Weisenstein** works in Roland Berger's Detroit office. He gained a degree in economics at the University of Michigan and his MBA at the University of Chicago. Prior to joining Roland Berger in 2004, he gained extensive industry experience working at Thomson, Daimler and Toyota Motor Manufacturing. He specializes in process improvement, procurement, growth strategies, corporate restructuring, post merger integration, and the Toyota Production System implementation in the automotive, engineered products, and manufacturing industries.

**Michael Zollenkop** joined Roland Berger in 1999. He gained a degree in business administration from the Friedrich-Alexander-University Erlangen-Nürnberg, a master's degree in economics from the Wayne State University in Detroit and his doctorate in business studies from the Otto Friedrich University in Bamberg. His focus is on product creation strategies, product portfolio and business model optimization, and procurement strategies in the automotive, machinery, IT/telecommunications and healthcare industries.

**Marco Zurru** is a Partner at Roland Berger's Milan office. He advises clients in the aerospace and automotive sectors, and in government and public services on strategy, operations, sourcing, supply chain and logistics, manufacturing, and business process re-engineering. Before coming to Roland Berger in 2001, he worked for Booz Allen & Hamilton and various industrial companies. He gained his MS in engineering and his MBA from Politecnico in Milan.

**Roland Berger Strategy Consultants** are especially grateful to Florian Kaiser and Heidi Sylvester for their work in the preparation of this volume.

# LIST OF ABBREVIATIONS

| | |
|---|---|
| ABS | air-bearing surface |
| B2B | business-to-business |
| B2C | business-to-consumer/customer |
| CAD | computer aided design |
| CAE | computer aided engineering |
| CCR | comprehensive cost reduction |
| CEE | Central and Eastern Europe |
| CEO | chief executive officer |
| CFO | chief financial officer |
| CKD | complete knock down |
| CMMS | computerized maintenance management system |
| COO | chief operating officer |
| CPL | corporate procurement and logistics |
| DFMA | design for manufacture and assembly |
| DRG | diagnosis related groups |
| DtC | design to cost |
| EADS | European Aeronautic Defence and Space |
| EAI | enterprise application integration |
| EBIT | earnings before interest and taxes |
| EMEA | Europe, Middle East and Africa |
| ERP | Enterprise Resource Planning |
| F&A | finance and administration |
| FDI | foreign direct investment |
| FMEA | failure mode and effect analysis |
| GAP | good–average–poor |
| GCL | global commodity leader |
| GDP | gross domestic product |
| HSSEQ | health, safety, security, environmental and quality standards |
| HWPM | heavyweight product managers |
| IPO | international purchasing offices |
| IS | information systems |
| KPI | key performance indicator |

| | |
|---|---|
| LB | local buyer |
| LCC | low-cost country |
| LEG | lead engineering group |
| M&As | mergers and acquisitions |
| MbO | management by objectives |
| MRO | maintenance, repair and overhaul |
| OEM | original equipment manufacturer |
| OPEX | operational expenditure |
| P&L | profit and loss |
| P2P | peer-to-peer |
| PEP | Purchasing EmPowerment |
| PM | purchasing manager |
| PPC | production planning and control |
| PPP | public–private partnership |
| R&D | research and development |
| RCL | regional commodity leader |
| REACH | registration, evaluation and authorization of chemicals |
| RFQ | request for quotation |
| ROCE | return on capital employed |
| SAP | Systems Applications and Products in data processing |
| SC | supply chain |
| SCM | supply chain management |
| SFP | site fitness programme |
| SKU | stock keeping unit |
| SUVs | sport utility vehicles |
| TCO | total cost of ownership |
| UNSPSC | United Nations Standard Product and Services Code |
| VDC | vehicle development centres |
| WHU | Wissenschaftliche Hochschule Für Unternehmensführung |

'It's not through inventions but through improvements that
fortunes are made.'

— **Henry Ford**

Achieving operative excellence is an important endeavor for all companies –
it is the golden path that leads to increased value over the long term.

By applying operative levers systematically and managing them
correctly, companies are doing everything in their power to ensure that
they follow their selected corporate strategy. It helps them answer some
critical questions: What value should my company create itself and what
should be achieved by external parties? Where are my company's end
production sites located and which key technologies and products take
center stage? How does my company manage innovation and where is it
supported? Where is the company's supplier base mainly located and how
can we steer the supply chain with maximum effect?

*Operations Excellence* takes up these questions. The authors provide
answers based on their extensive consulting experience, gained while
working with leading industrial sectors over many years. When answering
these questions, the authors keep two things in mind: What do leading
companies do? and What can be learnt from their approach? Bear in mind
that operations excellence, ultimately, is not a question of geniality – it is
more a question of an appropriate approach and fit to strategy, and of
continuous improvements as Henry Ford Snr knew very well.

At the beginning of the twentieth century, Henry Ford developed modern
assembly lines for the mass production of cars, which marked the beginning of a decisive and formative paradigm shift. These days the principle of
operations excellence has spread far beyond traditional manufacturing
industries and now shapes entirely new sectors. McDonald's, for instance,
extended the main features of operations excellence and made them relevant
for the restaurant sector. Toyota, which is currently the No. 1 automotive
player in the world, broadened the scope of mass production and started
applying its expertise in this field to the housing market. With its Toyota
Home, the carmaker has created a completely new business. Thanks to
explosive growth rates for prefabricated and terraced houses, it has created

for itself an additional growth motor. Even in traditional sectors, change is seeping in. Machinery producers such as Trumpf, whose processes in the past were often organized as stand-alone workshops rather than serial industries, are implementing industrial manufacturing processes, as mass producers have for quite some time.

Companies that have the correct operative strategy and are prepared to make sometimes difficult changes in order to improve their business are acknowledged as best-in-class. It is these that reach best practice status.

## The best things come in threes

There are three levels to operations excellence, and this book provides insights into groundbreaking developments in all three levels.

- The first level – that of strategy – provides companies with information on how they should travel their own path to best practice and the milestones they should see on their medium- and long-term horizons.
- The second level is that of performance improvement. It provides answers to questions such as: Which service level must my company reach in order to be competitive and leading edge? What requirements should my company expect from asset productivity and what should be the cap for our various cost types?
- The third level concerns enablers. This level answers questions about the correct organizational form, best processes, most appropriate human resources and key performance indicators, as well as infrastructure excellence fields such as IT.

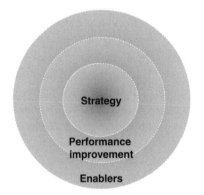

**Operations strategies**

... tackle the fundamental operational challenges of the future

**Operations performance improvement**

... transfer performance drivers such as cost structure and asset productivity into best practices

**Operations enablers**

... help to support, measure and control all operational enabler issues such as organization, processes, IT and KPIs with tangible values for companies

**Figure I.1**   Our approach – three levels to create operations excellence

**Figure I.2** Four fields of action to create operations excellence

## Operations excellence – four fields of action

This book tackles four fields in some detail: research and development, purchasing, manufacturing, and supply chain management. The authors are experienced consultants, professors and practitioners from all major industrial nations.

- In Part I approaches and cases from the area of R&D are introduced and debated
- Part II is dedicated to trends and approaches in the area of sourcing and purchasing
- Part III examines developments in the field of manufacturing
- Part IV deals with improving supply chain management; covering aspects such as comprehensive process optimization, reducing complexity and improving working capital.

We hope you enjoy reading this insightful book. Moreover, we hope you stumble across many helpful suggestions that enable you to achieve operations excellence within your own company.

ROLAND SCHWIENTEK
AXEL SCHMIDT

# PART I

# Research and Development

# Introduction

# What is successful product development?

*Thomas Rinn and Kai Bethlehem*

No one would doubt today that markets are becoming progressively more global. The rise of Eastern Europe, the upturn in Latin America and, of course, the entrance of China *et al.* into the global marketplace have significantly increased the numbers of suppliers for almost every kind of product. With competition rising, it is more important than ever before for companies to find and highlight their unique selling point, to offer something that singles out one company from the crowd.

'Innovation' is considered the magic word with which to rise to this challenge. Companies wish to create products or processes that lead to cheaper and better products, and innovation is the key to achieving this. Yet, innovation does not happen by chance: it has to be planned. The environment for excellence in innovation has to be actively established and fostered.

These lessons are part of all undergraduate classes in business administration or engineering. Yet, we continue to see many managers struggle to put this knowledge into practice in a systematic fashion, even though they are fully conversant in the theory of innovation.

The task is not an easy one. There is no one best, easy-to-apply strategy for successful and efficient innovation. Indeed, the opposite is true: each industry and segment requires a tailor-made approach to reach the best possible results.

A recent Roland Berger study[1] on the globalization of R&D organizations shows that there are several clusters to which companies and their R&D structures typically belong. Within each cluster, there are many ways to be successful. While there is 'no one single best way' to be continuously successful, product development is the area that is always most in need of improvement in order for a company to flourish, irrespective of the cluster or industry.

But what exactly should be the target of such improvement? What is successful product development?

This can be best answered by a comment by one of our clients, the head of R&D with a global blue-chip company recognized as being an innovation leader, during a workshop we moderated in early 2007. He said: 'When looking at the company from an external perspective, successful product development means that the new product fulfills or exceeds its targets concerning profitability, that it is different from other products, creates value-added for customers, and meets any other target that has been defined for this product. Looking from an internal perspective, however, things are different. Development is successful if R&D fulfills all its initially set targets regarding timing, money spent, smoothness of the process and quality of the result.'

In fact, this company sometimes had issues with developments and products not running well, leading to sales levels significantly below target and negative business results. This raised the question as to whether the company correctly focused its resources and whether it took appropriate steps once developments got off track or circumstances changed.

The important underlying questions are: how can companies stop projects that are clearly going to fail, and would a company be more successful if it stopped projects bound for failure early on?

Based on our experience, the answer is yes. By stopping a project in a timely fashion, resources, time and money can be channeled to other, potentially more successful, projects that might bring a greater overall benefit, as intellectual capital is allocated to developing products with the best business case for the entire company.

Thus, stopping a probably unsuccessful project as early as possible is central to improving overall innovation performance. According to our study, those companies that have the courage to stop previously very appealing product developments stand out from the crowd, and experience greater success.

Courage is not enough. In order to stop product developments early on, companies must have a clear strategy, fact-based performance measurements, and rigid quality gates.

In Part I, which focuses on product development, we thus examine different kinds of measures and methods to steer, control and optimize a product development project. Looking at R&D strategy, Michael Zollenkop explains how business model innovation is dependent on product/service innovation and how this fosters excellence in product development. Following this, Ralf Augustin and Kai Bethlehem reveal the levers that can be applied during product development. Jochen Gleisberg and Kai Bethlehem complement this section with their thoughts on the challenges of global development organizations. Then, Stefan Pötzl, Thomas Kohr and Dr. Michael Zollenkop take a closer look at a couple of enablers, starting with an innovation toolkit that has been proven to work and easy to implement. Ken Mori and Satoshi Nagashima round off this section by providing an example of a very successful Japanese approach to setting up smart engineering processes within a global organization.

## Note

1. Roland Berger Strategy Consultants (2007) 'Globalization of R&D – Drivers and Success Factors'. Study, ESB Research Institute, Reutlingen University, June.

# CHAPTER 1

# Changing business models and their impact on product development

## *Michael Zollenkop*

### Introduction

This chapter will examine how changes in the business model – whether in a company or an entire industry – can affect the process of product development. First, I define the precise nature of a business model, and how it should be used as a steering instrument for a company. Next, the chapter explores how business models develop over time and how these developments can be viewed as part of a lifecycle model. Following this, the question is discussed as to how companies can initiate and manage these innovations. Finally, a case study illustrates how generating scenarios for future business models can help companies to see what action they need to take now in terms of product development.

### The business model – corporate strategy in action

A number of factors, both internal and external, can influence the type, scope and direction of a company's product development. Corporate strategy determines the methods that a company employs. It also determines the contents of a company's innovation strategy. Corporate strategy is thus responsible not only for the underlying competitive strategy – for example, cost or quality leadership – but also for the overall form of the company's business model.

In simplified terms, the business model can be seen as the 'day-to-day living' of the corporate strategy, or a description of a company's activities. The business model comprises three interrelated components, which are shown in Figure 1.1.

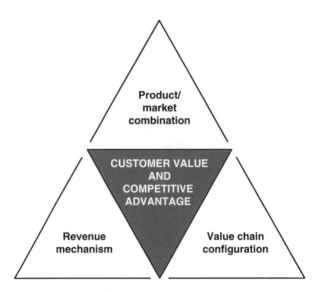

**Figure 1.1**    Components of business models

The first component is the product/market combination, which describes the customers that the company aims to serve, its markets and its services. Key elements here are the products and the scope of additional services the company will offer, the type of transactional relationship (that is, B-2-B, B-2-C or P-2-P) and the relevant market, defined according to functional, demographic, regional and other criteria.

The second component of the business model is how the company's value chain is to be configured and applied. This describes the degree of company internal value-added, the basic type of company configuration and the design of functional strategies. In terms of the company's configuration, the company must choose between vertical integration, specialization in particular functions, or coordination of the value chain.

The third component of the business model is the structure and relative weighting of the company's sources of revenue. Revenues can be transaction-based or non-transaction-based, and might come directly from users of the company's primary service offering or indirectly from users of a secondary service. Important elements here are customers' willingness to pay and the company's pricing strategy.

A company's business model lives or falls on the interdependence between these three components. Achieving a good fit is a prerequisite for generating superior customer value and, ultimately, competitive advantage. The following example from the airline industry will make this clear.

## Example: The airline industry

Most scheduled airlines – such as Lufthansa, for example – pursue a strategy of quality leadership. They aim to provide the best possible service and comfort combined with a global flight network. By contrast, low-cost carriers – Ryanair, for instance – aim for cost leadership. They proclaim that flying is an integral part of people's leisure activities and should be affordable for all. According to their philosophy, flights are in competition with other means of transport or other types of leisure activity. In this way, low-cost carriers are responsible for what may be called the commoditization of flying – a type of customer value that differs fundamentally from that offered by traditional scheduled airlines.

These two contrasting business strategies find their reflection in two differing business models. Both business models are internally consistent and, therefore, successful.

Traditional scheduled airlines target a mixture of business travelers and tourists. They offer a wide range of regional and international routes – their product/market combination. They have a hub from which they operate intercontinental flights; short-haul flights between major cities function as feeders for their intercontinental routes and are not generally designed for point-to-point transport (configuration of the value chain). Scheduled airlines' revenue comes in the form of payment for the transportation of passengers and cargo. A wide range of tariffs is available for tickets (the revenue mechanism). The business model is based on service, customer loyalty, and offering an international flight network.

Low-cost carriers have a very different business model, one that is based entirely on cost. Ryanair targets cost-sensitive tourists and only offers flights within Europe, with no in-flight meals (product/market combination). To keep costs to a minimum, Ryanair uses remote airports that often owe their very existence to it. Consequently, the standing times at these airports are very short, especially as flights are used for point-to-point transportation (value chain configuration). Low-cost carriers' revenues come not only from the sale of tickets, but also from areas such as on-flight purchases, data mining and advertising. Ticket prices vary according to when they are booked and the number of seats remaining at the time of purchase (revenue mechanism). All three components of the business model are directed toward cost optimization.

In both business models, the individual components fit well together. Yet, a number of companies – the KLM subsidiary 'Buzz' and the British Airways subsidiary 'Go' for example – were unable to achieve this level of consistency in their business models. They were the first victims in the low-cost carrier market.

In fact, even successful business models are subject to change. How this happens forms the subject of the following section.

## Change and innovation in the business model

Today, more than ever, competition between companies is driven by the increasing speed of technological and market change. As the pace of innovation steps up and market cycles shorten, more and more companies are redefining the basis of their business fundamentally, repositioning themselves as the providers of comprehensive solutions rather than as the manufacturers of specific industrial or consumer goods. The same goes for service providers. They, too, are expanding or adjusting the range of services they offer on the basis of functional and other criteria in order to exploit their own specific competitive advantages. The days are gone when competition was restricted to the home industry and to traditional competitors. Traditional boundaries between industries are rapidly dissolving, and companies are increasingly operating across a variety of different markets and sectors.

The construction and plant engineering industry is a good example. The industry is currently witnessing a shift in business models. Increasingly, companies are achieving customer value and competitive advantage by offering comprehensive solutions rather than specific products or individual services.

The construction company Bilfinger Berger, for instance, has added the Multi Service Group to its title. Industrial, power and facility services generate around €2.6 billion, or more than one third of the group's total revenues. Also, the services it provides extend well beyond the field of construction – including, for example, the maintenance and hiring of pumps to chemicals and pharmaceutical companies. Many plant construction companies now sell services using an operator or pay-on-production model. Linde, for instance, operates an air separation plant at the site of Finnish steel producers Avesta, supplying them with oxygen, argon and nitrogen. The German compressor manufacturer Kaeser currently generates only half its revenues from the sale of compressors; the remainder comes from sales of compressed air. In the automotive industry, Eisenmann, a manufacturer of painting systems, generates revenue by painting car bodies for its client Ford, while the KUKA Robot Group is paid for the number of auto bodies it welds at one particular Chrysler plant.

According to a study published by the Fraunhofer Institute for Systems and Innovations Research ISI,[1] around one fifth of producers of industrial goods have brought their business model into line with the 'complete solution' approach and now offer operator models: this pays off. Average pre-tax operating margins for companies with operator models were 6.8 percent, compared with 5.9 percent for companies without.

In infrastructure projects where the cash-strapped public sector is involved, companies are at a distinct competitive advantage if they are able offer additional services, such as the management of buildings or institutional facilities under a public–private partnership (PPP) model. Bilfinger Berger, for example, expects a return on equity of between 12 and 13 percent from its respective service business.

While corporate strategy remains as relevant as ever, changes to a company's business activities such as those outlined above have a far-reaching impact on its products, markets, value chains and revenue mechanisms. Business models change and develop over time. Particularly with the benefit of hindsight, it is possible to see quite different business models in a single company or industry as time goes by (see Figure 1.2).

One sector that has recently experienced major changes to its business model is the biotech and pharmaceutical industry. These changes are, for instance, reflected in how the business model of the company Mologen has developed over time. Mologen, originally a spin-off of the Free University of Berlin in the field of bio-informatics, moved into the area of molecular medicine. Its focus turned particularly to the research and development of drugs based on DNA structures, which are used, for example, in the fight against cancer. This area of activity, also known as 'genetic immunization', represented Mologen's product/market combination. Over time,

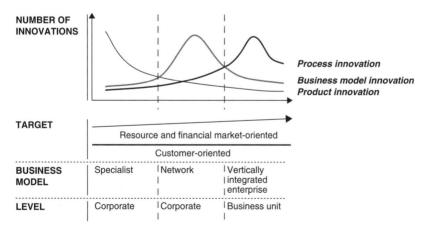

**Figure 1.2** Development of business models over time

Mologen gradually extended its area of activity from veterinary to human medicine. In terms of the value chain, its original configuration when it was still operating in the field of bio-informatics was that of an integrated company. The side step into molecular medicine brought with it, first, a specialization model and, later, building on this, a network coordination model. In a number of cooperative projects, Mologen initially concentrated on producing its own patented, DNA-based technology platforms. As time progressed, however, the company took over the coordination of the value chain in areas such as development and the functions of production, marketing and distribution, depending on the line of business, in cooperation with various partners. Today, the company enjoys even greater vertical integration, especially in the areas of production and distribution. Whereas its product/market combination and value chain configuration have undergone a number of mutually-dependent transformations, the revenue mechanism has remained transaction-based.

Changes in the business model such as those described above either come about in a planned way – the product of decisions made by top management – or they simply emerge as a result of actions taken by middle management. The constant changes in the environment, plus the fact that business models can readily be copied and imitated, make it important that companies consciously engage in this process of business model innovation, actively shaping the development of the company. Technological innovation is a key component of rapidly changing environments. Just as much as demographic change, new technology can change the basis of a company's operations, making existing business models obsolete. This is particularly true when it comes to technological convergence, which almost always brings in its wake a convergence of products and sectors. Functionalities that were formerly independent start to merge and previously distinct products draw closer in terms of their technology. As a result, products' value chains also become more and more similar. One present-day example is the competition between consumer electronics and the computer industry, with both areas battling it out over leadership in the area of access to digital services.

Essentially, business models can be imitated wherever barriers to market entry – such as physical resources that require building up over time – are low or non-existent, and wherever the often complex quilt of relationships between different components of the business model can be disentangled and transferred to other companies, markets or businesses. In the case of electronic commerce, for example, imitation is not difficult. Moreover, the fact that the companies themselves all strive toward the same benchmarks and best practice, and industries undergo consolidation following mergers and acquisitions, further contributes to the process of imitation and, ultimately, the consolidation of business models. It is exactly for these reasons that innovation and continuous product development are necessary for those companies that intend to stay 'removed from the crowd', to be special, to enjoy a strong reputation and lead in their respective market segment. With innovation and progress lacking at a company, the field will soon have caught up and leveled any kind of advantage that such company might have had a few years before.

Nike has long been regarded as a prime example of a company with a successful business model, a benchmark of effective business management in the sporting goods manufacturing industry. The company focuses its value creation on product development and brand leadership, outsourcing production to third-party providers. In terms of its product/market combination, Nike positions itself in the high-quality lifestyle/sporting goods segment, where items carry high price tags. Nike has also opened up a number of its own elaborately designed department stores – known as Niketowns – where the purchase experience becomes a leisure activity in itself. This model has been widely imitated throughout the industry. Today, all the major players, including the German companies Adidas and Puma, employ a similar business model. These two companies were in crisis at the beginning of the 1990s as a result of excessive costs, a stale brand image and an outdated product mix. Both managed to move themselves away from the brink of disaster, largely by adopting the best practice modeled by Nike. As the then Adidas CEO Robert Louis-Dreyfus himself admits, they did so by engaging in 'large-scale imitation' of Nike's successful model.[2]

## Business model lifecycle – the basis for innovation

The question is now – how can companies recognize the need to innovate in their business model and how may they determine when best to do this?

As we have seen, business models change over time. Just as products, technologies and industries do, business models pass through stages of formation, growth, maturity and decline. Put simply, they have a lifecycle. However, business models can be very complex. A large number of different factors can influence them. So, rather than trying to grasp this complexity in one attempt, it is often easier to look first at the lifecycles of the three components that make up the business model – the product/market combination, value chain configuration and revenue mechanism – and then draw conclusions on the overall lifecycle of the business model.

The indicators for different lifecycle stages are based on criteria and appropriate models taken from the discipline of innovation management. These indicators are different for each component of the business model. For the product/market combination, there are dozens; we have to select the right criteria from among those, bearing in mind the particular business model in question. In general, criteria for assessing market potential and penetration, innovation rate, degree of product or component standardization, customer adoption, and satisfaction of customer expectation by the market are particularly relevant. For the value chain configuration, criteria such as technological development, its influence on company costs and performance, and factors determining the development of the sector are important. The key criteria for the revenue mechanism are purchase criteria, price elasticity of demand, and changes in market participants' willingness to pay.

By examining these criteria, we can develop a picture of the lifecycle of each component of the business model, and how this influences the overall lifecycle of the business model. The relationship between the different components and how they interact with each other is also highly significant. To a large degree, this determines how well the business model fits together and, hence, how successful it is. The key question therefore concerns what the consequences are for the overall business model lifecycle if the indicators for each component show that they are in different phases, or when one component enters a different lifecycle stage (see Figure 1.3).

Accordingly, top management needs a tool for early recognition of the need to take action or innovate in the business model, which will help them to generate different options for change. This tool must provide top management with enough information sufficiently early in the process without deluging them with unnecessary data. Ideal, for this purpose, is a combination of an early warning system that senses any alterations in the indicators for the business model lifecycle and a system of what are known as 'weak signals'.

The indicators relate directly to the company's competitive environment, while the weak signals relate to the general environment in which the company operates. The competitive environment determines the attractiveness of the industry or business model and refers to suppliers, customers, relations with industry, rivalry between market players, newcomers to the market, and substitute products. The general environment relates to technological, macroeconomic, socio-cultural, ecological, political, and legal factors. These factors are shown on Figure 1.4. An example will elucidate the point.

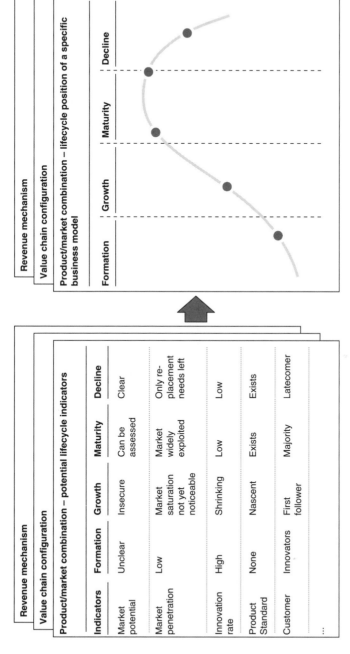

**Figure 1.3** Lifecycles of business model components

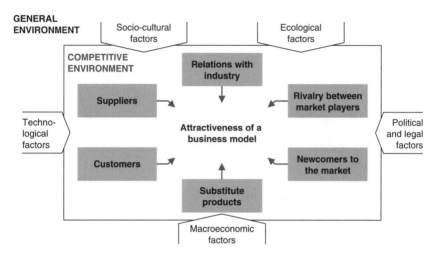

**Figure 1.4**   Indicators for business model attractiveness

## Case study: The music industry

The music industry – comprising companies being involved in the production, marketing, and distribution of audio media – has produced a number of early warning systems for its business models in recent years. The industry is vertically integrated to a large extent. Its products are CDs and suchlike, containing a selection of titles by a particular artist or in a particular genre, and offered within a constant price spectrum across the industry. In the past, four major labels formed an oligopoly that accounted for some 80 percent of worldwide sales. However, between 1997 and 2003 these four big players experienced revenue losses of approximately one third. Initially, the reason was music-swapping services such as Napster and Kazaa; later on, legal online platforms appeared such as iTunes, from which customers could buy individual tracks as MP3 files rather than having to purchase whole CDs.

Indicators had appeared in both the industry and competitive environments that the CD-based segment had reached its mature phase and an innovative business model was on its way. In terms of technology, there were unmistakable signs of forthcoming change: digitalization, the emergence of the MP3 format, and the rapid spread of Internet use with ever-faster transmission rates. In terms of socio-cultural change, the popularity of competing leisure activities (media such as DVDs, computer games, PlayStations, and so on) among young people – the key customer segment – was bringing about a significant shift in behavior. These factors in the overall environment led to an increase in the power of performing artists in the competitive environment. No longer were artists forced to work exclusively with a label for the purposes of production and distribution. The changes also led to an increase in consumer power. Now, fans could buy the particular track they wanted rather than a CD put together by the label.

Weak signals also appeared early on that changes were afoot in the music industry. Back in the early 1990s, leading figures such as MIT Internet guru Nicholas Negroponte and inventor of the MP3 format Karlheinz Brandenburg were already talking about the threat of digitalization for the music industry. Indeed, the former head of Universal in Germany describes the situation as follows: 'The early tremors of the digital revolution could be felt in the music industry well over a decade before the earthquake hit – that is, if one wanted to feel them.'[3]

Yet, many companies that had traditional business models did not want to feel the earth move. For many years, they failed to react either to the indicators and early warning signs or to the arrival of Internet file-sharing services. Instead of developing a consistent strategy, they tried to take legal action – first, against the file-sharing services and, later, against their users. Apple, an industry outsider, understood the signals better. Its reaction was to launch iTunes, the first and, to date, most successful seller of tracks via the Internet.

Generating business model lifecycles in this way gives top management an early warning system. When this system indicates that the business model is entering into a period of decline, or shows that other, superior business models are possible, top management knows that they must do something about product development. What exactly it is that they should do – and how scenarios can help them find out – forms the subject of the following section.

## Product/service innovation – the prerequisite for innovation in the business model

The information that early warning systems generate forms the basis for drawing up scenarios. Top management can then use these scenarios to test potential business models for durability and robustness. The scenarios themselves give a picture of what the complex systems of the future could look like. They must be produced in a systematic fashion and be entirely plausible in nature. Their purpose is to create transparency over possible future competitive conditions and different factors affecting the success of business activities. The scenarios form a key component of a company's business planning and development, as well as serving to generate potential future business models.

The process of drawing up scenarios consists of three stages: scenario field analysis, projections, and scenario building. This process is preceded by a stage of scenario preparation and followed by scenario transfer. In the scenario field analysis stage, key factors are determined for the entire system. In the projections stage – the core phase of scenario management – appropriate projections are made for the key factors determined in the initial phase. These projections are then bundled into draft scenarios, visualized and described. Ideally, companies should draft two or three scenarios with different constellations, so that the actual development falls somewhere between the more extreme scenarios. In the case of innovative business models, it can again be helpful to run this procedure for each of the three components of the business model first, and then combine the three to form appropriate scenarios. This ensures a good fit in the future business model.

According to expert opinion in recent years, three main scenarios exist for the future of the music industry. These scenarios are 'equilibrium between online and offline services', 'dominance of online distribution' and 'the end of the music industry'. In one extreme scenario, 'equilibrium between online and offline services', the product/market combination will consist of CDs and suchlike, accompanied by an attractive, legal download service. Online and offline services will be offered as additional services when customers buy CDs. The value chain configuration will involve major labels gradually running down their vertical integration in favor of cooperation with specialized players. The revenue mechanism for this scenario will be a combination of various online and offline components in the revenue stream. In the other extreme scenario, 'the end of the music industry', music will simply become another type of digital content. The convergence of contents and hardware will lead to sections of the value chain – such as distribution and marketing – being taken over by the companies formerly responsible for bundling and selling content or producing hardware: these might be Internet portals, mobile telephone companies or media firms, or hardware manufacturers such as Apple. In this scenario, labels will become redundant.

Clearly, companies need to be prepared for the new conditions arising in the competitive environment. They must be in a position to implement a business model that can face these new conditions robustly. They need to know what wheels they should set in motion in their product or service development process, their value chain configuration and their revenue mechanism. To do this, two activities are vital: companies must carry out a gap analysis to determine what needs to be done, and they must determine the correct timing for initiating action. It is essential that they manage the transition from the old business model to the new one in a fluent manner.

The gap analysis should check what potential resources lie in the company and whether these resources are sufficient to meet the needs of the future product/market segment. This means that companies should examine what technology they currently have, how this compares with what will be required in future, and what new skills they need to develop. Companies must ask themselves what their current capacity is, and how they should prioritize their resources between the two goals of keeping up existing product development (for example, supervising current series production) within the framework of the present business model, and closing the development gap with respect to the future business model. One possible solution is for companies to buy in external know-how – finances permitting.

Google, Yahoo! and eBay are good examples of companies that continually acquire start-ups with promising technological developments or existing business models. Their aim is to shorten development times, which are often more relevant than costs when it comes to competition over innovation. At the same time, by buying up start-ups they guarantee themselves an excellent starting position as fast followers or even first movers. For instance, eBay bought up Skype, a service that makes it possible to make free telephone calls via the Internet. Similarly, Yahoo! acquired the photo management and sharing application Flickr, and even made Flickr's founder its own vice president.

Apple has taken a different approach. Heeding the early warning signs, Apple looked at what it needed to do to build up the requisite skills and designed an attractive spectrum of future services. Ultimately, Apple was able to generate a new field of business for its iPod hardware through its download service iTunes. The rumors that Apple's hardware business cross-subsidizes its software business persist. But, ultimately, Apple's success is enough to quell any criticism. The new business field of iPod and iTunes now accounts for 49.5 percent of Apple's revenues, compared with just 6 percent in 2003. The company's revenues were up by 211 percent in 2006 compared with 2003, and profit was up by 2,780 percent.

Determining the correct timing for initiating action means making the most of windows of opportunity before product standards, dominant designs and business models have crystallized and established themselves.

One key aspect of good timing is apparent in the strategy of graduated reaction. As information becomes more concrete and the direction of change clearer, companies' preparations for the future should – indeed, they must – become more and more committed. Companies must be constantly looking at the latest information available from the early warning systems and using it as a basis for initiating actions aimed at closing the resource gap. This up-to-the-minute information can also serve as the basis for drawing up technology and innovation roadmaps.

## Outlook

Business models are a key component of corporate success. To a large extent, they decide the type of service provided by the company, as well as how it delivers this service. This, in turn, determines a significant portion of the customer value generated by the company and the competitive advantage to which it aspires. Innovative business models therefore play an important role in stimulating product development. Consequently, management information systems must be geared toward monitoring indicators and weak signals, giving companies the chance to recognize the need for action early on – whether in the form of risks to the current business model or opportunities for future models.

## Notes

1. *Frankfurter Allgemeine Zeitung* (2003) 'Mit Betreibermodellen neue Märkte erschließen', 21 July.
2. See comment made in Boldt, Klaus; Hirn, Wolfgang (1997) 'Der Spielführer', *ManagerMagazin*, 12: 81. Spiegel Verlag.
3. Renner, Tim (2004) *Kinder, der Tod ist gar nicht so schlimm! Über die Zukunft der Musik- und Medienindustrie*. Frankfurt am Main: Campus Verlag: 9.

## Further reading

Christensen, Clayton M. (1997) *The Innovator's Dilemma. When New Technologies Cause Great Firms to Fail*. Boston.
Knyphausen-Aufseß, Dodo zu; Meinhardt, Yves (2002) 'Revisiting Strategy: Ein Ansatz zur Systematisierung von Geschäftsmodellen',

in Bieger, Thomas; Bickhoff, Nils; Caspers, Rolf; Knyphausen-Aufseß, Dodo zu; Reding, Kurt (eds), *Zukünftige Geschäftsmodelle. Konzept und Anwendung in der Netzökonomie.* Berlin: 63–89.

Knyphausen-Aufseß, Dodo zu; Zollenkop, Michael (2007) 'Geschäfts-modelle', in Köhler, Richard; Küpper, Hans-Ulrich; Pfingsten, Andreas. *Handwörterbuch der Betriebswirtschaft.* Stuttgart, 6th edn, cols 583–91.

Meier, Horst (ed.) (2004) *Dienstleistungsorientierte Geschäftsmodelle im Maschinen- und Anlagenbau. Vom Basisangebot bis zum Betreibermo-dell.* Berlin.

Meinhardt, Yves (2002) *Veränderung von Geschäftsmodellen in dyna-mischen Industrien. Fallstudien aus der Biotech-/Pharmaindustrie und bei Business-to-Consumer-Portalen.* Wiesbaden.

Zollenkop, Michael (2006) *Geschäftsmodellinnovation. Initiierung eines systematischen Innovationsmanagements für Geschäftsmodelle auf Basis lebenszyklus-orientierter Frühaufklärung.* Wiesbaden.

# CHAPTER 2

# Innovate to win: how clever cost approach design can outsmart competition

*Ralf Augustin and Kai Bethlehem*

## Introduction

Most of us know it, but few are willing to admit it freely: innovation and progress in technical products hardly ever provide sufficient leeway to increase prices to a considerable degree. The pressure from competing products or alternatives on offer around the world is simply too high. Innovation is something customers expect from well-known companies. It is a given – not a sign of outstanding performance.

Innovation is not about the ability to raise prices but, rather, how to avoid having to lower them. At the same time, innovation is a costly matter requiring manpower, research, and certificates. Companies cannot pin their hopes on price increases in order to finance innovation. Bearing this in mind, it is valid to ask whether companies are at all wise to invest in innovation and R&D. The truth is hard and simple: companies no longer have a choice. If your company does not innovate, your competitor will; and any profits your company might have made through saving on R&D expenses will be hacked away as you become forced to sell 'outdated' products at a lower price.

History is a minefield of companies, industries, and even whole countries that lost the battle for customers when their products fell below technical standards. Income in hard currency in the former Soviet Union and all affiliated countries dried up during the 1980s as their products became more and more inferior and, thus, less attractive to western markets. The Eastern Bloc's substantial basic wealth of oil and mineral resources could not prevent it from sliding into bankruptcy and political turmoil.

This example might be heavily influenced by market-averse political philosophies, but there are plenty of other examples to draw on. Think of the once flourishing fabric industry in Great Britain, Germany's consumer electronic industry, or the 15 or so car manufacturers France had after the war. As the balance between innovation and cost competitiveness became unstable, all of these industries fell by the wayside.

The other side of the coin shows companies and countries that achieved impressive turnarounds when they started to provide the right innovation at the right price. Consider, for example, Japan's automotive industry – or Korea's in its younger days for that matter, the Silicon Valley's computer industry, or current solar panel production in Germany. These examples prove that innovation, when it fits perfectly with the right cost figures, does pay off.

Offering innovation at competitive prices is the key to success. But how can companies produce innovative products sufficiently cheaply to cover their R&D cost and price them no higher than the predecessor model? The answer is 'design to cost' (DtC). Combined with Roland Berger's 'comprehensive cost reduction' approach (CCR), DtC covers more than merely the four typical levers that are usually applied to tackle cost.

## Setting the points: reducing cost is – above all – a mindset

Mindset is the first obstacle that needs to be overcome when trying to implement any sort of DtC approach. This is as true for engineering as it is for other professional fields. The word 'engineer' is derived from the word 'genius'. Miraculous inventions and brilliant ideas spring to mind when we think of genius. Down-to-earth aspects such as bookkeeping and savings realizations tend not to enter the imagination in this context. It is no surprise, then, that few of us actually think of making things cheaper while wondering how we can make them better. But an engineer's prestige is not lowered when his new solution is cheaper, faster or more efficient to produce. The opposite is true – it actually enhances his image. Improving the cost situation is a sign of genius. Cost saving must be a *conditio sine qua non* for any innovation undertaken.

All of this should be common sense. Unfortunately, many people both within and outside R&D still believe that commercial aspects are best left to the purchasing department (if not bookkeeping) once miraculous ideas have materialized into products. Strangely, this thinking continues to be widespread, even though 80 percent of a product's cost is already determined in the R&D phase.

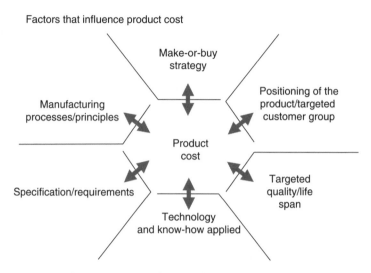

Factors that influence product cost

**Figure 2.1**   Product costs are influenced by several surrounding factors

R&D alone, however, should not bear the sole blame should costs get out of hand. There are at least six main areas that significantly increase the cost of a product: positioning of the product, targeted quality, technology and know-how applied, specification, manufacturing processes and principles, and make-or-buy strategy.

## Positioning of the product

This element depends on the image that a company has to maintain. In many ways, every targeted market segment requires a product to offer a certain number of features that might prohibit material savings. A high-end fountain pen needs to have a certain weight to feel right and be accepted as a luxury item. Similarly, expensive furniture may not be made out of artificial leather.

## Targeted quality

The second area that increases the cost of a product is very similar to the first aspect, with the exception that the difference between quality and inferior materials is not just skin-deep. Here, we are referring to quality that only makes itself apparent after years, such as jeans that retain their color when others have long faded, or a chair that is still comfortable when others have already started to squeak and fall apart. Developing and manufacturing products that are built to last is, in itself, an art. Making these sorts of products does not give manufacturers a license to stop caring about cost but, rather, a healthy dose of respect that certain things simply cost.

## Technology and know-how applied

This third aspect affects a product's cost. There are sometimes invisible barriers that should not be crossed in a DtC approach. In many companies, there are certain parameters that prescribe the use of certain solutions for intellectual property reasons or owing to a certain image. Sometimes, it is simply because someone important in the company invented something – for example, the one-arm 'hopping' windscreen wiper of Mercedes cars during the 1990s. Once the inventor retired, the 'hopper' went out of action. In cases such as these, it is more productive to accept the barrier and change it at a later date. It is important, however, to calculate and communicate the cost of the 'protected' product.

## Specification

The cost of a product is largely affected by specifications, which is our fourth aspect. In ideal terms, a product specification simply means quantifying the wish of a targeted customer. In reality, however, this is rarely the case, especially since a customer's wishes are strongly influenced by the sales force, marketing gurus, product planners and such. There is often a discrepancy between what customers think they want and what they really want. Examples of products that have flopped on the market are endless. Wishes might be misinterpreted, customers misguided. Thus, a specification should never be accepted as being carved in stone. One of the first steps in a DtC approach, therefore, should be close examination of the reasons behind the need for specific costly solutions.

## Manufacturing processes and principles

Manufacturing principles, too, can significantly shape the cost of a product, especially when second thoughts arise during the R&D process. Barring cases where expensive processes are deliberately chosen purely for the sake of it, there is generally a great deal of interdependency between product design and manufacturing principles. Certain technical solutions or specifications simply require certain manufacturing methods. It is of utmost importance to keep the production process in mind when designing a product. Whenever meticulous, time-consuming and error-prone manual work is necessary, there is a high probability that the product design has not been optimized for efficient production. The same is true whenever production is hampered by bottlenecks.

## Make-or-buy strategies

In this area, in particular, emotional aspects often color rational decisions. Core competencies that should not be lost, the will to keep the workforce employed, and doubts about whether the quality and flexibility can be guaranteed once processes are outsourced are all factors. While such decisions might involve less emotional energy in modern blue-chip companies, emotional factors will probably play a considerable role in traditional, family-owned enterprises, especially if the founder is still deeply involved in the business.

We have chosen to illustrate these six general factors that affect product cost right at the beginning because it cannot be stressed too much that the engineering, purchasing or accounting functions alone are not responsible for fully optimizing cost. Each function has to become involved. Only if these and other departments participate actively is there a likelihood that a product will meet its target cost.

## Cost drivers in detail: the quartet that sets the stage

The cost of a product is influenced by more than the pure material or production cost. There are overhead costs – which will not be dealt with in this chapter – and there are value chain factors. A close inspection of factors along the entire value chain reveals that the cost of a product is largely influenced by the four following aspects: sourcing, manufacturing, product design, and supply chain.

## Sourcing

In addition to negotiations concerning certain materials and components, sourcing encompasses aspects that need to be regarded during the product's design phase. For example, materials, components or modules that are easy to obtain; whether substitutes could be used to allow for sourcing from a market with strong competition.

Overlap exists here with aspects of product specification. Consider, for instance, certain technical parameters such as geometrics, strength and weight that predefine whether companies must select from molded, stamped/forged or machined parts; or whether plastics, metals or laminates could/must be used. Clearly, there is less competition for injection-molded, fiber-reinforced metals with an aerospace certificate (making it difficult to achieve any competition in the supply base) than for simple, stamped, sheet-metal parts (where setting up a sound supplier matrix would be comparatively easy).

To deliver the best possible results, intelligent sourcing needs to start with the design phase of a product. This targeted interaction between R&D and the purchasing department can be achieved using one of two set-ups. In an 'institutionalized' set-up there is a dedicated 'upstream' purchasing group whose sole purpose is to accompany all relevant developments from the sourcing point of view. In contrast, in a project-based set-up engineers and 'normal' purchasing people meet in core teams to discuss and align innovation and the sourcing strategy.

Irrespective of the set-up selected, a true DtC approach needs to take into account potential suppliers, markets, duties, and certificates. Only if the purchasing department is given sufficient freedom to activate its purchasing and negotiation levers, can satisfying results be obtained.

## Manufacturing

Of equal relevance to the sourcing aspects are the manufacturing aspects. Again, the design of a product stipulates the kind of manufacturing that will be necessary to produce a particular product. Involving manufacturing experts early on will help ensure that manufacturing or production processes are chosen that are well mastered by the company. This ensures, in turn, that capacities and existing machines, or even tooling, can best be utilized.

In many cases, engineers in R&D are largely unaware of the processes and techniques in a company's production line. This is especially true for those companies in which R&D and production are not located at one site, as is so often the case with huge companies or global firms. In these cases, it is essential to include a representative of the manufacturing department in the development process. Companies can thereby avoid preprogramming production issues into the product. Examples of such issues include massive production limitations due to bottlenecks arising from new processes, machines standing idle or lost flexibility following the outsourcing of production steps.

A DtC approach that focuses on manufacturing and production aspects always needs to zoom in on the balance of techniques, processes, and materials mastered by the company. Production steps that cause obstacles due to poor quality, bottlenecks or other negative factors need to be addressed.

## Product design

The importance of the product design has already been touched upon. Its importance should never be underestimated. About 80 percent of a product's cost are defined during the development phase of a product, and 'errors' committed here can rarely be rectified in later steps. Besides its influence on purchasing and manufacturing, there are further cost factors that are influenced by product design: the most important is the quality of the product, which is decisive for recall expenditures, guarantee cost, and cost to keep exchange parts in stock.

As legislation to protect the rights of customers becomes ever stronger, recall expenditures and guarantee cases – especially in the automotive industry – have risen significantly over the past decade. While debate rages about the damage or improvement to a company's image resulting from a recall, the cost is a factor today that no company can omit when calculating a business model for a new product.

The introduction of the first aluminum mass-market bicycles in Germany forms a cautionary tale. The reputation of the bicycle producer HSK quickly became sullied when its bicycle frames began to crack. Only by offering a ten-year guarantee on its bicycles, could HSK make customers return to its stores. The characteristics of the material used for the frames were obviously not sufficiently known and did not align with the product design. At the product design stage, it should have been clear that a better design or reinforced aluminum tubes would be required. As a result of this mismatch between design and material, HSK's image was significantly harmed, as was the business case of these revolutionary bicycles.

How easily a product can be scaled up is another aspect of cost influenced by design. By this, we mean the potential to develop derivatives or a whole product family from the initial starting product. The design of platforms in the automotive industry is illustrative here. For instance, using common platforms Volkswagen builds cars ranging from Seat to Skoda and Volkswagen and to Audi.

Yet another aspect of designing products to cost is the ability to use externally available knowledge. This encompasses the tapping of external R&D capabilities and know-how; it also means using certain modules or functional groups that can be put into an article as a ready-made black box rather than being produced anew. The Dolby function in home-entertainment serves as an example. Only very few manufacturers (mostly in the up-market segment) continue to braze the electronics using discrete components. Most prefer to use the ready-made chips widely available on the market that can simply be put onto the circuit board to perform the required function.

Companies need to have certain rules in place that stipulate when external know-how can be used. Areas regarded as core competencies should not be outsourced. Considered from another angle, this means that companies need to ensure that areas defined as core competencies are so competitive that it is not possible to find an adequate replacement in the market.

## Supply chain

The fourth aspect that DtC usually focuses on is the supply chain. Attention is paid here to the physical handling of goods, both inward and outward bound. Incoming inspection plays a major role in production efficiency, as undetected gaps in quality might cause severe obstacles during production or, worse, in customers' hands. The management of warehouses and stock is also important and, typically, the cost for warehousing, inventory, and moving of goods is underestimated. Fully optimizing them can free up cash quickly. Switching stock into consignment stock is another option, and having suppliers that own, manage, and look after a warehouse adjacent to the production line is the dream of every logistics manager.

Logistics clearly demonstrate how interlinked processes in modern companies are. An engineer who intentionally selects parts from a best-price supplier that offers consignment stock or even a warehouse close to the production line would be a treasured member of any core DtC team.

The importance of pursuing DtC with a global view cannot be over-stressed. Only when all factors are considered can the best possible result be achieved. This is not an exercise that can be done piecemeal. Instead, it should be institutionalized throughout a product's entire lifecycle – from the cradle to the grave, so to speak. In a project set-up, DtC can possibly fix some aspects, but to exploit the entire savings potential, a fully-fledged approach influencing the basic product design is better suited. How this can best be achieved is illustrated in the following section.

## The comprehensive cost reduction approach – ten facets of a gem

Implementing DtC thinking in a company is no easy task. This is all the more true if DtC has to be performed swiftly in order to help alleviate a burning cost issue. In such challenging situations, a proven methodology is required.

Roland Berger's comprehensive cost reduction (CCR) approach has been tested and refined on numerous occasions. Five key features ensure the successful use of this tool: holistic perspective, fact-based neutrality, complete coverage, openness to change, and inclusion of all stakeholders.

As the approach strives for a holistic perspective, the total cost of ownership and production is investigated rather than only the purchasing cost. All levels of a product are analyzed: parts, components, modules, systems, and finished products. The fact-based neutrality of this approach means that rather than relying on gut feeling, this method uses thorough data analysis, employing tools such as bottom-up and top-down cost calculations. With its complete coverage, not only are internal processes covered, but also every step of the value chain, from suppliers to the product's customers. The approach's openness to change means that the fact-based analysis uncovers all optimizing potential, with disruptive changes as well as incremental improvements being options that might be pursued. Lastly, all stakeholders are included: not only purchasing and R&D, but also sales, marketing, production, and logistics are involved in the process when necessary.

At the very heart of the CCR is an analysis tool-matrix as shown in Figure 2.2.

On the y-axis, the ten tools to be applied are listed. The checks to the right indicate the departments and stakeholders that are typically involved in each action. Further to the right, indications are given for typical savings that could be achieved by professionally applying this tool under normal circumstances. An indication of the effort usually required to execute the tools is also provided.

## Tool 1: Technical benchmarking/DFMA

This is basically the 'disassembly' of competitive products to analyze the materials and manufacturing methods used. Given certain knowledge, it is possible to calculate the cost for the competitor to build the product, deduct his margin and, thus, understand his cost position. Following from

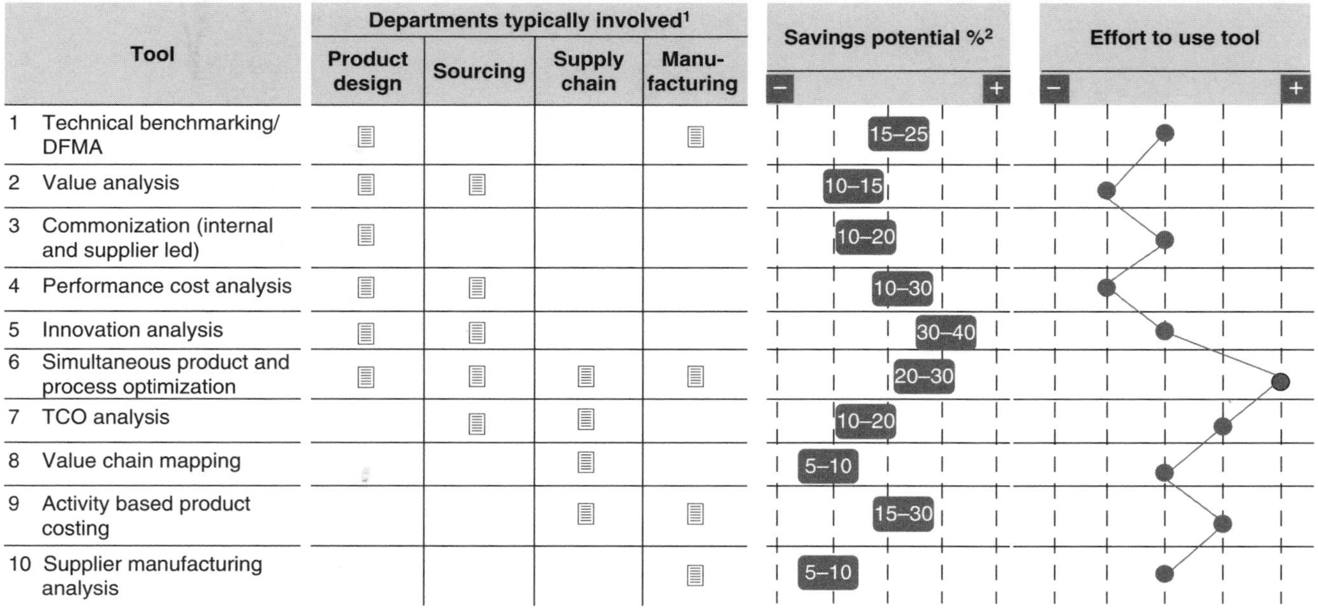

| Tool | Departments typically involved[1] | | | | Savings potential %[2] | Effort to use tool |
| --- | --- | --- | --- | --- | --- | --- |
| | Product design | Sourcing | Supply chain | Manu-facturing | | |
| 1 Technical benchmarking/ DFMA | ▦ | | | ▦ | 15–25 | |
| 2 Value analysis | ▦ | ▦ | | | 10–15 | |
| 3 Commonization (internal and supplier led) | ▦ | | | | 10–20 | |
| 4 Performance cost analysis | ▦ | ▦ | | | 10–30 | |
| 5 Innovation analysis | ▦ | ▦ | ▦ | | 30–40 | |
| 6 Simultaneous product and process optimization | ▦ | ▦ | ▦ | ▦ | 20–30 | |
| 7 TCO analysis | | ▦ | ▦ | | 10–20 | |
| 8 Value chain mapping | | | ▦ | | 5–10 | |
| 9 Activity based product costing | | | ▦ | ▦ | 15–30 | |
| 10 Supplier manufacturing analysis | | | | ▦ | 5–10 | |

**Figure 2.2** The comprehensive cost reduction approach covers the complete value chain

Notes:
1 Indicative, pending adjustments for certain industries, company setups, etc.
2 Savings for the system components addressed.

this knowledge, it is possible for a company to generate ideas on how to optimize its own design, manufacturing process and/or assembly. It is also possible to gain profound knowledge about the competitors' competencies.

## Tool 2: Value analysis

This tool aims to define the cost of each functionality a finished product offers. The goal is to single out the most expensive functionalities and find ways to replace them with more attractive alternatives. This tool is also excellent in the framework of market/consumer studies as it helps companies to understand what a consumer would be ready to pay for a certain functionality and, thus, to discover the 'profitable'/unattractive functions of a product. An example for the value analysis of a power window module in a car is provided in Figure 2.3.

## Tool 3: Commonization

The goal here is to use as many parts or components from existing products as possible. This method is extremely valuable for articles that are utilized or manufactured in limited numbers, and also with products that are similar in general but different in detail. Here, it is helpful to imagine the merger of two competitors who want to reduce costs by using as many common parts as possible.

## Tool 4: Performance cost analysis

This tool is based on the belief that cost and characteristics (performance, power, weight, dimensions, and so on) of similar products are somewhat linear. This means that it is possible to extrapolate target costs for a product by knowing the cost of similar products. This approach requires the availability of a series of products that serve as the basis for a 'curve' on which the respective product is placed (see Figure 2.4).

## Tool 5: Innovation analysis

This tool aims at reducing cost by using the latest technologies, materials, processes or solutions. Companies might use more powerful computer chips

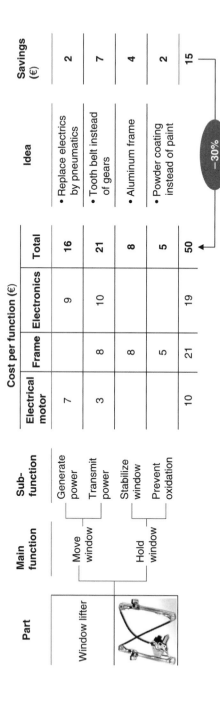

| Part | Main function | Sub-function | Electrical motor | Frame | Electronics | Total | Idea | Savings (€) |
|---|---|---|---|---|---|---|---|---|
| | | | **Cost per function (€)** | | | | | |
| Window lifter | Move window | Generate power | 7 | | 9 | **16** | • Replace electrics by pneumatics | 2 |
| | | Transmit power | 3 | 8 | 10 | **21** | • Tooth belt instead of gears | 7 |
| | Hold window | Stabilize window | | 8 | | **8** | • Aluminum frame | 4 |
| | | Prevent oxidation | | 5 | | **5** | • Powder coating instead of paint | 2 |
| | | | 10 | 21 | 19 | **50** | –30% | 15 |

**Figure 2.3**   Value analysis – vehicle window lifters

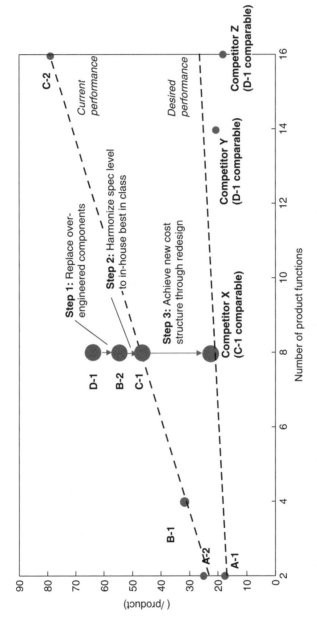

**Figure 2.4**  Performance Cost Analysis – Cost comparison by most important function
*Note:* A-1... D-1 own products (different families).

to allow functionalities to be integrated more tightly on a lesser number of chips; they might produce concentrates, as do detergent makers to reduce packaging, logistics and sales cost; or they might replace light bulbs with LEDs. Revamping products, especially those that have been around for some time, is often an excellent way to cost-optimize a product.

## Tool 6: Simultaneous product and process optimization

This entails a systematic analysis of the product and process cost of both a company's own and competitive products. What is unique about this tool is that it should be employed with several strategic or key suppliers. In fact, the cost analysis and calculation will mostly be undertaken by the suppliers, as they will have more expertise in calculating cost on component or part level than companies themselves. Moreover, having several competitors calculating the same range of products will create greater confidence in the prices estimated. To use this method, companies require suppliers that can be trusted and that are ready to become involved in the endeavor. This creates a challenge for suppliers, because such an exercise might set the target price for products they supply to the company.

Figure 2.5 illustrates the results of such an approach, with five suppliers having calculated costs for five competing articles. Although the price estimates vary, certain trends can be identified.

## Tool 7: Total cost of ownership

Total cost of ownership (TCO) is already a 'classic' among DtC tools. The goal of this lever is to quantify all costs of a product over its full lifecycle (development, series production, and after sales). TCO strives for an overall cost optimization. It is especially applicable in cases when production machines, parts or components used in own products incur further cost during their lifecycle. This tool is applicable mostly when designing processes or services.

## Tool 8: Mapping the complete value chain

This is one of the most comprehensive approaches with which to understand and reduce cost. The individual aspects to be regarded in this approach are shown in Figure 2.6.

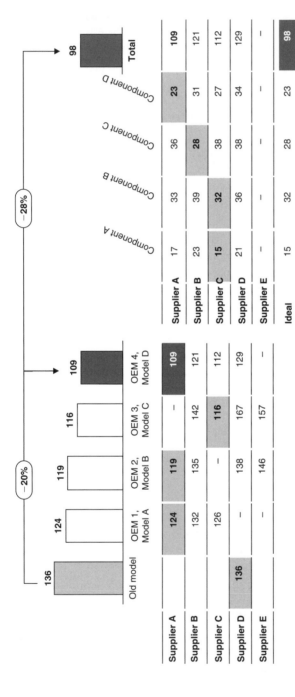

| | OEM 1, Model A | OEM 2, Model B | OEM 3, Model C | OEM 4, Model D |
|---|---|---|---|---|
| **Supplier A** | 124 | 119 | – | 109 |
| **Supplier B** | 132 | 135 | 142 | 121 |
| **Supplier C** | 126 | – | 116 | 112 |
| **Supplier D** | 136 | 138 | 167 | 129 |
| **Supplier E** | – | 146 | 157 | – |

Offers by five supplies for four different seats (competitor models) are requested and compared with own current product design
First benchmark reveals lowest cost design (model D), which is 20% less expensive than old design (module cost of € 109)

| | Component A | Component B | Component C | Component D | Total |
|---|---|---|---|---|---|
| **Supplier A** | 17 | 33 | 36 | 23 | 109 |
| **Supplier B** | 23 | 39 | 28 | 31 | 121 |
| **Supplier C** | 15 | 32 | 38 | 27 | 112 |
| **Supplier D** | 21 | 36 | 38 | 34 | 129 |
| **Supplier E** | – | – | – | – | – |
| **Ideal** | 15 | 32 | 28 | 23 | 98 |

Detailed analyses of model D cost structure for each supplier reveals further potential from process improvements
Best model D component proces cherry-picked form all suppliers reveals target cost of € 98 (28% below current model)

**Figure 2.5** Simultaneous product and process optimization example car module – vehicle driver seat (EUR/vehicle)

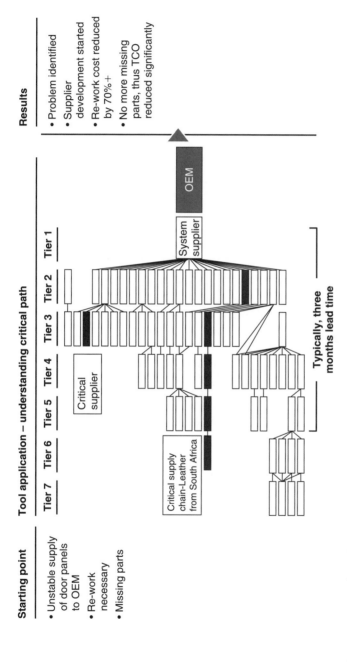

**Figure 2.6** Value chain maps help to identify critical branches and to focus supplier development – passenger car door panel example

40

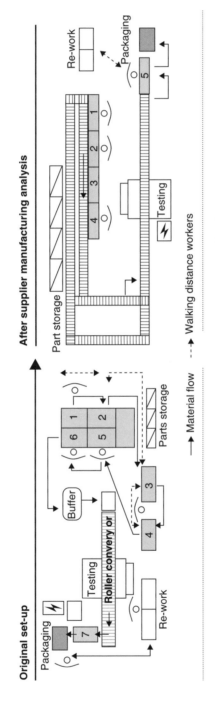

**Figure 2.7** Supplier manufacturing analysis: component assembly – lamp manufacturer

This process requires the involvement and cooperation of all participants in the value chain, from suppliers to retailers. Parties involved mostly welcome this approach as it helps them to optimize their own products or processes in a joint approach. In many cases, such 'external' pressure helps the affected party to push through changes in a process that they would find hard to achieve on their own. This approach is best performed with experienced people from the companies involved. They should have an educated eye and be able to spot possible bottlenecks, complicated work-flows or costly processes at the supplier during a visit.

## Tool 9: Activity based product costing

This lever is based on a 'well-educated guess' to define target cost. The trick is to use the guessed cost to open up discussion with the supplier, and to encourage him to prove that his costs are in fact different from the guess. This approach is suitable for situations in which internal staff from R&D and the purchasing departments meet with the staff from the supplier's R&D, production, finance, sales, and product departments. This lever should be pulled aggressively, especially when previous discussions have come to a standstill.

## Tool 10: Supplier manufacturing analysis

This tool builds on improving processes at the supplier, whether by unblocking a production bottleneck, helping to lower investment cost, supporting a DtC session on-site, or seeking to reduce the waste and zero-quality level in production. Frequently, an external view will help suppliers to detect outages in processes that were not previously apparent. Figure 2.7 shows how productivity could be significantly increased by readjusting the load balance between workers on a manual assembly line at a supplier.

### Case study: Comprehensive cost reduction in the automotive industry

A project team helped one of the top global vehicle manufacturers when its cost pressure became almost unbearable. The company faced a difficult situation in two of the three global regions where it was present. It was suffering in Asia, where competitors reduced prices after they had implemented smart cost reduction programs; in the United States, a hefty price war had dramatically eroded margins. The manufacturer had already executed a series of mainly commercially focused initiatives, yet lacked the final step to reach the desired cost level.

In this situation, a six-phase CCR process was conducted to address the situation and help the company to take steps to reduce costs.

The first phase, which involved forming a solid, factual database, set the foundation for all later steps. Necessary data was collected and analyzed, calculation rules were agreed upon that were to be used for reporting savings later on, and cross-functional core-teams were established.

In the second phase, ideas were generated, and processes and cost structures were detailed, based on the results of the initial data analysis. Creativity and fresh ideas ruled thinking at this stage. It was important, in this phase, to create a spirit of trust among the teams and to foster belief in the success of the project. Evaluation and censorship of ideas and thinking were banned.

In the third phase, those creative, fresh ideas were examined for their feasibility. In several cases, this led to mining and working down through details and issues, and finally to an excellent understanding of the limitations and opportunities of a certain production step.

The fourth phase was used to compute and analyze ideas 'mathematically', and to build calculation and business models. In short, it quantified the ideas that had been generated in previous phases. By clearly separating idea creation from idea calculation, team members – depending on their mission – were able to keep their creative spirit or their feel for numbers.

Phase five, although a separate stage, actually spanned the entire twelve weeks of the project. Project management was the task of this module. During this phase, it was essential to ensure ongoing communication between all teams and to make sure that information was flowing freely between stakeholders and management. This module or phase also served as an escalation path when issues appeared to be getting out of control. It was also a good means by which to obtain swift decisions. As people who were not involved in the other areas undertook the work in this phase, political issues were kept apart from the financial and creative aspects.

In phase six of the project, action steps that had been created, calculated, and verified were carefully planned and organized. A thorough action plan with responsibilities, target dates, and controlling tools to monitor the savings implementation was created. Once carefully documented, the plan was put into action and steps that had been specifically agreed upon were implemented.

Looking at the time necessary to execute such comprehensive work, it may be said that a CCR project can be completed within ten to thirteen

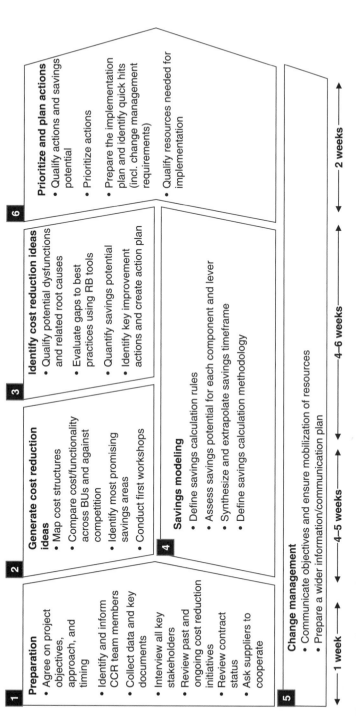

**Figure 2.8**  The CCR phase for diagnosis and drafting an action plan takes roughly 10–13 weeks

weeks, provided that a handful of people can commit 80–100 percent of their time to the project. The ability to complete the project within this period also requires strong support from top management. The timeframe is shown in Figure 2.8.

Looking at the work completed in each phase, the initial analysis phase is often seen as being lengthy and uncomfortable. In fact, this phase can be accomplished relatively quickly, provided that the required data (for instance, in an SAP system) can be retrieved. Usually, data always exists in modern companies. If accessing this data was previously unsuccessful, political reasons are to blame.

## Discussion and perspective

The number of competitors is increasing as more and more companies and suppliers enter the global market. This leads to relentless cost pressure. Products are needed that are sufficiently innovative to attract customers even at a certain price.

This chapter has illustrated how prices can be shaped during the R&D phase, and how they can be trimmed, optimized or tuned at a later stage, if necessary. By using a comprehensive DtC approach such as CCR, experienced managers are given the tools with which to optimize products and cost. The sooner managers become involved, the more that can be achieved without harsh and disruptive consequences.

The main advantage of the CCR approach is that it examines processes so carefully and in such detail that it will always detect a product's hidden cost drivers or bottlenecks in a production line. As the focus is quite wide, important aspects at the very front or very end of the process are also considered. Equipped with the right tools to optimize the cost side of a product, team members can be confident that their efforts will pay off.

## Further reading

Augustin, R. and Arndt, H. (2006) 'Produktion 2020 – Globale Netzwerke als Erfolgsfaktor', *Industrie Management*, 22.

Augustin, R. (2007) 'Not all roads lead to China', *Executive Review*, 1, ISSN 1617-4194.

Boutellier, R., Gassmann, O. and von Zedtwitz, M. (2000) *Managing Global Innovation: Uncovering the Secrets of Future Competitiveness*, 2nd revd edn. Berlin.

# CHAPTER 3

# Global development made successful: lessons learned by the automotive industry

*Jochen Gleisberg and Kai Bethlehem*

## Introduction

We are living in a globalized world. This, of course, places each individual as a buyer of goods in an advantageous position, yet it has also put enormous pressure on all companies, worldwide. In response to ever-increasing global competition, far-reaching change has taken place at many companies over the past decade. Hierarchical organizational structures, once very common throughout industry, have given place to decentralized leadership concepts and global company networks.

Leadership concepts that are both efficient and tried-and-tested are sought after as never before. The question as to whether or not to 'go international' has passed its use-by date. The issue today is, rather, how a global organization can best be managed.

During the first decades after World War II, internationalization rarely meant anything more than opening sales channels in neighboring countries. Today, globalization takes place on a much grander scale. Over the past years, an increasing number of companies has moved entire departments to locations abroad, or alternatively built up new departments in these locations. Even core functions, such as R&D, have not been spared. Decentralized or polycentric structures, worldwide cooperations between units, and strategic alliances with external partners around the globe have become everyday reality in many industries. This new environment poses significant challenges and is characterized by complexity and change.

As the automotive industry is at the forefront of this new environment, we will use it as an example to evaluate the trends and reasons that lead to international engagement. We then look at how an international or global R&D organization can best be managed in daily business. Lead engineering – one of the best-practice organizational concepts used in the running of global R&D activities – will then be presented, followed by a section showing how lead engineering might be implemented in a company. A real-life example for lead engineering implementation will also be given, before perspectives and discussion bring the chapter to a close.

## Global product development – *status quo* and trends

Customers of the automotive industry today are better informed and more demanding than ever before. Their expectations are high. They seek innovative, high-quality products that are ecological and individualized. At the same time, they expect these products to come with an affordable price tag. Delivering better and cheaper products is a major challenge for car manufacturers. Price and R&D capabilities are the keys to rising to this challenge.

While cost cutting has historically been the central focus of the purchasing department, it has long been an open secret that R&D plays an even greater role when it comes to lowering product cost. Decisions made in R&D departments determine up to 80 percent of the cost for production, quality and repair. This function also influences how much money is spent on testing, tooling and guarantee cases.

Global customers have led to R&D processes that span the world, which turns complexity up another notch. The potential advantages of a global R&D organization – making use of 'local' knowledge, fulfilling local content expectations, tapping low-cost workforces, and so forth – can be undermined if organizations are not well structured. Clearly defined workflows are essential.

## Organization is what really matters in a global world

As a 2007 study by Roland Berger Strategy Consultants, entitled 'Globalization of R&D – Drivers and Success Factors', shows, around 190,000 employees at original equipment manufacturers (OEMs) work on developing a rapidly increasing number of vehicle models. Today, about 90 percent of these employees are still based in Europe, North America or Japan. Yet, this number is expected to change, especially because today's fastest growing vehicle markets are located outside these regions. Employees at manufacturers in the 'old' countries will soon welcome new colleagues from China, India or Eastern Europe into the fold. As this happens, complexity increases even more.

The challenge will be organizing such complexity and properly managing globally connected development departments.

Unfortunately, stagnating R&D budgets – a typical scenario at many companies – do not help the situation. A company's survival chances are strengthened if it organizes its R&D in an optimal fashion and is able to use best practice approaches to ensure the greatest efficiency of employees. 'Doing more with less' is just as important as being able to serve local expectations with a globalized product.

The classic approaches used to reach these goals at present are:

- to bundle and standardize parts (a car, for example, can be considered as the sum of standardized modules)
- to set up innovative, efficient workflows and processes in order to increase output per employee
- to establish local development centers to offer 'localized' products that respect the individual taste of regional consumers.

## Tailoring global product development to ever evolving circumstances

The importance of the traditional home market is decreasing. A fully integrated, global development network – consisting of various technical centers, strategic alliances and fully linked in-lead suppliers – is appearing on the horizon.

With R&D becoming global, companies also need to revisit other departments. While global purchasing departments already exist, a global production set-up is just on the verge of becoming widespread reality. In such a set-up, standardized modules of a vehicle are produced in a few plants – sometimes even in one plant alone – and then shipped to various assembly plants around the world for use by either one manufacturer or an alliance of manufacturers.

Although standardization is critical, regional differences should be neither forgotten nor overlooked. Customers around the world continue to have different tastes. Moreover, legal and geographical differences call for products that are tailored to regional needs. Companies therefore need to differentiate between those parts that can be standardized internationally and those that need to be tailored according to regional requirements. 'Individualized standardization' is the term often used for this.

48

**Status quo:**
**Coordinated, multinational development**

**Coming decade:**
**Integrated, global development networks**

| | |
|---|---|
| **Global commonization** | • Low/medium, mostly selected components or platforms |
| **Global specialization** | • Low, with lots of redundancies in the network |
| **Global coordination** | • Coordinated development activities, yet strong local autonomy |
| **Emerging markets** | • Mostly 'me-toos' with limited development activities/capabilities |

| | |
|---|---|
| • High, with global platforms, systems/modules, components and technologies |
| • Medium/high, specialized technical centers with specialized development focus |
| • Fully integrated lead concepts with little regional autonomy |
| • At the same level in specialized technical areas |

**Figure 3.1** Trend towards integrated global networks

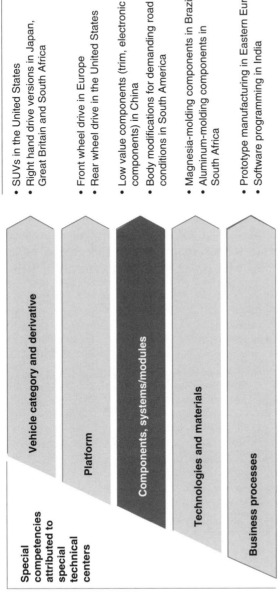

**Figure 3.2** Allocation of core competencies in a global R&D network

Ultimately, this will lead to regional technical centers that are responsible for developing and manufacturing globally required modules. Yet, these very same regional technical centers will also be in charge for making the adaptations necessary to sell a global product successfully in a regional market. In many cases, the allocation of global core competencies is centered on certain regional and 'special' requirements, as Figure 3.2 indicates.

There is no single perfect strategy for car manufacturers to follow when it comes to splitting R&D activities among sites. The choice depends on the targeted regional markets, the product portfolio, and the particular history of each technical center. Depending on the 'maturity' of a local technical center, various levels of responsibility might be allocated to the regions. In regional offices that have only been established very recently (often referred to at that stage as 'local antennas'), the focus will initially be on supporting sales activities, helping with technical issues or starting some kind of local assembly.

The next level of maturity and growth for such local antennas is to become a 'local satellite', with the key R&D responsibility still being held with the manufacturer's head office(s). The local satellite, however, might already be in charge of designing and executing modifications necessary to adjust a global product to local requirements. This kind of structure is typical for manufacturers with strong R&D competencies in their home

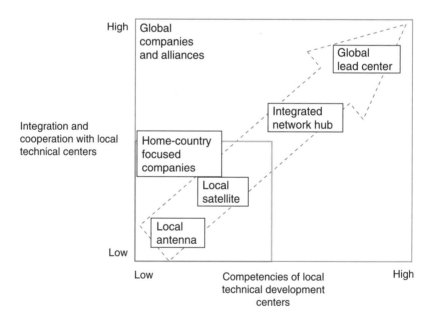

**Figure 3.3**   Integration and competencies of local technical centers

country – such as Porsche or BMW, both of whom still complete most of their R&D work in Germany.

Companies with a more international set-up tend to be structured as 'integrated network hubs' or 'global lead centers'. At an alliance such as Renault–Nissan, only the basic concept or lead car is developed centrally. Cars within respective family groups are finalized in individual regions. Regional centers are even allowed, sometimes, to develop individual, local derivates of the initial basic concept. Global lead centers, having reached the most mature state of the ladder, are often highly specialized in their areas of responsibility. They are also fully integrated within the global network, allowing them to steer and make use of R&D capacities worldwide. Modules for car systems are developed in these global lead centers and tested by a global team of engineers located at various technical centers around the world and managed by the respective global lead center.

When organizations have reached this state, there is typically no more home country. On the contrary, core competencies, manpower, and testing and development facilities are spread all over the world. The global lead centers act as gravity centers to steer and maneuver all R&D activities completed throughout the company. Through this combination of 'thinking globally and acting locally', it is possible for car manufacturers to reach the highest levels of standardization on a global scale, and to adapt universal products for regional markets when necessary.

There are numerous risks that need to be addressed in this kind of international R&D set-up. Coordinating and harmonizing all parallel R&D activities is essential. Only if all sub-systems, irrespective of where they are developed, fit seamlessly together to make a great product, can this whole set-up be as productive as initially expected. Knowledge management and exchange of ideas, data and technical information are essential to reach that goal. Creating the technical means to communicate is not, by itself, sufficient: the mindset counts, too. Ultimately, it is people that do business.

So, the questions are: Can this whole process be managed successfully? What is the best way to reach this goal? Lead engineering is probably the best answer to this kind of question.

## Lead engineering: the basic concept and how to implement it

Lead engineering is a concept developed for companies that have split their product development by regions or business areas, or for companies who develop goods in a strategic alliance. In these cases, R&D departments are

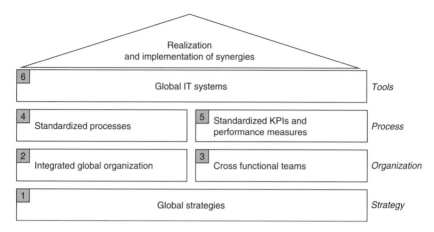

**Figure 3.4**   Six key elements of the lead engineering concept

not geographically united; this also applies to the people working on assigned topics. This situation usually makes synergies hard to tap.

This is even truer in global R&D set-ups, where not only physical distance, but also language and time zone differences can create significant communication barriers. This leads to two main questions: How can synergies be created and savings be realized? How might the need for standardization be reached, considering the urgency to develop individualized solutions for regional customers?

Figure 3.4 highlights the six key elements of the lead engineering concept.

## Global strategies

With lead engineering, universal solutions are developed that utilize common system architectures, components, and modular construction concepts. In other words, one common product strategy exists across business areas, alliance partners and regions. This point cannot be overemphasized. Without such common ground, all further activities will lack orientation and failure will be inevitable.

The creation of this one strategy is the central task of the nominated lead engineer. He is responsible for defining the best possible structure to split up all parts of a product and allocate them to individual work teams. It is his responsibility to find the best balance between standardization and regional or customer-related aspects. An overall strategy that acts as the backbone, providing orientation for all R&D activities, is therefore required. Sound overall strategies address savings targets, lifecycle, facelifts, number of variants, potential suppliers, and many other aspects from the very beginning of a project.

The lead engineer can be considered as the intellectual leader of a project. He mediates conflicting interests, and is the troubleshooter when projects threaten to verge off track. Depending on the size of a project, the lead engineer might be one very knowledgeable, well-recognized person, or a team of people sharing this task.

## Integrated global organization

One prerequisite for global development teams is a suitable integrated structure across all centers. The composition of multi-national teams should be so organized that hierarchical structures and areas of influence are clearly delineated. Individual engineers are then clustered in 'lead engineering groups' (LEGs): for example, they could be responsible for exhaust systems or a vehicle's braking concept. The early involvement of departments such as purchasing 'lead buyers' in such LEG activities is highly recommended.

For each individual LEG, the roles of leadership are then individually defined. There are three levels of coordination: mandate, leadership, and local execution.

**Mandate approach**   One business area or technical center takes over full responsibility for developing a certain component or module. In this case, all

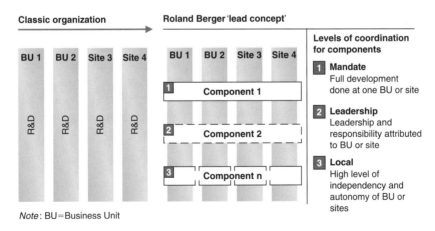

*Note*: BU=Business Unit

**Figure 3.5**   Three coordination options

required know-how is bundled in one competence center, and the involvement of people from other areas or regions is not required. This kind of organization is typically chosen for components that do not require any local adaptation, but can be used globally in one standardized execution.

**Leadership approach**  One region takes over the lead for a LEG, but engineers from other technical centers are fully integrated members who form one team. Each regional engineer contributes specialized, local knowledge and, possibly, takes on responsibility for defining localized executions of a basic global standard. This kind of set-up is especially effective when it mirrors a purchasing organization that also acts via lead and regional buyers.

**Local execution approach**  Development exclusively addresses regional needs for parts or variants with limited (or no) need for global standardization. Local development is undertaken by regional technical centers that exchange ideas with colleagues from other regions.

## Cross-functional teams

To speed up the innovation and development process, it is important to work on various aspects of a product development in parallel. This is true not only for engineering and developmental activities, but also for areas such as purchasing, production, marketing, and sales. Making sure representatives of such functions are included very early on in the development process is strongly recommended, as is their involvement in the work being done by the LEGs.

To achieve this, the LEGs are given central support by the lead engineer. He is linked to other departments (such as purchasing, production, and sales) through cross-functional teams, reflecting the whole value creation chain of a company. Ideally, the lead engineer assigns one representative from each of the purchasing, production, and sales departments to each LEG. For example, one lead buyer might be assigned to one or several LEGs, ensuring that all developmental activities are backed up by a supply base that will be able to support deliveries for a new vehicle on time.

## Standardized processes

Common processes are a prerequisite for harmonizing component and vehicle development, using efficient work plans and introducing quick decision-making routines. Equally as important are well-defined escalation and mediation processes, together with change management procedures and standardized data warehousing. The lead engineer is the driver of communication for his LEG. He will coordinate and harmonize the different activities within the group, and will make decisions wherever necessary. While doing so, he will respect the input of his counterparts to make sure that regional needs are well reflected in his decision and in the overall LEG strategy.

The lead engineer also sets the pace for the LEG, and is responsible for phasing the activities of his LEG into the overall development plan. To ensure that there is a common pace for the overall development process and to ensure that signals are well understood down to the most minor subproject, milestones and quality gates need to be standardized by the lead engineer and reflected in each LEG's work plan. The same is true for technical specifications, whereby common definitions and wording are required to make sure that parallel developments do not get out of control.

## Standardized KPIs and performance measures

To implement and anchor the described processes and structures in the organization, it is important to introduce common target setting and management by objectives (MbO) measures. Defining globally applicable key performance indicators (KPIs) has proven to be a very powerful tool to ensure top performance across the organization.

Common targets and measures need to be implemented for lead and local engineers and also, ideally, for their counterparts, lead and local buyers. While defining measures, it is essential that companies set quantitative targets (meeting of cost targets, deadlines, and so on) that can be easily quantified at set times. Setting only qualitative targets (such as 'adherence to global processes') is unsuitable for fostering trust and cooperation between international colleagues. Only if a transparent system of targets, KPIs, bonuses, and premiums is introduced, can companies expect people from all regions to cooperate.

## Global IT systems

Communication between global colleagues is of the utmost importance. Yet, good language skills and company-wide telephone books alone do not guarantee open communication channels. More important is the implementation of linked IT tools that allow for seamless data exchange and transparency between all sites. Attention should be paid to the compatibility of IT, unified groupware solutions and the sharing of knowledge.

**Compatibility of computer systems or data formats**   An example of this is introducing SAP company-wide as the sourcing and bookkeeping standard, or selecting one global CAD standard. Compromises might be necessary. It will probably be more important to install a system that enables barrier-free communication than to have a system that is the best of its kind, yet lacks communication and data transfer capabilities.

**Unified groupware solutions**   E-mail, e-conferencing, net meeting, data warehousing, and workflow management systems need to be standardized and harmonized in order to enable trouble-free, automated communication between all sites.

**Sharing of knowledge**   The creation of a know-how database in a central, unified format is recommended in order to make know-how accessible company-wide. The tendency to 'reinvent the wheel' must be avoided – but is, however, seen so often in large, international companies.

Since establishing a comprehensive data warehouse requires a significant amount of manpower, topics to be stored in the data warehouse should be screened, gathered and prioritized with care. IT solutions will never completely replace personal interaction between colleagues from different regions. One of the duties of lead engineers is to create the time for periodical group reviews or meetings that address overall work progress and upcoming challenges. Recognizing and rewarding success in a face-to-face context is a duty, too.

## Implementing the lead engineering concept

All six key elements of the lead engineering concept need to be individually adapted when being implementing at a company, or in an alliance or R&D network. To ease that adaptation, companies should discriminate between the short, medium and longer-term steps that need to be taken.

In the short term, the logic of a product's structure – separation into modules, systems, sub-systems and parts – needs to be standardized. This should always be the very first step. Only if the perimeter/separation of a sub-system is commonly defined, is it possible to work in parallel on sub-systems without interfering with the adjacent sub-systems. For example, does a car-radio include the connection wires to the loudspeakers or do they belong to the dashboard or even the loudspeaker/amplifier/sound system module? Based on this common understanding and structure of a system, LEGs will be able to their work to maximum efficiency.

In the medium term, harmonizing business processes and the organization of departments should be the primary goal. Escalation paths need to be defined to permit rapid decision-making when conflicts arise. The introduction of standard targets and balanced scorecards is the best means by which to support the harmonization process.

In the longer term, a vision should exist to harmonize all business processes and to introduce standardized IT solutions. Departments such as purchasing and sales also need to be reorganized to ensure that they reflect, at least to some degree, the R&D organization's common structures.

All of the above steps must be fully backed by the top management and the HR department. Top management will need to take active steps to steer, lead and communicate all changes, and to express clearly the goals that will be reached because of the reorganization. In parallel with the steps taken by the top management, the HR department should work out a detailed personnel plan that includes educational aspects for all employees. Cultural training to help employees avoid culture clash is particularly helpful in the early stages of a newly established international partnership or alliance. Furthermore, rotation programs provide staff with a greater understanding and deeper knowledge of their new partners. To ensure productive and amicable interaction company-wide, KPIs, MbO programs, bonuses, and premiums need to be aligned.

There is a price to pay for implementing the lead engineering concept. Accomplishing it will take time and effort. It cannot be tackled as a secondary exercise. The concept cannot be implemented successfully without detailed planning, sufficient budget and the full-scale involvement of the top management. Political maneuverings can easily topple the lead engineering concept, if the proper support is not given from the beginning.

## Lead engineering in real life

Roland Berger designed, adapted and implemented the lead engineering concept at one of the world's major vehicle manufacturers, which has three business units on three continents. Each of the three business units produces similar products with their own individual R&D departments. The expectations for savings through the introduction of a lead engineering concept were high, as the vehicle manufacturer expected substantial savings to occur by unifying and rationalizing the R&D workforce.

## Example: The automotive industry

In a first preparatory step, cross-functional 'pilot' project teams were defined, including representatives from the engineering and purchasing functions. These teams were then asked to analyze the technical similarities between the different products manufactured and to compare cost-per-function data for certain selected components. Saving potential was calculated and the implementation of changes commenced.

As the savings implementation in these areas was convincing, the manufacturer decided to move beyond the 'pilot' teams and to roll out this kind of core-team structure through all of its R&D organizations around the globe, which proved to be a very ambitious task. Different strategies, concepts, technologies, materials, and philosophies had to be compared, harmonized, and adapted before a lead engineering concept could be implemented. This was to be integrated with the lead buying organization already in place.

The client agreed to a common product structure, which divided vehicles into groups of functional systems and components. Each system and component was assigned to a permanent core team of three engineers, one from each business unit. One of the engineers acted as a lead engineer and was responsible for defining the overall strategy, developing a modular construction system in line with the overall system architectures. His task was also to control diversity, technical concepts, and the applications that were within his scope of responsibility.

To institutionalize the integrated approach between lead engineering and lead buying, the lead buyer was made a permanent member of the lead engineering team. Experts from other functions (such as the product planning, sales, and legal departments) joined the teams as required.

Major savings could be achieved with the integrated lead buying and lead engineering approach. In addition to commercial savings, up to 9 percent of purchasing volume could be reduced via technical modifications and standardization. Additionally, between 15 percent and 40 percent of the number of parts per component or system could be eliminated, and the number of suppliers was finally reduced by 30 percent.

The integrated lead engineering/lead buying approach convinced the client of its efficacy. 'The introduction of this integrated concept with the aligned organization provides us with a competitive edge that has to date been unique in the history of our company', he said.

## Outlook

In a world of multinational companies, cross-country alliances and strategic partnerships between manufacturers from all regions of the world, the lead engineering approach has proven to be a valuable concept. It enables companies to channel communication, improve internal cooperation and steer global development. In the hurly-burly of change, it provides guidelines and orientation, helps companies tap synergies within global R&D structures, and enables the rapid realization of savings.

While the lead engineering concept acts as a compass for companies to navigate an ever-changing environment, the concept itself forces change upon the organization. The previous authority of historically grown structures, home turfs, and spheres of political influence are no longer valid. The willingness to embrace this change is decisive for the success or failure of the project.

Looking at the automotive industry, lead engineering will be a necessary concept in the years to come. It is expected that up to 60 percent of value created during the production of a vehicle will, in the future, be done at OEMs, so these need to be increasingly linked and integrated within the vehicle manufacturers. Borders between OEMs and suppliers will become increasingly invisible, with competencies spread between the two. IT systems will allow for seamless integration and barrier free communication. Yet, these interactions need to be managed. Chaos and failure will result when communication and processes are not managed properly. Lead engineering has already proven its value in the automotive industry.

Without a doubt, other industries will benefit from the lessons that car manufacturers have already learned.

### Further reading

Aberdeen Group (ed.) (2005) 'The Global Product Design Benchmark Report: Managing Complexity as Product Design Goes Global'. Boston.

Fecht, N. (2005) 'Global Footprint statt Nomadentum', *Automobil Produktion*, 7: 52–3.

Jürgens, U. (ed.) (2000) *New Product Development and Production Networks: Global Industrial Experience*. Berlin.

Roland Berger Strategy Consultants (2007) 'Solving the Powertrain Challenge'. Stuttgart.

Roland Berger Strategy Consultants (2007) 'Globalization of R&D – Drivers and Success Factors'. Stuttgart.

Zetzl, R. (2004) 'Engineering Collaboration in der Produktentstehung: Mehr Wertschöpfung aus besserer Zusammenarbeit', *ZWF – Zeitschrift für wirtschaftlichen Fabrikbetrieb* 99, 12: 698–701.

# CHAPTER 4

# Success factors and levers for best practice in innovation management

*Stefan Pötzl, Thomas Kohr and*
*Michael Zollenkop*

## Introduction

Innovation is becoming increasingly important for companies in many industries. Companies today are often so dependent on innovation that, if they were to fail to bring products to market, they would risk losing substantial market share at a rapid pace. Phonak, the Swiss producer of hearing devices, considered a 'hidden champion', makes 65 percent of its turnover with products it has brought to market in the last two years. This philosophy applies in more traditional industries, too. For example, Wittenstein, a German producer of gearboxes, generates 85 percent of its turnover with products fewer than five years old. To survive global competition, most companies simply have to innovate.

The question is whether it pays off. Are innovative companies really more successful than others? The answer is 'yes'. According to a sector report on innovation published in 2006 by the Centre for European Economic Research, ZEW, companies with a young product portfolio have a significantly higher return on sales. This trend is consistent across all industries. The reason for this is clear: companies with many innovations either lead a whole market segment or, at least, dominate their 'niche'. This is more profitable than the average me-too or mass markets, particularly where companies can only rehash what other companies have already created. Most companies have recognized this fact and have made 'being innovative' part of their strategy. Nevertheless, not all companies are equally successful in turning their target into reality. Many innovations continue to fail.

This chapter puts the spotlight on the success factors for innovation and shows how the best companies tackle them. We will also talk about an

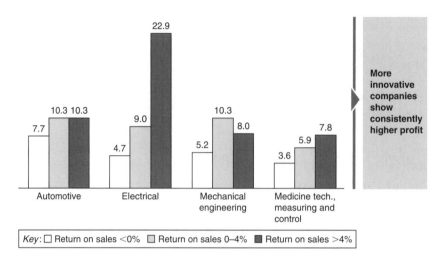

**Figure 4.1** Share of sales with original product innovation in different industries (%)
*Source*: Center for European Economic Research (ZEW), Sector Report, 'Innovation', May 2006.

innovation toolbox developed by Roland Berger, which is a proven set of tools and levers to be applied during the different phases of a development project. We will also discuss a project during which this toolbox was successfully used.

## The challenge of innovation: how to manage it in a business context

In most companies, idea creation is not a problem. Most employees have excellent ideas. The problem is to distinguish between good and mediocre ideas, and how to foster the one and shelve the other.

Based on our experience, the major challenges in innovation management are:

- Prioritizing the right ideas and allocating the right level of resources
- Conducting the correct 'make-or-buy' decisions in innovation
- Meeting shrinking development budgets
- Realizing shorter development lead times
- Maintaining increasingly high quality standards
- Providing a more customized product portfolio with more variants

- Successfully managing market launches
- Meeting customer requirements regarding function and price.

During the innovation process, focus on the customer is often lost. While customer involvement is usually high in the early and late phases of development projects – when defining the first specifications and launching the product – involvement dries up during the detailing phase and the various change procedures.

A survey amongst R&D leaders in mechanical engineering conducted recently by Roland Berger confirms this problem. When asked about the major reasons for failed innovation, 38 percent ranked 'missed market requirements – the technically perfect solution' in first position (see Figure 4.2). Other answers, especially the 'me-too product' or 'products with competitive disadvantages', also hint at missed customer needs. Far too often, technical perfection has the upper hand, leading to over-specification and overly expensive products.

The right approach would be to:

- undertake a clear analysis of the functions required by the customer
- define their value to the customer and their target cost
- design the product features accordingly.

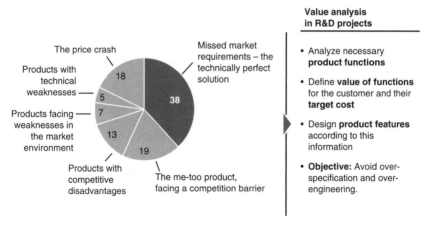

**Figure 4.2**   Innovation in the mechanical engineering industry – failure reasons in commercialization (% of answers)
*Source*: Survey among R&D leaders in mechanical engineering conducted by Cooper–Roland Berger.

This process is called value analysis. Involving the customer is vital.

Examples of failed innovations are endless. One of the most spectacular examples is the aircraft Airbus A380 whose market introduction was delayed by almost two years. The financial damage to EADS, the parent company of Airbus, was substantial. It suffered from significant market capitalization loss, increased development cost, delayed and lost sales, penalty payments and delayed break-even not only of the A380, but also of other projects. The damage to reputation and customer trust is much harder to quantify but most definitely not of minor importance.

### Example: Airbus A380

The heart of the problem was a technical issue: construction errors in electrical wiring. Different computer aided design (CAD) systems in the engineering sites in France, Germany and Spain are a probable reason for the wrong construction. Inadequately identified responsibilities in the complex R&D network and limited competence to handle smaller problems on a working level created the real problem. The internal coordination process was extensive and time-consuming, and the existing company culture led to many people not addressing issues rather than dealing with them. Thus, the project leaders were often not informed of a problem until very late in the product-creation process; the problem was left to escalate for too long and a solution was not defined early enough.

Solving the technical issue was cumbersome, as engineering data had to be manually converted between the different CAD systems, causing a further delay of several weeks. Finally, production of the correct electrical wires started much too late and production capacity could not be increased sufficiently to make up for the delay. To put it in a nutshell: innovation management at Airbus failed, causing the company significant damage.

Another industry that is often in the media due to problems in the innovation process is the automotive industry. Almost every original equipment manufacturer (OEM) has had to conduct costly safety recalls, which damage reputation. The reasons for this become clearer when one looks more closely at how innovation performance requirements have changed in the past years (see Figure 4.3). Model proliferation is tremendous. Each year, increasing numbers of niche models, each bearing a long

Textbox 4.1
Airbus A380

The Airbus A380 is one of the most prestigious industrial projects ever – the largest commercial aircraft in the world, boosting the efficiency of passenger transport. On January 18, 2005, Airbus introduced the A380 to the public. The initial delivery date had been planned for March 2006, to Singapore Airlines. Technical problems led to various delays. The first aircraft was finally delivered in October 2007. After announcing another major delay in October 2006, shares of EADS (the parent company of Airbus) dropped short-term by 10 percent, according to a report in the Swiss newspaper *NZZ*. Increased development cost, penalty payments and lost orders were the consequence. Overall, Airbus estimates the additional cost caused by the delay at roughly €5 billion. In addition, the development of the A350 is significantly affected due to engineering capacities bound for the A380. Today, the company is still struggling to recover from both the financial impact and the damage to its image.

list of equipment options, are introduced on the market. At the same time, development lead times – from concept approval to the commencement of production– have shrunk. This has happened even though R&D capacity is stable. Suppliers have become more involved in development as OEMs focus on their core competencies, but also the efficiency of OEMs has risen significantly. Intelligent product architectures, a clear development organization with defined cross-functional processes, and application of virtual engineering methods are just some of the issues OEMs have tackled.

Despite these advancements, too many product launches continue to fail. Mercedes also experienced this with its last E-class model. After the launch of the new model in 2002, various technical problems occurred. The most critical one affected an innovative electro-hydraulic braking system. Some 1.3 million vehicles had to be recalled at a cost estimated at €325 million. Sales for the E-class, the most profitable Mercedes model for years, dropped drastically and did not recover for several years. The company even considered renaming the new model in an attempt to avoid long-term damage.

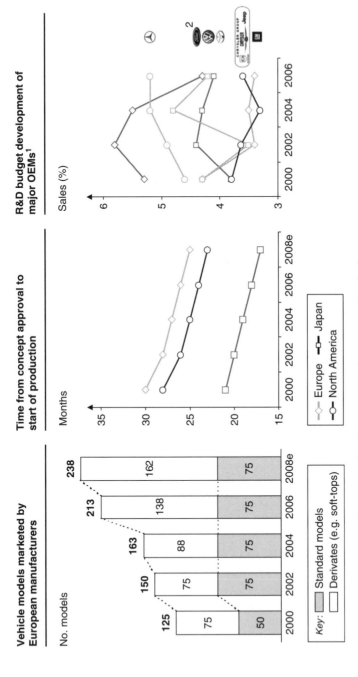

**Vehicle models marketed by European manufacturers**

No. models

**Time from concept approval to start of production**

Months

**R&D budget development of major OEMs[1]**

Sales (%)

Key: Standard models
Derivates (e.g. soft-tops)

Europe  Japan  North America

**Figure 4.3** Innovation performance development in the automotive industry
*Notes:* 1 Includes product development, corporate research.
2 Without financial services.

Yet, the company reacted: Daimler is the first OEM to date to have developed a series vehicle – its new Mercedes C-class – using a fully integrated digital prototype. By simulating all major characteristics of the vehicle, this prototype helps save development time, solves goal conflicts and enables the company to test the overall vehicle concept in a virtual stage. In the case of the C-class, not only crash safety and passenger protection have been simulated and tested with the digital prototype, but also comfort (noise, vibration, roll-off), operational stability, energy management, air conditioning, and aerodynamics. These virtual methods have existed, in theory, for several years. However, they were not systematically applied in that integrated form until the C-class. IT systems performance is still a critical aspect here.

Failed innovations, in most cases, are notched up to wrong decisions and the behavior of individuals: this analysis is too easy. Individual mistakes are made in all environments. It is the task of the innovation management system to minimize mistakes, as far as possible, and to make sure when something goes wrong that the issue is detected early – guaranteeing that the problem can be solved in the most efficient way.

So, what distinguishes strong from weak innovation management? What can companies learn from the best in innovation management? According to our analysis and experience drawn from various projects, the following criteria are important:

- Consistency – innovation strategy, performance targets, and the necessary enablers need to be aligned
- Holistic approach – innovation organization, innovation process, supporting systems/tools, and innovation culture need to be considered
- Cross-functional approach – innovation is not a pure R&D issue, all functions need to be involved.

## Roland Berger Innovation Toolbox

The Innovation Toolbox contains all the tools needed to ensure that the criteria listed above can be fulfilled. It addresses all aspects of innovation management with a specific set of levers and enablers that can be applied flexibly according to the company and its specific business situation. The toolbox consists of an integrated set of strategy, performance, and enabler tools.

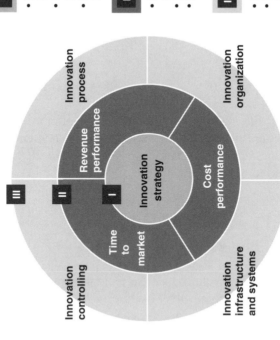

**Innovation strategy**

- Links innovation initiatives to corporate strategy and its targets
- Gives clear guidance on expectations and innovation performance targets
- Determines innovation effectiveness (doing the right things)

**Innovation performance**

- Covers all aspects of value creation; that is revenue optimization, cost optimization, and time-to-market
- Describes a comprehensive set of innovation levers
- Determines innovation efficiency (doing things right)

**Innovation enablers**

- Foster the sustainability of innovation optimization
- Describe preconditions for innovation effectiveness and efficiency

**Figure 4.4** Roland Berger Innovation Toolbox

## Innovation strategy

Innovation strategy should be viewed as the starting point for all innovation activities. Ideally, it is derived from corporate strategy, thus ensuring a close link with the intended corporate development. Corporate strategy sets the scope of action by defining parameters such as future market positioning, corporate growth targets or targeted future product portfolio. Innovation strategy defines the targets and key guidelines for innovation activities, including parameters for:

• The innovation project portfolio
• The innovation value-added
• The prioritization of projects with respect to financial and human resources
• Key performance indicators (KPIs) for innovation activities.

Innovation strategy ensures that the focus is set on the right issues, directing all corporate innovation activities into the most effective areas.

## Innovation performance

Innovation performance – the second tool for successful innovation management – is crucial for making innovation activities efficient. The Innovation Toolbox contains a comprehensive set of thirty levers with which to optimize performance with regard to revenues, cost, and time-to-market. In a development or innovation project, levers are selected based on their ability to bring the right sort of change for a particular company. First, the relevant levers are determined according to current weaknesses in innovation management and the project target. Second, the optimal portfolio of levers is selected based on the scope of changes and the resources available to apply them.

Both the potential effect and the effort required to apply levers vary widely. In general, the higher the effect and the lower the effort, the more quickly the optimization measures should be tackled (quick wins). The higher the effects and the effort of application, the more management attention is required to select and implement the levers. For the ratio of effect and effort, industry characteristics and company-specific circumstances need to be considered. A general overview is provided in Figure 4.5.

**Revenue performance levers** aim at creating higher rates of innovation compared with a turnover increase reached via innovation. The most

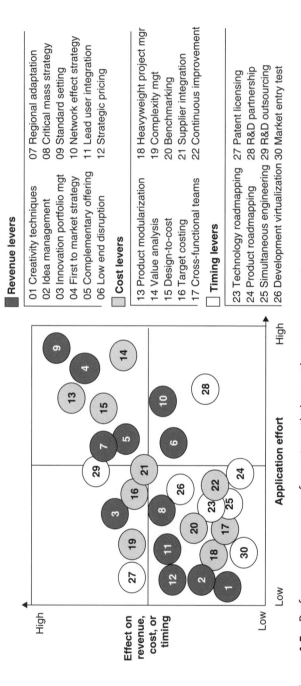

**Figure 4.5** Performance measures for systematic innovation management

powerful levers include 'innovation portfolio management' and 'first-to-market strategy'. Balancing the project portfolio in terms of revenue potential, cost, risks, and timing of market entry is vital for foreseeing future cash flows and revenue development. This is the goal of the 'innovation portfolio management' lever. The lever 'first-to-market strategy', on the other hand, is crucial for winning early adopters of an innovation as customers. This often creates the basis for market leadership in the long term. Further important revenue performance levers include modifying and tailoring the portfolio to additional markets (new regional markets, low-end markets such as emerging or developing countries, or complementary products for existing markets) and measures for the diffusion and adoption of innovation (for reaching critical mass rapidly, setting standards, and creating external network effects).

**Cost performance levers** aim at generating innovation more cost efficiently. Here, product modularization (with toolkits for product modules) and complexity or product variant management play an important role to ensure that companies avoid reinventing the wheel in product development. All modules lacking the potential for differentiation, which is appreciated by customers, need to be examined and evaluated carefully so that development cost can be allocated to a higher number of products, thus reducing the cost burden per unit. Moreover, methods such as value analyses, design-to-cost, and target costing contribute to cost efficiency by scrutinizing either the value to customers of certain product functions or by challenging the intended technical solution for those functions.

**Timing related levers** form the third performance category. In innovation management and product development, timing is crucial. On the one hand, time-related issues are often more important than cost-related aspects since timing – especially of market entry – largely determines the remaining time within the product lifecycle for amortizing the incurred development cost. Time saving technologies such as simultaneous engineering or virtualization of development processes (virtual prototyping or testing, for instance) might be decisive for the overall commercial success of an innovation project. Levers – such as partnerships in R&D, or even outsourcing part of the development work – also need to be considered for time-efficient product development. On the other hand, the right timing often depends on external events. Windows of opportunity need to be grasped for optimum success. Technological maturity, the development of market requirements or competitor action need to be monitored in order to determine the appropriate point for market launch, product differentiation or changes in pricing strategy. Technology and product roadmaps based on weak signals external to the company and on company specific scenario planning are important levers for the best possible preparation in terms of timing.

## Innovation enablers

Innovation enablers, the third category of tools, are a prerequisite to ensure performance optimization is effective and sustainable in the long term. The Innovation Toolbox examines issues and success factors in four dimensions:

- Innovation process – that is, a quality gate system, effective interface descriptions and coordination between the concerned corporate functions and departments in product development
- Structural organization – that is, level of (de-)centralization and business unit specific activities, and the global footprint for product development
- Infrastructure and systems – that is, tools such as CAD, virtualization techniques, and rapid prototyping
- Innovation controlling – that is, innovation KPIs, an innovation scorecard, and project management tools for individual projects.

The toolbox is a treasure trove of levers, success factors, and cross industry project experience that enables us to combine the appropriate actions for any innovation-related challenge a company might face – whether it be on corporate or on business unit level – and for all stages in product development. We show how the toolbox works in the following case study.

### Case study: 'Innovation to cash' at a leading European utility company

Roland Berger has successfully applied the Innovation Toolbox in various projects. This approach was used recently when working with a leading European utility company. The company had already established the framework for successful innovation management. A Corporate Innovation unit had been installed that was responsible for managing and driving innovation in the group. The internal collaboration with the three business units had been roughly defined, an external network to suppliers and universities had been structured in a dedicated forum, and a group-wide technology plan had been established.

The questions, however, were:

- Are the current innovation efforts focused on value?
- What does the 'ideal project portfolio' look like?
- What is the ideal innovation process and innovation management methodology to capture the full value of innovation?

The core question was, in fact, how innovation could be used to a maximum extent to reduce the company's cash-out for the distribution business.

In the first phase, the project team carried out an audit of the existing situation. The team examined the current innovation process and analyzed the existing innovation portfolio, with a special focus on the distribution business unit. External benchmarking, focusing on both the innovation processes and portfolio, completed the diagnosis. In the second phase of redefinition, the Innovation Toolbox played a major role. Several levers were selected and customized to the client's situation, in order to establish and steer an entire innovation portfolio and manage innovation projects. Recommendations on how to adjust the current innovation portfolio with regard to relevant technologies and focus areas were worked out. The third and final project phase focused on defining an implementation plan for the defined concept.

The results of the audit phase showed clear deficits in the innovation process:

- No clear trigger for idea evaluation and prioritization
- No formal project set-up; projects started by coincidence or by CEO's order
- No standard project planning and reporting, each project 'reinvents the wheel'
- Missing commercial focus of projects – for example, no business case
- Missing checkpoints and deliverables/KPIs along the innovation process
- No clear decision point for implementation/investment, despite decisions about huge investment as a result of innovation projects
- No systematic review of project success and gathering of lessons learned.

Overall, the company lacked a systematic way to manage and materialize on innovations.

Using the Innovation Toolbox, the project team defined a holistic concept of innovation management, which is shown in Figure 4.6. At the heart of the concept is the quality gate method for managing projects. A structure of six quality gates was introduced that clearly defined the major decision points in an innovation project, including

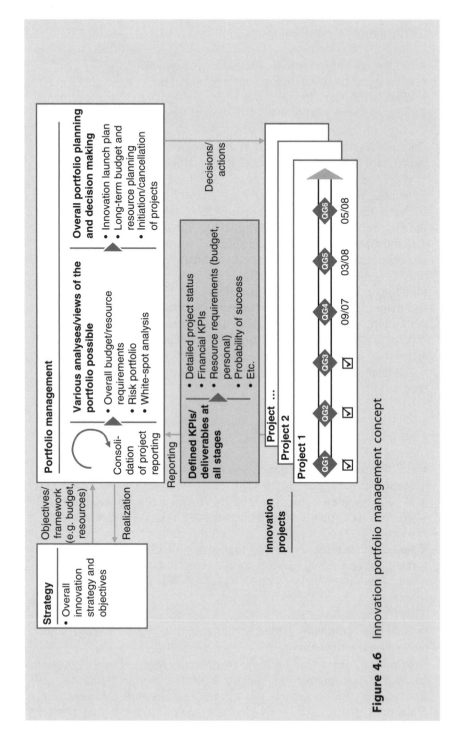

**Figure 4.6** Innovation portfolio management concept

detailed deliverables. Standardized reporting templates were created that today form the basis for consolidated innovation portfolio reporting. These standardized inputs from the projects, which can be led either by the Corporate Innovation unit or another business unit, form the basis for a portfolio management function. This should become one of the core functions of the Corporate Innovation unit. This function is responsible not only for portfolio reporting, but also for the active steering of the launch and cancellation of projects, and for regularly releasing the corporate innovation launch plan – an item that is significantly important for shareholders.

For the analysis of the innovation portfolio itself, the first step was to map the entire innovation portfolio in the company, analyze the alignment of the innovation projects with the strategically set priorities, and check the impact of the projects in relation to the big cash-out blocks.

The results of the analysis were surprising to everyone. The running projects neither aligned with the strategic objectives, nor did they systematically address the major spend blocks. Projects with the highest budgets focused on very little optimization potential, whereas very significant fields of cash-out had not been addressed systematically at all. A missing portfolio management function was clearly responsible for this situation.

Based on these results, a plan was introduced to shift the focus from pure asset-driven innovations to process items such as maintenance or breakdown processes, which had not been considered before.

In the final phase of the project, a detailed implementation process was defined. The quality gate structure to be implemented across all business units was demonstrated in pilot projects. The adjustment of the current innovation portfolio in distribution was started immediately, focusing on the major innovation projects first.

Overall the project was a tremendous success. The Innovation Toolbox supported the project team in the complete redefinition of innovation management and the innovation portfolio of a major European utility company in barely three months.

## Outlook

The existence of many companies is closely linked to their ability to manage innovation successfully. Companies are obliged to innovate, and experience shows that there is a clear correlation between a company's innovation performance and its commercial success. Managing innovation on a global scale is vital to remaining a first league player.

## Textbox 4.2
## Globalization of R&D – success factors

Innovations play a key role in helping companies to remain competitive and to grow in a globalized economy. To meet customer requirements on a global scale and to harness all available know-how and technologies, companies need to internationalize their innovation process. This often involves globalizing R&D activities.

Roland Berger Strategy Consultants conducted a study, together with the ESB Research Institute, which examines the strategic aspects of R&D relocation. Over 100 companies from six different industries were surveyed and additional expert interviews of key players in these industries were conducted. Five guiding questions formed the basis of the survey:

1 What drives companies in globalizing their R&D?
2 How do companies pick their R&D locations?
3 How do companies organize their R&D network?
4 What tools do companies apply for managing the global R&D process?
5 How do companies communicate and exchange know-how globally?

Based on the degree of importance of access to the market and technology, companies can be grouped into four clusters: globalization leaders, global marketers, technology hunters, and opportunistic players.

**Globalization leaders** view access to the market and to technology as being of equally high importance. They create a network of central research and local development centers. Activities are coordinated throughout the entire global R&D network.

**Global marketers** view access to the market as being more important than access to technology. They generate basic innovations and product platforms in global research centers. These are transformed into products for local markets in local development centers.

**Technology hunters** view access to technology as the main reason for globalization. They focus R&D efforts on a small number of global research centers that specialize in individual research areas. Local customization of products is limited.

**Opportunity players** are not driven to globalize R&D systematically but, rather, base their globalization policy on specific and individual business requirements. They drive their R&D efforts mainly out of their home base. Global efforts are limited and typically driven by individual client or product requirements.

Six success factors could be distilled from the information gathered:

1 **Start from corporate R&D strategy**. Companies need to assess whether it is technology, market access or opportunistic cost reduction that drives the globalization of R&D.
2 **Concentrate technological know-how as much as possible**. Leveraging global know-how is more effective when a critical mass is reached in single places. Bundling of know-how in one place is necessary.
3 **Develop market know-how in decentralized units**. Local knowledge requires a certain degree of autonomy to be an effective innovation driver. Central units should provide basic research, the overall strategy, and should monitor R&D activities.
4 **Be pragmatic in applying R&D management methods**. Tools for managing R&D processes – such as stage gate or quality gate processes, R&D cycles, project controlling or IT platforms – are necessary in any global R&D, and have become standard in most companies.
5 **Manage burdens of historical growth**. R&D networks need active management. Historically, grown networks are seldom efficient if the organizational structure is not planned or controlled according to the corporate strategy. Clear directions and guidelines are necessary.
6 **Implement organizational changes carefully**. Transition and change processes need to be handled carefully to avoid losing key personnel. Know-how is predominantly bound to people. Radical changes can make it more difficult to retain experts and the carriers of knowledge.

Innovation clearly has to be on the agenda of every CEO. It has to involve all areas of a company, not merely the R&D department. The good news is that there is a proven set of tools – the Innovation Toolbox – that might help to improve the efficiency of innovation projects.

## Further reading

Heidtmann, Volker (2007) 'Gewusst wo! Forschung und Entwicklung passgenau globalisieren', in Roland Berger Strategy Consultants, *Executive Review*, 2: 18–23.

Kerka, Friedrich, Kriegesmann, Bernd, Schwering, Markus G. and Happich, Jan (2006) *'Big Ideas' erkennen und Flops vermeiden – dreistufige Bewertung von Innovationsideen.* Institut für angewandte Innovationsforschung e.V. (iAi), Bochum.

Leysieffer, Hans (2005) *Innovationsmanagement bei der Phonak AG.* Vortrag Swiss Innovation Kongress 2005, http://www.zpeportal.ethz. ch/events/ swissinnovation/downloads.

Roland Berger Strategy Consultants (2006) 'Innovation in Mechanical Engineering – Failure Reasons in Commercialization', Survey among persons in charge of R&D in mechanical engineering.

Roland Berger Strategy Consultants (2007) 'Globalization of R&D – Drivers and Success Factors'. Study, ESB Research Institute, Reutlingen University, June.

Zentrum für Europäische Wirtschaftsforschung GmbH (ZEW) (2006) *ZEW Branchenreport Innovationen Elektroindustrie, Fahrzeugbau, Medizin-/Mess-/ Steuertechnik, Optik, Maschinenbau.* Jahrg 13, 2, May.

# CHAPTER 5

# Smart engineering processes: 'made in Japan'

## Ken Mori and Satoshi Nagashima

## Introduction

When people hear 'operations excellence in Japan', manufacturing inno-vations instantly spring to mind. This is not surprising considering the revolutionary concepts 'just in time', 'cell manufacturing', and 'total quality control', all of which bear a Japanese hallmark. Operations excellence in Japan, however, is not limited to manufacturing but spreads into other areas, such as cost control, supplier management, and product development too. This article concentrates on tried-and-tested product development strategies that originated in Japan, such as front loading, lead time reduction, and cost planning. The focus is turned sharply on the automotive industry, the birthplace of these groundbreaking R&D organizational processes.

To understand operations excellence in product development in Japan, we have to take a short step back into history. In the early 1990s, two professors – Dr Takahiro Fujimoto and Dr Kim Clark – analyzed the efficiency of product development at various automotive manufacturers in Europe, North America and Japan. They found that Japanese firms had significantly shorter lead times, a lower defect level, and better manufacturability than their competitors in these other regions. According to the professors, one of the reasons for the high efficiency of Japanese firms was the process led by what they called 'heavy weight product managers' (HWPM).

The product development organization of all automotive manufacturers in Japan comprises functional departments such as design, body, chassis, power train, electronics, and testing. The importance of the HWPM becomes clear when one realizes that if those functional organizations are considered as the vertical axis, then the HWPM is the horizontal axis. An HWPM is completely responsible for a vehicle model and works closely

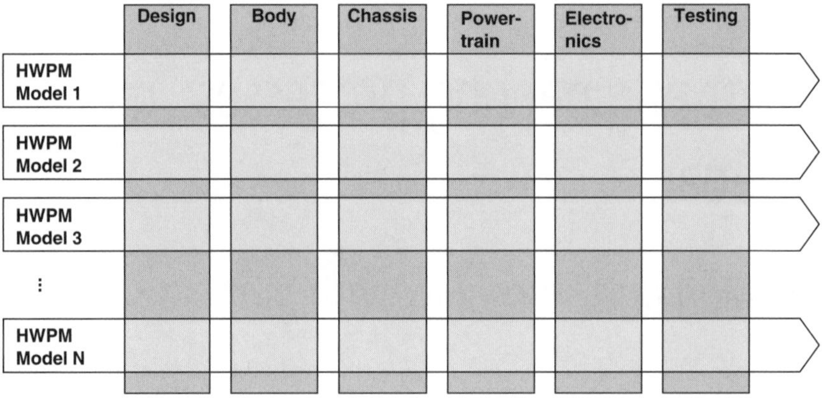

| | Design | Body | Chassis | Power-train | Electro-nics | Testing | |
|---|---|---|---|---|---|---|---|
| HWPM Model 1 | | | | | | | |
| HWPM Model 2 | | | | | | | |
| HWPM Model 3 | | | | | | | |
| ⋮ | | | | | | | |
| HWPM Model N | | | | | | | |

**Figure 5.1**  Matrix organization

with all of the functional organizations, even though he does not belong to any of those functional departments. This is a version of what is known as matrix organization, shown in Figure 5.1. By integrating different functions such as design engineering, manufacturing engineering and marketing, the HWPM facilitates the speedy completion of a project.

## History of HWPM

It is generally accepted that Toyota was the first company to introduce the concept of HWPM. An earlier form of these product manager heavy-weights had existed at Toyota since 1949, when President Kiichiro Toyoda appointed Kenya Nakamura to the position of *Shusa* (chief) after having decided to develop a pure Japanese car. 'A *Shusa* is the representative of the President and has the ultimate responsibility for developing a new vehicle,' the President said as he inducted Kenya Nakamura to this elevated position. From its very inception, the position of HWPM has been synonymous with ultimate responsibility. Holders of this position are granted enormous power from top management.

What Nakamura did once he was appointed as *Shusa* characterizes product development in Japan to this day. He listened to potential users. Since taxi companies were the typical customers of passenger cars in 1949, Nakamura visited them and spoke directly with the drivers to find out their needs. This practice is still alive at Toyota and other automotive firms in Japan. An HWPM always speaks with potential customers, and sometimes even lives with them to gain a thorough understanding of their real – but often hidden – needs and requirements.

Toyota continued to use these special product managers to develop other cars, and a matrix organization was created. Rather than having the matrix organization designed by top management, organizational specialists, or even management consultants, it was created naturally by recreating Kenya Nakamura's team in the functionally formed organizations. Learning from Toyota, the product development organizations at all Japanese automotive manufacturers now have a similar set-up.

## How can the HWPM be successful?

Although the shape of the organization resembles a matrix, the organization concept underpinning Japanese automotive companies is a little different from typical matrix organizations elsewhere. A member of a matrix organization generally reports to two bosses. Yet, engineers at Japanese automotive companies report officially to their functional department heads only. They do not report to the HWPM.

The HWPM has his own small team, often consisting of about ten engineers. The HWPM does not have authority over HR issues such as performance evaluation or promotion decisions. Despite this, he still needs to be able to lead the vehicle development program and manage hundreds of engineers. How is this possible? There are four main factors.

**Strong empowerment by top management**   The president of Toyota set the standard when he bestowed immense power on his *Shusa*. All other Japanese automotive companies followed that pattern. Many western automotive firms, particularly American ones, later introduced the HWPM concept. Unfortunately, they rarely attained their objective of improving product development practices. Part of the reason for their failure rests with power: HWPMs in the United States were not given sufficient clout by top management. Without this, they could not reach the desired goals.

The HWPM has the ultimate responsibility for each program's results, and he is the ultimate authority on key decisions. An engineer who officially reports to his functional head and wants the program to be successful has no choice but to follow the HWPM's directions. When he develops technology that is specific to his own field, the engineer needs to follow directions from his functional head. In the vehicle development program, however, it is the HWPM's voice to which he should listen.

**Representative of customers**   Once the design has been agreed upon, the engineering organizations of Japanese automotive companies stop interacting with the market, with the exception of focus group interviews and consumer clinics. The HWPM is the only voice they hear in their daily engineering work. He represents the customer. Since employees at Japanese automotive manufacturers are trained to be customer focused, they cannot neglect the voice of the HWPM, who speaks for the customer and reflects his innermost needs.

This is in stark contrast to the beginning of product development, when concept planners, designers, marketers, engineers, and the HWPM travel through cities and towns in Japan and in other parts of the world to gain a sense of the market and to understand the desires and requirements of users. They do not rely on consumer trend data. Instead, they speak face-to-face with consumers, and even stay with the target users for weeks in some cases.

**Well-defined processes**   HWPM's often cite well-defined processes for their success. It is more the company's well-defined process and less the official human resource authority that helps them attain their goals. At each design review, items to be discussed are clearly defined and HWPM approval is required at each event.

We asked an engineer why he worked so hard for the HWPM who was not his official boss. He answered: 'Because I saw my predecessors (*sen-pai*) work hard for their HWPMs'. This sense of tradition is alive at Japanese car manufacturers. While all Japanese original equipment manufacturers (OEMs) change their processes, especially to shorten development lead time, the fundamental philosophy remains the same. The HWPM is the driver of the process. He has ultimate responsibility and authority.

**Capability of HWPM**   When asked for the reasons why their HWPMs are so successful, Japanese engineers at automotive companies often refer to their capability and personality. Put simply, only the tried-and-tested have a chance of becoming a HWPM. These heavyweights have often worked as a member of the HWPM team for 15 years or more before being considered for the position. The skills, negotiation style, and personality of potential HWPMs are scrutinized over years. The very existence of the 'Ten *Shusa* Requirements', a set of commandments of sorts, provides an indication of how high Toyota's expectations of a *Shusa* are.


## Practices derived from the HWPM concept

An HWPM oversees the entire process of product development and all related functions. Several practices were developed, based on the initiatives of HWPMs, to improve product development efficiency and effectiveness. These smart engineering processes include front loading, lead time reduction, and cost planning.

## Front loading

Companies have much greater freedom during the early stages of product development than in later stages. More than 80 percent of product costs are determined in the concept development phase. Taking this knowledge to heart, Japanese automotive manufacturers and their HWPMs have made efforts to improve front loading, which means investing more engineering resources in the earlier stages of the processes.

The 'set-based process' is a general practice followed in Japanese firms for front loading. Some say that it is a Toyota practice: this is not quite true. It is a practice that most Japanese manufacturers have followed for decades. If a team develops a component, the simplest and most natural procedure is to design the component, test it, identify problems, fix the problems, and improve the product design. In this process, a single product is improved continuously, which is why this process is called the 'single design method'.

Japanese firms, in contrast, develop a set of several components with different specifications; different levels of performance for some components, and different shapes in other components. At the same time, engineers responsible for adjacent components do the same. They also develop several designs with different parameters. Together they evaluate the 'fit' with adjacent components, assess the attainment of objectives, and select the better options. They narrow the parameters. They then develop a few designs with a narrower range of deviation in parameters. After a few trials, they reach the final parameter. This method requires greater resources allocation in the early stage, but allows savings later.

Translated for non-engineering experts, the difference between the two processes can be explained using an analogy. Three busy businessmen are trying to set a meeting. In the world of the 'single design method', Mr A suggests a time slot, Mr B says 'no', then Mr A suggests the next one, Mr B agrees, but Mr C rejects it. This is a protracted process. In the 'set-based' world, all three gentlemen put available time slots on the table, and select a few slots. They then narrow down the selection – the earlier is perhaps the better option, or perhaps the longer option is better, and so forth.

Another example of front loading is the willingness to stop listening to customers after the concept has been chosen and following design freeze. Considered from a different perspective, this means that while Japanese automotive manufacturers invest more time when developing the concept and during the design phase, they need less time for implementation.

Some companies start engineering work when the concept is still undecided and then create numerous significant design changes due to modifications in the concept. To avoid this, successful Japanese firms devote more time to developing the concept. This does not mean that engineering work is not conducted in the concept and styling development phase. A great deal of analysis, design, and testing are performed in order to ensure that the concept and styling are realistic in terms of structure, quality, manufacturability, cost, and so forth. Thanks to front-loading activities, change requests that might affect product concept and styling are extremely rare at Japanese automotive companies.

Computer aided engineering also contributed to the dominance of front loading. Even in the styling phase, engineers can begin to conduct a preliminary analysis of crash tests. Digital mock-ups require a great deal of data creation work in the early stage but save extremely significant amounts of time in the later phase. Japanese automotive manufacturers were not necessarily the first to use digital tools but, once they started working with these tools, they became adept at integrating them in traditional human-based processes. They do not attempt to complete everything in the virtual world. Instead, existing processes are complemented with digital tools in order to further advance front loading.

## Lead time reduction

In the 1990s, automotive manufacturers worldwide found that the requirements and preferences of consumers were considerably more diversified than in the past. There has been no slowdown or reversal of this trend to date. Companies felt – and continue to feel – that they needed to launch more products with greater variety to respond to this change. A shorter lead time was desired, especially after the design freeze phase. To satisfy diversified customer preferences, styling of the car became more crucial than ever to win customers, especially since technology and quality gaps among automotive manufacturers have become increasingly smaller. Car styling is finalized at 'design freeze'. If the design freeze happens four years before the start of sales, planners and designers need to predict consumer preference four years in advance. If the process is shorter, say 18 months, prediction is easier and the probability of a 'big hit' is higher. As a result, automotive companies started to compete with each other in the 1990s to shorten product development lead time. The Japanese won hands down. In the late 1990s, Japanese automotive manufacturers attained 18 months process as standard, with 12 months for 'hurry up' models. Players in North America still required more than three years.

Figure 5.2 shows the typical process taken by Japanese automotive manufacturers up until the middle of the 1990s. Typically, it took 24 to 36 months to put a car on the market, from design freeze to start of production. Figure 5.3 shows the shortened version – 18 months in this example.

There were several enablers for the reduction in lead time. Here, we outline the four most important:

**Engineering tasks**  More engineering tasks were conducted before design freeze than ever before. They performed underbody engineering work such as power train and chassis as early on as possible. Regarding upper body engineering, the basic body structure was designed and validated before design freeze, thanks to extensive use of computer aided engineering (CAE). Basic designs for dies and tools were also started before design freeze.

**Prototype evaluation**  The prototype evaluation process was dramatically simplified to one step. Most Japanese car manufacturers used to have a three-step approach to evaluate prototypes. The new process often has only one step. This reduces lead time by four to five months.

**Die manufacturing**  Die manufacturing was dramatically shortened. Many Japanese companies now try to reduce manufacturing time further by abolishing prototype dies. They aim to build prototypes by using dies for mass manufacturing. By doing this, they do not need to spend time developing mass production dies in the production preparation phase.

**Trial production**  The number of trial production stages was also reduced. At many firms, there used to be two stages now, they conduct trial production in one stage. They use as many mass production dies as possible for prototypes, thereby shifting workload during trial production to an early stage. Another enabler was the use of simulation tools.

## Cost planning

To control the cost of new products, Japanese automotive manufacturers introduced a practice that is often translated as 'target costing'. However, 'cost planning' – which is the direct translation from Japanese – seems to express the practice more accurately.Manufacturers say that this practice is not only about reducing costs; cost planning involves creating a philosophy for a new cost structure.

During product planning, the cost planning department (the name of this department varies from firm to firm) defines the total target cost by

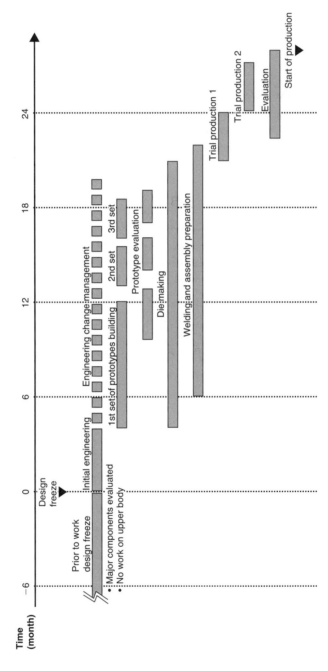

**Figure 5.2** Product development lead time

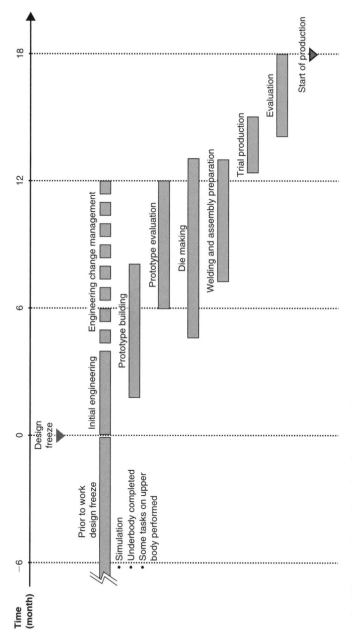

**Figure 5.3** Shortened product development lead time

analyzing target performance, price and performance of existing products, potential rival products of competitors, and so forth. At the same time, the cumulative costs of the new product are calculated by estimating the cost of each component. Usually, the latter cost is higher than the former, and the cost planning department allocates target costs for each component so that the cumulative total cost does not exceed the total target cost. Engineers design components that can satisfy performance, weight, and cost targets. If a certain component will exceed the target cost, then the cost planning department reallocates the target cost by component after discussion with the HWPM and relevant engineers.

In addition to complying rigorously with the cost planning process, each firm has developed its own way to manage product costs. For example, Toyota has been working on the construction of cost competitiveness (CCC21) initiative. One of the particularities of CCC21 is the concept of 'absolute cost'. Toyota has developed a database consisting of global suppliers. In the database, the absolute cost for each part is calculated by summing up the lowest material cost, the lowest process cost, and the lowest overhead cost. The absolute cost is the ultimate target for Toyota and its suppliers.

## Initiatives for change in HWPM organizations

The HWPM system has been a very powerful and effective mechanism for Japanese automotive firms. While processes have been improved, organizations also have been modified. One big change at Toyota occurred in 1993. Compared with the very early days of Kenya Nakamura and his successors, the product development organization of Toyota had expanded dramatically. The number of engineers and technicians had risen to 12,000 in 1993. This put a heavy burden on HWPMs, since they needed to spend considerably more time on coordination than their predecessors. Toyota then divided its organization into four vehicle development centers (VDCs). VDC1 is responsible for rear wheel drive cars, VDC2 for front wheel drive cars, VDC3 for commercial vehicles, and VDC4 for major components. The chief engineers at Toyota said that their productivity improved significantly following the introduction of this organizational change.

Two other interesting changes in the HWPM organizational structure should also be mentioned: the concept planner of Toyota, and Nissan's team management.

## Toyota's concept planner

At Toyota, a HWPM is assigned as soon as the top management decides to start a new vehicle development program. The HWPM leads the program from the development of the concept all the way through to the start of production. He is involved in minor changes that take place over the next few years, and even in the next full model change. Far-reaching as this role already is, Toyota concluded that it was not enough. To create truly innovative cars, Toyota thought capable engineers should start concept planning from a much earlier stage. To fulfill this requirement, the company created a position called the 'concept planner'. Concept planners develop concepts for 'dream cars', 'super eco cars' and other future vehicles. They talk intensively with engineers and researchers working at the Toyota Central Laboratories and other research arms of the Toyota group, major universities, and researchers in other industries, in order to come up with their ideas and visions. They also discuss market trends with the Research Division and other relevant organizations within Toyota. Following Toyota tradition, they also travel worldwide to see, talk with, and grasp the needs of potential customers. After successfully developing the concept, the concept planner is assigned to the chief engineer (HWPM) of the vehicle. Toyota expects the concept planner to bring unprecedented creative ideas and concepts, which can later be directly developed and realized by the same person without any gaps between the concept and the product.

## Nissan's team management

Nissan used to have a similar management model as Toyota. At Nissan, a HWPM was known as a *Shukan*, rather than a *Shusa* as at Toyota. After forming an alliance with Renault, Nissan abolished the position of *Shukan* and created teams that have ultimate responsibility for vehicles. A team consists of five people: chief product specialist (product planning), chief vehicle engineer (manufacturing), product chief designer (design), chief marketing manager (sales and marketing), and program director (overall coordination). This team has wider responsibility than a traditional HWPM who, typically, does not have responsibility in sales. This team is responsible for every factor determining the success of vehicle. The success of Nissan in the early 2000s was largely attributed to this management practice.

## Further challenges

Product development practices in Japan are still evolving. There can be no stop to this activity, especially as companies face new challenges and hurdles. The shortage of engineers is a headache for most companies in Japan. The number of engineers at Japanese automotive companies has not kept pace with the speed with which new models are launched. The shortage is especially severe in the electronics field. To respond to this situation, automotive manufacturers are trying to utilize the engineering capabilities of their suppliers. They have started to engage engineering service providers – mostly European firms – that have not previously played a major role in Japan.

The globalization of product development is another challenge. To satisfy local requirements, a certain amount of product development must occur locally. Japanese firms have historically conducted product development in Japan only. Striking the right balance between local and Japanese organizations, and ensuring sufficient communication between the two, is a big challenge.

Companies now manufacture some global products in different places in the world at the same time. Manufacturing engineering, including trial production, must be performed simultaneously all over the world. This exacerbates resource problems. In the past, a group of manufacturing engineers conducted work in Japan before moving on to the next country. Companies now need those same people in different parts of the world at the same time. One way to resolve this is by global development of talent with the same capability; another way is to utilize IT tools to conduct manufacturing engineering centrally from Japan. Each firm takes its own approach to resolve this challenge.

Japanese automotive manufacturers will face many more challenges in the future. Manufacturers in other industries and other regions would be wise to watch and take note of their reactions carefully.

## Further reading

Aoki, M. (2007) *Toyota Seisan Kojo No Shikumi. Nihon Jitsugyou Shuppansha.* ISBN 978-4-534-04246-0.

Hino, S. (2002) *Toyota Kiei System No Kenkyu.* Diamond. ISBN 978-4-478-38040-6.

Morgan, J. and Liker, J. (2007) *The Toyota Product Development System.* Nikkei BP. ISBN 978-4-8222-4570-2.

Kato, Y. (1993) *Genkakikaku, Nikkei.* ISBN978-4-542-13048-4.

# PART II

# Purchasing

# Introduction
# Strategic trends and challenges for purchasing

*Roland Schwientek*

The purchasing of material and services has undergone significant change since the middle of the 1980s. There has been a complete switch from purchasing being a traditional, reactive administrative function to becoming active cost management. In many companies, purchasing has been responsible for cost awareness being established comprehensively throughout whole organizations. Successful approaches such as reverse auctioning, target costing, value creation or supply chain management – all of which were considered innovative, in their time – were often initiated in purchasing departments and first gained widespread acceptance there.

Particularly in times of upheaval or recession, purchasing activities have contributed significantly to company results. However, irrespective of whether the economy is facing an upturn or a downturn, the importance of purchasing is not diminishing: it is, rather, extending.

The gradual reduction in vertical integration that has come about as industries concentrate on core competencies and key technology in order to position themselves strategically on the market drives this development. The relative share of external procurement costs to total internal costs in western Europe has increased by almost 1 percent annually since 1990, despite a continual decline in prices in almost all industries.

Although the pivotal role played by purchasing is widely understood, it is deployed with varying intensity from industry to industry. Sectors that have traditionally judged purchasing as being of secondary importance – utilities, banks and insurance, and construction – are now viewing it more favorably. Significant effort is being made by companies in these sectors to latch onto the type of success enjoyed by early procurement supporters, such as the automotive industry.

For leading purchasing industries, optimizing pure material costs was just the beginning. They had already started to improve their entire purchasing process many years ago. Key suppliers are integrated into company processes, from development to production. Laggards are now haphazardly employing innovative approaches in an attempt to reach the top. Seldom have they done enough homework to establish which approach would suit them best.

A critical examination of these activities reveals that while these innovative approaches are largely known in theory, they are applied in a half-hearted fashion. Owing to inaccurate interpretation or the defense of vested rights, applying these innovative approaches will, sometimes, even lead to undesirable developments. Only those companies that can clearly formulate their purchasing strategy, arrange the purchasing process to function flexibly and realize bundling effects without falling into a functional mindset or building up 'purchasing empires' will be able to sustain the dynamic necessary to remain innovative in the long term. Purchasing must capitalize on the significance it has already gained to keep driving processes that span across functions.

Understanding and adapting quickly to changing environments – whether customer expectations, competitive conditions, new technology or general social or political change – is decisive for success. Current trends that influence the strategic direction of purchasing include:

- *The increasing globalization of industry and society*

  Rapid advancements in IT and communication technology give this trend additional strength. Synergies that have been recognized but not yet realized could spark the creation of international partnerships that go beyond the purchasing function. By taking on a more cross-divisional functional role, purchasing could contribute to greater adhesion throughout the entire company.

- *The increasing pressure to concentrate on core competencies, not only in companies' own competitive playing fields but also in those of customers and suppliers too*

  As duties are handed over to external parties, it becomes even more essential to have comprehensive outsourcing know-how in purchasing. The closer suppliers become to core competencies, the more important it is to capture favorable suppliers – those that bring their own value into the entire process – before the competition does.

- *The necessity of strategic alliances along the value chain*

  The concentration on core competencies means that strategic alliances will become even more important in the future. These are still viewed skeptically today, especially by medium-sized companies. The optimal orientation along the entire value chain will be important in order to remain competitive in the future. This is true even for 'virtual' companies, in which many productive value-chain functions are taken care of by external parties.

- *The increasing pace of action, whether implementing innovations or reacting to customers' wishes*

  Changes in the competitive field and within companies will speed up. Processes will face increasing demand and the production lifecycle will become shorter. As vertical integration becomes lower, partnerships with suppliers will become even more intense.

- *The ability to use innovation as a competitive differentiation factor*

  Companies must bundle their own power for innovation with their suppliers and use this combined power for their own benefit. The task is to win the best and most innovative suppliers, to build up a joint competitive position and to make sure that new ideas and developments bring your company gains. This will safeguard your company from competitors.

  There is no singular one-fits-all approach that allows purchasing to gain the upper hand over all these trends and make purchasing more professional. Companies need to realize at what stage of development they are, before embarking on an improvement strategy.

  For this purpose, Roland Berger Strategy Consultants developed Purchasing EmPowerment, a comprehensive approach that helps purchasing reach performance excellence. Part II describes this approach. In Chapter 6, Michel Jacob and Gabriel-Assad Singaby look at key trends in purchasing best practices and examine the impact these have on purchasing strategies. They go on to examine the strategic direction purchasing is likely to take in the future and the role strategic partnerships might play. Chapter 7 examines the different facets of the approach in its entirety. It looks at the short and medium-term cost reductions that are possible in procurement values through systematic commodity management, and how companies can optimize external direct or indirect spend through appropriate innovative optimization levers and by managing suppliers more effectively. In Chapter 8, Tobias Franke takes a closer look at different organizational frameworks in order to find the one that works best for mastering future challenges.

# CHAPTER 6

# Key trends in purchasing best practices and impact on purchasing strategy

## *Michel Jacob and Gabriel-Assad Singaby*

### Introduction

As competitive pressure intensifies in most industries, CEOs are increasingly putting procurement at the top of their agendas. The corporate world is dealing with an onslaught of modern challenges, ranging from globalization, to the entry of new competitors, through to rising material prices. Purchasing, which is viewed as a way to master these challenges, is shaping up to develop even further into one of the hottest corporate topics of the next decade.

The purchasing world, in its endeavor to adapt to this changed and changing external environment, is reworking its own DNA. For a long time, the major concern of purchasing departments was to buy goods and materials at the lowest price possible. Faced by increasing globalization and business volatility, companies these days are adopting a more holistic perspective, and purchasing is being considered as part of the entire corporate strategy. Price alone is no longer the unique key performance indicator, but one of many aspects of sourcing excellence, along with anticipation, quality, total cost of ownership (TCO), industrial footprint consistency, and sourcing security.

These key performance indicators generate a new complexity that companies must address in order to gain, and then maintain, a competitive edge. Although developing a powerful purchasing strategy is now a 'must' for companies that want to succeed, it is a complex and sophisticated exercise. Experience gained from projects with clients shows that increasingly more companies are designing purchasing plans that span several years, and which attempt to anticipate major business moves and shifts.

In this chapter, we outline how purchasing practices have evolved over the past decades, and analyze the main challenges that companies are confronted by in the new purchasing environment. We then look at the key trends that are vital to achieving purchasing excellence, and show how companies can build up a purchasing strategy that will let them achieve that sort of excellence. These key factors have been distilled from assignments Roland Berger has conducted for major global companies as we assisted them to structure their three-to-five year purchasing plans. At the end of the chapter, we discuss a real project in depth.

## Where is purchasing today?

Based on experience working with companies from a large number of industries, it is clear that purchasing organizations, especially those belonging to large companies, go through three stages of maturity along their lifecycle.

In the first stage, companies are concerned primarily with negotiating prices, and with developing professional buyers and a new, more structured approach to purchasing. When companies focus on improving the purchasing process during this phase, they focus almost exclusively on commercial negotiations. This improvement typically generates a savings potential of approximately 5 percent (percentage of annual spend – operational expenditures + capital expenditures). One can safely say that companies in all industries have advanced beyond this first stage.

In the second stage, which is based on bundling volumes, companies centralize sourcing functions and geographically extend their sourcing. Thanks to economies of scale, this lever yields a 5–10 percent cost improvement from suppliers based on unit price. Volume concentration has become a key lever for producers of manufactured goods. By and large, almost all industries have now deployed this lever, and the most advanced companies have been fully utilizing it for decades already. As a result of bundling volume, strong purchasing organizations developed. These organizations have a clear mandate and have carved their own niche at the corporate level.

The third stage involves far-reaching organizational change, as it entirely redefines a company's relationships with its suppliers. This stage is much harder to complete and companies should consider it a medium-term task. Although this phase calls for more effort, and might initially push companies beyond their comfort zone, the benefits are immense. By entering partnerships and alliances with suppliers, both company and suppliers can improve their processes. When buyers together with internal users of purchased goods and services become involved in product

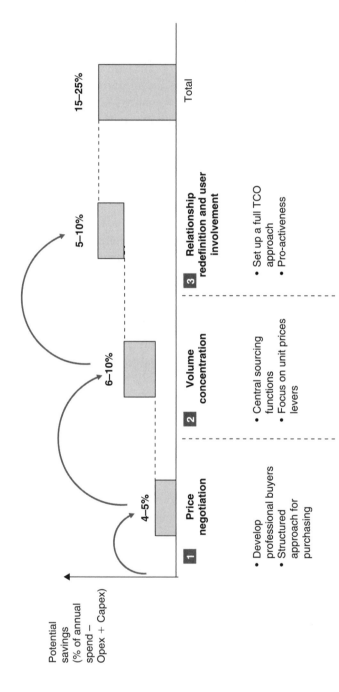

**Figure 6.1** Maturity steps at purchasing organizations

specifications, a full TCO approach has usually emerged. It is at this point that the philosophy of purchasing changes radically. It shifts from being reactive to proactive. Savings of between 5–10 percent are the norm. The automotive and aerospace industries are typically leaders in this approach.

## Challenges that still need to be addressed

Irrespective of what stage of development a company has reached, a handful of challenges affect all purchasing organizations. The only difference between purchasing late-comers and purchasing organizations that perform strongly is that the latter have already dealt with several of these challenges or have introduced long-term strategies to remedy them. These challenges are discussed below and shown in Figure 6.2.

Centralized and centrally-led purchasing models are now commonplace, but companies need to find ways to sustain these models. By centralizing purchasing, organizations gain efficiency and effective processes. The advantages of centralization are varied and well known: goods are purchased using standardized criteria, buying is concentrated, best practices are adopted between sites and regions, tasks are no longer duplicated, staff generally become more professional. Yet, a specific sort of organizational structure is required for centralized models to function properly. Another form to benefit from the effects of centralization without losing contact with the base is the lead buying model, as detailed in Chapter 8 by Tobias Franke – organizations drive strategy and performance. Information

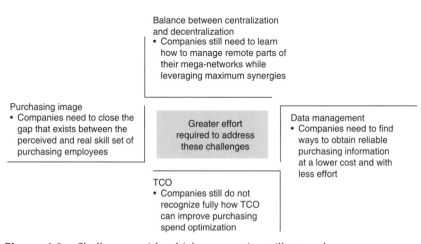

**Figure 6.2** Challenges with which companies still struggle

technology systems and information flows need to be designed with precision, too. Without the correct structure and information flows, problems arise. Companies might suffer from a lack of coordination, or the purchasing department might fail to take adequate account of the needs of local business units. Additionally, as companies become more global and expand, the challenge of managing remote parts of 'mega networks' while avoiding building central 'ivory towers' also increases.

A second challenge revolves around the perceived and real skill set of purchasing employees. Over the past years, the career track within purchasing and the skills and competencies of purchasing managers has developed considerably. Top management is increasingly becoming involved in purchasing, and it is attracting the attention of CEOs. Unfortunately, many people in business remain blind to this reality. At too many companies, the purchasing function is not viewed as a company's core business. The image of 'tactical' purchasing – focused on short-term profitability improvements, which had been the dominant model for years – is etched into minds. Unfortunately it overshadows the new reality of 'strategic' purchasing, which aims to secure competitiveness over time. Finding a way to close the gap between reality and the image that persists about purchasing professionals remains a pressing challenge for many companies. While the job market has reached a low point for professionals with tactical purchasing experience, there is a talent crunch for strategic purchasing jobs. These jobs are being created faster than they can be filled.

With that said, many companies realize that some of their purchasing staff do not have an adequate skill set to complete the work that is demanded of them as the purchasing function develops. With a tailored training program, this gap can be closed relatively quickly. In addition to having staff with basic skills and soft skills, purchasing departments these days also need purchasing employees with operative and strategic purchasing skills. The sorts of operative skills required span interface management – dealing with internal customers and international internal customers and making cooperation between them work – over the controlling of purchasing activities through to contract management. This latter criterion increasingly demands international contract law knowledge and expertise. Strategic purchasing skills include commodity management, supplier management, project management and risk management experience.

Total cost of ownership (TCO) is a third challenge. TCO helps companies assess the direct and indirect costs of purchases for their entire lifecycle. Many internal users and prescribers have not fully comprehended the consequences of the TCO-based purchasing revolution. As a result, they have not been able to adapt fully to the expectations of this new world order. Too many companies have failed to consider how this new paradigm fits into their organization and, consequently, do not give users and prescribers incentives to contribute to improved purchased product and service specifications. There is a lack of open discourse with suppliers. But companies underestimate the importance of TCO at their own peril. The higher the follow-up costs relative to the cost of acquisition, the more important the TCO concept becomes. In the engineered products industry, follow-up costs average out at more than 100 percent of the cost of buying a machine in the first place. In some areas, these post-deployment costs actually exceed the initial purchase price many times over.

There are good reasons why TCO remains a challenge for most companies. Procurement departments focus on the purchasing budget. But the purchasing budget is burdened only by the cost of acquisition. Follow-up costs are charged for, and paid by, other cost centers. In many cases, they are not even carried as a separate item. Since buyers are required to optimize their budgets, the obvious thing for them to do is to minimize the initial cost of acquisition. Little or no account is taken of any costs that might be incurred once the good or service has been paid for. For TCO to be successful, the purchasing organization has to rethink and re-engineer its entire way of doing business. Additionally, a successful TCO approach must draw heavily on non-purchasing resources (the prescriber–user–buyer triangle). Companies tend to underestimate how many resources will be necessary. This creates bottlenecks when the TCO approach is deployed. (See Text box 6.1 for further information on the critical role of TCO for purchasing.)

Companies have warmly embraced performance measurements. But measuring and managing purchasing performance has become increasingly sophisticated over the past years and remains a challenge. The multiplication of relevant indicators for purchasing performance, beyond pure unit cost, creates additional complexity for companies. While unit price can be relatively easy to measure, purchasing and general management have a hard time identifying and implementing the measurement of new, more qualitative or complex indicators such as the quality and durability of the relationship with suppliers or the TCO. How should TCO be measured, for instance, before the product lifetime is actually finished? Moreover, the increasing volatility of prices, upward-oriented market trends, and the increasing diversity of stakeholder needs make it increasingly difficult to define an acceptable quantitative measure for purchasing performance. The additional debate on actual profit-and-loss and balance sheet impact resulting from any purchasing effort is far from being solved. Companies that want to keep up to speed with these developments in the long term have their work cut out for them.

Information knowledge and storage presents a similar challenge. While access to data has improved, companies must now learn how to obtain acceptable and reliable purchasing information at a lower cost and with less effort. They also need to find ways of storing complete, clean and quality data, as well as gain a better understanding of suppliers' costs and margins. Necessary tools and the underlying data for them are becoming increasingly complex as the number of parts and components increases. This complexity switches to an even higher level as the number of regions from which those parts and component can be sourced also increases. Supplier data must be brought together in a way that allows companies to minimize the time required for conducting supplier research and looking for contact information.

Catalog consultation must also be made more accessible, in order to reduce time and lower the risk of error. Economic data, whether it be tactical (prices of goods, suppliers agreements) or strategic (suppliers' costs and margins), must be tracked in a way that allows buyers to concentrate on their jobs and not have their attention diverted elsewhere. The massive deployment of ERP (Enterprise Resource Planning) systems and e-enabled tools has assisted companies a great deal over the past few years, but generally the investment has been massive. Worse still, current systems still manage to cause frustration because of their inability to keep up with the increasing speed and complexity of business life. They also fail to provide sufficient reactivity and transparency.

## New challenges

In addition to these current challenges, a number of new tests are also emerging as the purchasing environment evolves. These especially affect large multinational companies. When designing purchasing plans that span several years, it is imperative for companies to anticipate major business developments and calculate these in. Some of the trends or challenges have been around for a while; the importance of other trends is only just beginning to emerge. Figure 6.3 illustrates the top challenges that will affect companies over the next decade.

Clearly, the recent acceleration of globalization has caused considerable change in the business landscape. Purchasing, as it expands its strategic role within companies, bears the full brunt of this acceleration.

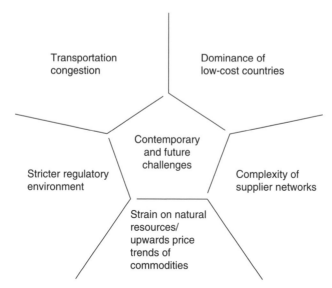

**Figure 6.3** Challenges that are reshaping purchasing

Each of the new challenges or trends can be traced back to the growing role globalization plays in the world economy. The challenge this creates for purchasing will continue, and even become greater in the medium term as the imbalance between EU-15 and emerging countries such as China and India becomes increasingly less pronounced. Certainly, new territories have appeared from which western companies can source. These span mature emerging countries such as China, India, and Eastern Europe, as well as countries in Africa. At the same time, ironically, world trade is becoming more and more regional, and new trade barriers are sprouting up between regions.

Globalization also affects the structure of supplier networks. Increasingly more suppliers and sub-suppliers are involved in the value chain. A complicated network of supplier relationships is commonplace these days. Making the situation more complicated is the inter-dependent relationship that has developed between suppliers and companies. Increasingly, companies are keen to involve suppliers, and this trend shows no signs of abating. While managing supplier relationships is not a new issue, thinking about how it will develop in coming years should preoccupy companies' thoughts.

A further challenge that companies must address is the strain on natural resources caused by rapid economic growth. As emerging countries develop, and mature markets fail to curb their dependency on natural resources, the cost of raw materials and energy explodes. In some cases, shortages even occur. Although the direction of the price development is fairly certain, it is unclear how strongly prices for natural resources will develop in the medium term.

The business environment is regulated to a degree not previously seen. Governments and inter-governmental agencies expect a degree of accountability from companies that is certainly challenging. Companies have to invest resources to ensure compliance, which contributes to price and cost increases. Upcoming regulations such as REACH (Registration, Evaluation and Authorization of Chemicals), a framework for the regulation of chemicals in the European Union, create new constraints, not to mention greenhouse-gas reduction.

Transport issues are a further challenge. While EU roads are becoming less congested, sea transport has become easier thanks to containers, and improvements are being made – albeit slowly – in rail transport, moving goods from one place to another will continue to keep purchasing departments on their toes. Transportation is a volatile industry riddled with heavy competition, tight capacity, and soaring fuel prices. Choosing transportation service providers requires an understanding of market dynamics across multiple modes, services and across thousands of domestic and international routes. It also offers companies an area of opportunity for significant savings.

## Spotlight on two major trends

We are now going to turn the lens slightly and focus on two trends or challenges with which companies, currently, are especially preoccupied. Companies very often turn to consultancies for help with dealing with low-cost country sourcing, and to manage supplier relationships. Low-cost country sourcing raises strategic issues and requires a deep understanding of the competitiveness from sources in emerging countries and how companies can leverage them while mastering the challenges of remoteness and consistency of quality. The second issue, supplier relationships, adds a new complexity to purchasing as it moves beyond internal cross-functional work. The main concern here is how companies can involve an external party that probably has interests that do not perfectly dovetail with their own.

Low-cost country (LCC) sourcing took off in the 1990s and has grown exponentially since then. While sourcing in LCCs makes the supply chain longer and more complex, it is a business reality for most manufacturing companies today. But generally there is more talk than action. Here, we wish to pay attention to how companies can achieve LCC sourcing on a large scale and not merely pursue it as a fashionable accessory to their sourcing strategy.

There are few symbols as powerful as China's 2001 entry into the World Trade Organization for the role LCC sourcing plays in today's global economy. China's admission to the WTO provided many companies with their first opportunity to test the LCC sourcing waters. Barriers to trade in other countries in the region have also collapsed, releasing a wave of procurement from these areas, too. GDP growth in most LCCs has outstripped western countries, as it has soared at a double-digit pace over the past 15 years.

China is the powerful new force of the LCC sourcing revolution. Companies that dare not source from this country risk exposing themselves to harsh criticism from financial analysts and other stakeholders. Although companies are quick to advertise their expanding involvement in China, most companies actually source only a small portion of purchasing requirements from this LCC heavyweight. Sourcing is limited to components with the least value-added. As economic pressure and competitive dynamics increase, companies will progressively feel forced to do more business there and in other LCCs, even if they are not entirely comfortable with this development.

What is the best way for companies to tackle this large step? How can they shift from their 'keeping up with fashion' sourcing strategy (less than 5 percent of sourcing spend) to adopting large-scale operations in LCCs? Given the immense pressure to source from China, companies should take the time to consider whether China is the most suitable place for their company to conduct this sort of business. Each LCC has its own set of advantages and disadvantages. It is important for companies to realize that significant differences exist in the various alternative markets. Different countries will best suit the particular sourcing needs of different companies.

Companies that choose to LCC source on a large-scale need to realize that this is a different ball game from the one in which they might be used to dabbling in these countries. Coordinating operations takes relatively little effort and entails minimal risk when 'only' 5 percent of a company's spend is at stake. Gaining access to commodities that are labor and material intensive – meaning those that require no sophisticated imported machinery – is generally the top priority of companies involved in low-intensity LCC sourcing. This makes it relatively easy for companies to change suppliers if the objectives are not met.

Companies that want to jack up the intensity of their sourcing from LCCs either have to purchase a larger number of commodities, or buy commodities that are module- or system-oriented or, alternatively, have key modules/systems with complex know-how requirements. When such complex components and parts are involved in LCC sourcing, their value and contribution to the final product is higher, and quality becomes even more critical. New, stronger organizations and processes are needed to manage these operations and the supply chain. Forerunners in LCC sourcing have noted that the local environment (legal, business, cultural) and extended distances make it difficult to control the output of the whole process. If quality control is not adequately addressed, sourcing projects are almost guaranteed to fail. As recent legal cases attest, the compulsory joint venture structure in China is not as risk free as people would like to believe.

There are six success factors that companies should keep in mind when embarking on their LCC sourcing adventure:

- *They should ensure that top management is behind the global sourcing initiative*
- They should set up a clear sourcing process and a high-level cross-functional team
- Companies need to focus on the most promising countries and commodities
- It is important to ensure quick wins to keep momentum high during a long process
- It is a good idea to set up and continuously enhance a regional sourcing presence
- Companies need to ensure proactive development of a local supply base.

Considering the extra hurdles that arise when sourcing from China, it is valid for companies to ask whether sourcing from China is the ideal strategy. While China definitely has a great deal of potential – and quality, reliability and price are likely to improve in leaps and bounds over the coming years – its basic industrial system has to be overhauled completely before it meets the requirements of manufacturers when it comes to large-scale and complex-goods sourcing. It needs to be said, however, that China's infrastructure, aided by strong governmental support, is far more advanced that some other low-cost countries in the region.

With so much attention paid to China, many other countries are unfortunately overlooked. For companies brave enough to venture out in their own direction, some of these other countries could potentially offer much more attractive sourcing opportunities and yield greater spoils. When drawing up a list of possible supply markets, companies must carefully analyze the benefits and risks of each region for a particular sourcing commodity. The main pitfalls are well known. Some additional important aspects that need to be considered are distance from plants (transportation costs are often underestimated), bilateral trade agreements, and the currencies involved in transactions.

Bearing these factors in mind, European companies would be wise to give greater priority to three low-cost sourcing regions closer to home: Central and Eastern Europe (CEE), the Middle East, and Africa. Near-sourcing is experiencing a renaissance as companies attempt to keep costs low by manufacturing and procuring goods and services close to their consumer market. Familiarity with the regions is certainly one argument for this renewal of interest, but another is the increased ability for companies to link forecasting and production more effectively. Some of the benefits of sourcing in CEE, the Middle East, and Africa are listed in Figure 6.4.

CEE is emerging as an excellent alternative to China for LCC sourcing, especially for European companies. Language barriers are lower and century-long business and cultural ties, although being neglected for some decades, have been relatively easy to re-establish. Austria was especially quick off the mark to start reigniting old networks with countries in this region. Many countries in CEE will become members of the Euro-zone over the next couple of years, which means that currency risk will be non-existent and there will be no need for spend to cover currency positions.

While labor rates in CEE might not be as low as in emerging Asian markets, transportation distances to other European countries are much shorter. CEE countries look back on a strong industrial tradition. They

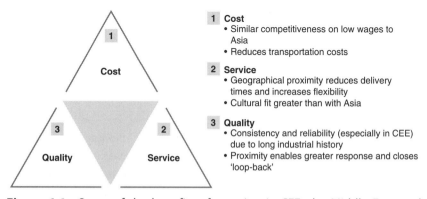

**Figure 6.4**    Some of the benefits of sourcing in CEE, the Middle East, and North Africa

also have a highly educated workforce that is fluent in various languages. This makes it a good choice for higher value-added sourcing. China, by contrast, is just beginning to enter this production territory and it will be some years yet before it reaches a comparable level. Many car manufacturers in Europe already source complex parts in the Czech Republic, Slovakia or Romania. This makes sense, especially because many have set up their own operations there. But Poland and Hungary have also established themselves as successful choices. Companies, lured by even lower labor costs, are beginning to look further afield into Ukraine, Bulgaria and Russia.

Setting up operations or finding a supplier for value-added products in Africa and the Middle East might be more difficult than in CEE, but cost advantages might offset this issue. While the Middle East and Africa lack the sort of industrial tradition that characterizes CEE, several countries in those regions have a qualified workforce and are taking steps to modernize their infrastructure. Production standards are improving dramatically in Africa. And, while the level of infrastructure varies significantly from region to region in this huge continent, advancements are being seen. Many countries have entered a second industrial phase, with a focus on value-added products in several industries. Whereas the US$ dominates many regions in the world, the Euro is considered an acceptable trade currency in the Middle East and Africa.

There is a compelling case for companies to consider the wider outskirts of Europe for their large-scale sourcing. Countries that are geographically nearer Europe are somewhat more costly than their Asian counterparts, but also more reliable. Considering the shorter transportation distances, companies can respond more quickly to developments and thus provide better service to the companies they serve. We recommend that sourcing initiatives be restricted to a few markets only. That way, companies can reach critical size while limiting complexity and overhead costs.

## Supplier relationships

Western companies can gain a strong competitive advantage by building smarter relationships with their suppliers around the world. Collaboration with suppliers is one of the hottest trends in purchasing to date. Partnerships and alliances with suppliers can take two different forms, depending on the technological intensity of the industry, and how critical an issue quality is.

A first kind of collaboration is the co-development of products. The reason for engaging in this sort of relationship is to improve the innovation process. Both parties seek to better leverage their respective technical, human, and financial assets from the alliance. Many industrial companies – such as car manufacturers (on interior trimming, for example) or aircraft manufacturers (on instrumentation or engines) – engage their suppliers in co-development relationships. These require the supplier to take full responsibility for the design, manufacture and warranty of their supplied parts.

By initiating a co-development project, a downstream company is able to influence the characteristics of the equipment, and the timing of its market entry. The upstream company benefits from the buyer's engineering capability. Its technological know-how also increases. As both partners bring their knowledge and capabilities to a co-development project, growing interdependence is a common sign of success in this relationship model.

A second kind of collaboration between upstream and downstream companies is supplier development, which aims at improving the supplier's performance on cost, quality, and delivery timing and reliability. It is a win–win relationship that benefits the two parties. Suppliers perform better and companies get the quality and delivery times they want. Although measuring supplier performance has been on the agenda for decades, studies continue to show that companies only continue to measure the performance of suppliers during the supplier selection phase and for special projects. This is not a sustainable strategy and will not result in supplier improvement.

Companies and suppliers could gain much more from these sorts of relationships. Companies should evaluate the performance of suppliers based on clearly defined processes and formal feedback, or they might introduce a quality certification program that leads to the number of inspections being reduced. Another common practice among forerunners includes company representatives visiting suppliers on site to help them improve their processes or, alternatively, inviting suppliers to a client's site in order to observe the use of their products. Best-in-class companies also recognize strong supplier performance by using an awards format or staff training.

Although the majority of OEMs have already implemented these sorts of supplier development activities, fewer than 50 percent of supplier development programs have achieved the targets initially agreed. Results have been 'at or below' expectations, according to a benchmarking study Roland Berger conducted among major car manufacturers and aerospace companies.

How, then, can companies truly enhance purchasing performance with supplier development programs? The steps taken by the best players in the automotive industry, especially Japanese automotive manufacturers, are instructive. They share a long-term commitment with their suppliers to improve each other's capabilities: the objective of this commitment being to lower costs and raise overall performance. The philosophy behind this approach is based on cost transparency and deep technical cooperation, as well as continuous improvement. For the car manufacturers, it results in acquisition costs 15 to 30 percent lower compared with those of a classical bidding process. This is due to higher supplier productivity, less re-engineering of products over their lifecycle, smaller purchasing structures for the car manufacturers, and lower warranty costs. The relationship also brings benefits for suppliers. The supplier earns a reasonable, fully agreed-on margin, as well as stable volumes. This is no small thing considering the difficult situation in which many parts suppliers have found themselves in recent years.

Such a close cooperation requires a joint process that is well coordinated. Once the costs of the suppliers are known, the car manufacturers help suppliers generate a manufacturing development plan, which aims at both decreasing cost and improving quality. It varies in its scope and depth depending on the supplier's process maturity. Objectives and key performance indicators (KPIs) are set based on industry benchmarks and the car manufacturer's experience of best practices.

Key success factors for this approach are long-term relationships (for example, through cross-investment) and joint teams; qualitative data, and a transparency pledge on breakdowns of cost; development and training of staff at all levels of the organizations; and organization alignment on all aspects. Although this approach is relevant for all industries that purchase manufactured parts and components, for cultural reasons it might be hard to implement. Cultural sensitivity is required, especially in companies with supplier networks that span several companies. To retain employees, companies should be particularly careful when designing objectives, and compensation and performance indicators.

## How it works in practice: examining trends to develop a long-term plan

Increasingly, companies are turning to consultancy firms to design long-term purchasing plans that span several years, in order to take into account expected purchasing trends. Roland Berger recently assisted a major global steel player to develop and formalize its five-year strategic purchasing plan. The company was obviously concerned about rising energy and raw material costs, but there was also a more general and unspecified unease with the fast pace of changes occurring within the purchasing world.

The project team developed a 'white book' that detailed the major relevant economical, political, and environmental changes that could be anticipated over the next ten years, and which could impact supplier markets and purchasing strategies. This white book provided fact-based insights on energy price trends, regulatory changes impacting future costs, development trends of emerging countries (including their economical potential), political stability, as well as potential capacity shortages on key markets such as ore, transportation, and strategic production equipment. The white book was used to stimulate discussion during the initial brainstorming process. This process marked the moment when the company started to develop a purchasing strategy.

In a second work module, the project team completed a comprehensive benchmarking exercise of major corporations in various sectors. This helped the team identify and document what leaders in the various industries considered good purchasing practices. It also helped the company to see what their peers were doing to tackle up-and-coming challenges and to prepare for the future. In a next step, face-to-face interviews were held between our client and these benchmarked companies. Information was exchanged openly.

The project team also completely reviewed the needs of internal users to anticipate changes in the specifications of future purchased goods and services resulting from programmed production process and product changes, but also from probable technology changes.

Structured workshops involving key internal users, prescribers, and purchasing commodity managers were then organized. During these workshops, formatted five-year purchasing plans were developed for each commodity. By integrating experts into these discussions, the purchasing plans were based on extremely thorough knowledge of supplier markets and the forecast evolution of internal needs.

This various information was used to develop a five-year purchasing plan that summarized all strategies. Based on optimizing the TCO of this company's purchased value, and a comprehensive risk management plan, a substantiated and quantified target of several hundred million Euros was agreed upon. This plan has become an integral part of the company strategy. Purchasing can now be managed better, both in the short and long term.

## Outlook

The days of simplistic purchasing strategies built on pure sourcing exercises and volume leveraging are gone. But, far too often, companies

Textbox 6.1

## TCO approaches – underestimate at your own peril

Simply stated, TCO (total cost of ownership) is a methodology for understanding the combined effects of first-time costs of equipment acquisition (whether leased or purchased) and the lifecycle costs (deployment, operation, support, and retirement) associated with operating the equipment. It provides companies with the true cost of doing business with a particular supplier for a particular good or service.

There is a real opportunity to further exploit TCO in all industries. Getting this right is critical for long-term success. The benefits of introducing the approach far outweigh the costs and difficulties. Companies that make full use of TCO are showered with numerous benefits which are closely related with and feed into one another, creating synergistic effects. These include improved supplier performance measurement, improved purchasing decision making, improved internal and external communication, and better understanding of purchased goods and services.

The overarching benefit of TCO is that it becomes a reference point for checking how matters are developing. It is an excellent tool for benchmarking, and thus offers a solid framework for evaluating suppliers as well as a clear-cut means to measure quality improvement. It improves purchasing as it forces staff to quantify trade-offs. Reliable data makes decisions on supplier selection easier and more informed. TCO provides data for trend analysis on costs, excellent data for comparing supplier performance and for negotiations, and provides critical data for target pricing. In addition, the long-term nature of TCO focuses the entire team on the big picture and helps them recognize non-price factors.

Despite its advantages, relatively few companies use a TCO approach. Special skills and a specific mandate are required for the successful introduction of TCO into a company. It requires a major change in purchasing resources, both quantitatively (in the sense of resources), and qualitatively (the experience and educational level of purchasing staff). The license to operate, by which we mean the ability to enforce supplier or specification changes, also requires significant reinforcement. Two last points need mentioning. No company can rely on TCO alone – traditional levers need to be applied in parallel. Finally, while collaborative approaches work, these partnerships are never easy or comfortable.

act immaturely when addressing the issue of purchasing strategy. They embrace 'trendy' approaches, such as LCC sourcing, before thoroughly assessing them and grossly underestimate, or even ignore, TCO approaches. No company that lacks a fully-fledged purchasing plan with a real strategic perspective can claim to have mastered purchasing. Purchasing functions that claim otherwise can expect to have their role as a main contributor to company strategy put in question. The challenges for purchasing are real, and evolving at an unprecedented pace. Long-term strategic plans that are flexible enough to adapt to these trends are a prerequisite for purchasing excellence.

## Further reading

Roland Berger Strategy Consultants (2006) 'Best Practices in Low-cost Country Sourcing'. Stuttgart.

# CHAPTER 7

# Purchasing EmPowerment: the way to achieve world-class purchasing

*Roland Schwientek*

## Introduction

Purchasing has grown considerably in stature in past decades. Its contribution to an organization's long-term success and strategy is increasingly well recognized. Increasingly more companies are aware of the importance of permitting purchasing to move away from being a cost-cutting function to becoming a strategic entity that helps companies achieve the highest performance standards.

Roland Berger's comprehensive approach, 'Purchasing EmPowerment' (PEP), helps purchasing to reach performance excellence. PEP moves beyond cost cutting, which is usually short-term in nature and focuses on specific actions or commodities within a distinct project, and hones in on long-term sustainable improvements along the process chain. In this strategic approach, the focus is on overall costs and company value. Procurement influences more than 50 percent of a company's total cash cost: depending on the industry and project aims, PEP can achieve savings up to 70 percent of important commodity or category groups.

For purchasing organizations to become first class, they need to estimate their current performance carefully. Development potential should be based on benchmarks to own and similar industries, competitors, and suppliers, as well as from internal resources. Although the prospect can be daunting, this enables a company to gauge its performance gaps. Only once this has been accomplished can a company develop an individually tailored, step-by-step plan for purchasing that charts out the optimal elements for reaching the desired goal.

Important steps along that path are the improvement of commodity groups, structure and processes, and working with suppliers. When assessing companies, project teams consider how much they spend on commodities, suppliers, and resources. This assessment can be carried out on a company, regional or divisional level. To gain a comprehensive view, an external assessment covering internal customers, external suppliers, competitor benchmarks, and additional stakeholders is conducted. This knowledge provides clues about the opportunities available to companies' purchasing departments, and their impact.

The initial step – managing commodities strategically – focuses on unit costs. Here, purchasing levers are examined to see whether they can be used in conjunction with a particular commodity for performance gains. The second step – optimizing purchasing organization processes – deals with process costs. It puts organizations in good stead by making processes leaner, establishing purchasing as an organizational function, making information transparent, and training as well as motivating staff. The final step – managing suppliers – deals with the entire value chain. Strategic supplier management improves the supply chain in both quantitative and qualitative terms.

Companies that work through all three steps tend to be more competitive than their counterparts. This article examines all three phases in detail. Project examples are given to illustrate how the changes can be implemented in real-life business situations and the benefits those changes can bring.

## Strategic commodity management – 6-lever approach to optimizing costs

Although the status of purchasing has increased in past years, all too often other functions underestimate what it can achieve. If purchasing consistently pushed through large cost-saving programs and communicated its achievements in driving down the cost base, its standing would improve. Numbers speak the clearest language in the business world.

One of the most successful ways purchasing can reduce costs is by properly managing commodities. Strategic commodity management is simply about finding the most relevant purchasing strategy for important goods. It is about applying a tailored set of differentiated procurement levers to commodities in the right sequence at the right time in order to reduce total cost.

To accomplish this, companies need to assess their sourcing behavior by segmenting the vast array of commodity groups within the portfolio. Each commodity or category is then assessed in terms of business impact and supply market challenge, and is placed in a matrix. Business impact is

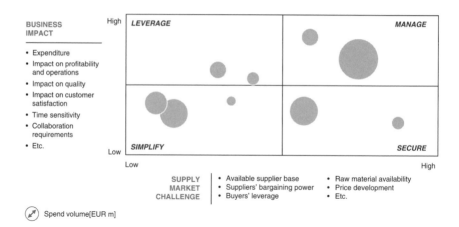

**Figure 7.1**  Each commodity/category is strategically assessed in terms of business impact and supply market challenge

determined by factors such as expenditure, and demands on product and process quality. Supply market challenge is determined by factors such as how many players are accessible, and what cost structures are encountered via suppliers. Each quadrant in the matrix represents a distinct sourcing strategy: leverage, manage, simplify, and secure. These are depicted in Figure 7.1.

If a commodity or category is characterized by a restricted supplier market but has a high acquisition volume – as would be the case for electricity in the aluminum industry – the commodity falls into the 'manage' quadrant. A commodity group such as packaging material – with its small acquisition volume, plentiful supply sources, and restricted business risk – would probably be found in the 'simplify' quadrant. For each strategy, there are six broad clusters of levers that can activate the right developments. These levers, which are shown in Figure 7.2, are clustered into price optimization, quantity leverage, process redesign, technical improvement, supplier integration, and functional adjustment.

## Price optimization

The potential for making significant savings when it comes to purchasing goods and services is commonly underestimated. Companies make this mistake at their own peril. Since improved procurement can bring savings of up to 70 percent, purchasing plays a vastly important role in boosting the bottom line. Purchasing has a number of commercial levers at its

**Figure 7.2**   The right mix of levers is key to finding the correct sourcing strategy for each strategic commodity/category field

disposal. The trick is to use them optimally for specific commodities. All levers in this cluster generate savings by focusing on price. It might be the case that looking closely at company prices at different locations brings about a moment of truth about best-price evaluation. Perhaps aggressively pulling the fixed-price contracts lever will do the trick.

Low-cost country sourcing is another lever. Companies need to ask themselves whether this much-lauded lever, which is also full of pitfalls and hurdles, will really activate the cost savings they want. Companies should have plenty of resources at their disposal – and patience – before pulling this lever. One of Europe's largest university clinics decided to concentrate its efforts on global sourcing activities. Commodity groups were assessed to see if reasonable sources existed in low-cost countries. The long list of countries that emerged was shortened by checking them against a series of criteria specific to clinics such as import regulations, technical clearance, and so forth. From this short list, five suppliers were selected, which were built up during a two-year development program. The low-cost sourcing lever does not bring quick wins.

## Quantity leverage

The second cluster of levers – quantity leverage – also plays an important role in optimizing sourcing costs: scale effects can be generated by increasing volumes by a certain amount in order to determine prices. This lever can be used to ensure that a certain volume is ordered or taken up in purchasing cooperations. Volume effects are not only achieved by pooling suppliers, but also by compiling a systematic compendium of requirements. Bundling volumes internally (for instance, subsidiaries within a group) and beyond the company (purchasing cooperations from independent companies) can bring significant savings potential. This potential is rarely tapped. When it is exploited, it is only undertaken in a half-hearted fashion. Companies are missing out. With this lever alone, an international group was able to attain savings of around 15 percent of the entire purchasing volume through pooling global volumes.

A financial service company also activated this lever, and benefited from doing so. In addition to establishing specific sourcing activities, the company also decided to build up a third-party business. It opened up its sourcing platform to other stand-alone financial service companies with low sourcing volumes. These third parties obviously benefited from the deal. For its part, the financial service company managed to gain significant scale effects too, by expanding its purchasing volume.

## Process redesign

Improving existing internal purchasing processes or redesigning them is not the focus of these levers: redesigning the process structure of suppliers is. Companies should ask themselves whether it makes sense to use a middleman or trader who dents trade margins but possibly generates volume effects that are almost unthinkable or closes attractive deals with alternative suppliers. Or is the opposite strategy a better option? Companies might find it preferable to have direct contacts and create internal structures to manage them. Levers belonging to this cluster include second-tier supplier sourcing, e-catalogs, e-sourcing, and the simplifying of accounts by introducing automatic credit memo procedures, for instance. One company achieved cost and quality improvements after it introduced catalog-based sourcing for roughly 40 percent of its sourcing volume, which was transaction-heavy but advisory weak. By pulling this lever, the company significantly unburdened operative sourcing, improved sourcing quality, and lifted the customer satisfaction rates of internal carriers.

## Technical improvement

This cluster of levers focuses on tapping the hidden potential within products by using consistent standardization and value-analysis programs.

The levers cover everything from applying alternative materials, to making finer specifications, through to purchasing modules and change process engineering. For these levers to work, the functions, customer use or customer value must be firmly in the foreground. Only in this way can costs be reduced.

An automotive supplier made cost savings of more than 40 percent by applying some of the levers in this cluster. Within the framework of a cost-optimization project for ABS finishing, the automotive supplier put various concepts and procedures under the microscope. Small changes resulted in large cost effects. By adjusting the pole kernels from turning part to beaten part, cost savings of 40 percent were achieved.

## Supplier integration

Integrating suppliers starts with product development. Levers in this cluster are aimed at enabling companies to unite the hidden creative potential of suppliers with their own specific abilities. By joining forces, companies can carve out a sustainable position for themselves. Concept competitions – a truly innovative lever in this cluster – encourage suppliers to find innovative product solutions. Companies can then use their suppliers' insights and knowledge to develop cutting-edge products and solutions. Supplier financing, consignment warehousing, and vendor-managed inventories are some of the levers found in this cluster.

A manufacturer of signal lights, for example, was able to develop a completely new solution for commercial vehicles by using a concept competition. One of its suppliers discovered that by using magnet valves, vehicle roofs would no longer need to be sawed through using the old cumbersome technology.

## Functional adjustment

Companies also have a set of functional adjustment levers at their disposal. These levers have more of a middle- to long-term impact, and usually change a company's value chain in some way. Make-or-buy options, in- and outsourcing options, backward and forward integration of value chain steps, and sale and lease back are some of the functional adjustments companies can undertake.

A benchmarking exercise at a machinery maker, for instance, showed a considerable tilt regarding manufacturing costs. A definite weakness was its vertical integration at 80 percent. Following close analysis, the company decided to outsource the prefabrication areas of turning and punching to specialists. Activating this lever resulted in a savings of 35 percent of total costs.

In each of the six category fields, various levers exist to improve operating cost performance. While some of these have been discussed, the entire list is shown in Figure 7.3.

Specific sourcing lever categories differ on average in their profit-and-loss (P&L) impact and implementation speed. The categories quantity leverage, technical improvements, and functional adjustment have a high impact on the P&L, but rank low on being quick to implement. The levers price optimization, process redesign, and supplier integration levers rank highly on both the implementation speed and P&L impact axis.

## Optimizing purchasing organization and processes

The second step companies need to take to make purchasing reach performance excellence is to optimize processes within the purchasing organization and the organization itself. Roland Berger research shows that most trading and service companies have still not properly embedded purchasing in their organizational structures. Only a tiny share of companies has a purchasing representative on the board or at general management level. Equally disappointing, far too few companies have a clear-cut organizational separation between strategic purchasing and operational procurement.

Companies need to focus on four main areas in order to lower process costs in a sustainable fashion: processes, organization, information, and know-how. These four areas are depicted in Figure 7.4. Processes need to be reshaped to make them more effective and leaner. Purchasing should be turned into a well-functioning, cross-disciplinary, organizational function. Information flows need to be made transparent, and employee know-how needs to be nurtured by training and motivating staff.

Purchasing processes do not exist in isolation and are not all of equal importance. Companies should give the highest priority to order-to-pay processes. It is critical that these work efficiently. Companies would also be wise to pay attention to processes that work in harmony with higher business processes.

Positive results are almost immediate, when action is taken to improve purchasing processes. For example, when purchasing redefines processes between companies and sites, and clearly defines competencies and interfaces between them, inefficiency and duplicated work is prevented. Similarly by

**1  PRICE OPTIMIZATION**

1.1  Best price evaluation
1.2  Tendering/(re)negotiation
1.3  Fixed-price contracts
1.4  Cost breakdown/cost disclosure
1.5  In-house costing/activity-based costing
1.6  Best-of-benchmarking
1.7  Linear performance pricing/Cost regression analysis
1.8  Target pricing
1.9  Global/LCC sourcing
1.10  Payment terms (accounts payable)

**2  QUANTITY LEVERAGE**

2.1  Volume bundling
2.2  Bonus agreements
2.3  Corporate supplier negotiation
2.4  Multi-year contracts
2.5  Lifecycle contracts
2.6  Purchasing cooperation
2.7  Demand management
2.8  Order management (batch size)
2.9  Transportation option (frequency)
2.10  Working capital optimization (inventory)

**3  PROCESS REDESIGN**

3.1  Value chain mapping
3.2  Total cost of ownership
3.3  Second tier sourcing
3.4  Hedging
3.5  Re-engineering the procurement process/reducing interfaces
3.6  Distributor
3.7  Avoid middle-man
3.8  e-catalogue
3.9  Web EDI
3.10  e-sourcing (tender, auction)

**4  TECHNICAL IMPROVEMENT**

4.1  Change materials
4.2  Commonization/standardization
4.3  Redesign/change of specifications
4.4  Value analysis/creation
4.5  Technical benchmarking/DFMA
4.6  Innovation analysis
4.7  Modular sourcing
4.8  Change process engineering

**5  SUPPLIER INTEGRATION**

5.1  Joint improvement program
5.2  Supplier manufacturing analysis
5.3  Consignment warehousing
5.4  Vendor-managed inventory
5.5  Supplier financing
5.6  Early involvement/collaboration through product development
5.7  Establish system supplier
5.8  Concept competition

**6  FUNCTIONAL ADJUSTMENT**

6.1  Make option
6.2  Buy option
6.3  In-sourcing option
6.4  Out-sourcing option
6.5  Forward integration
6.6  Backward integration
6.7  Sale and lease back
6.8  Deconstruction of the value chain

**Figure 7.3**  There are more than 50 sourcing levers for improving operating cost performance

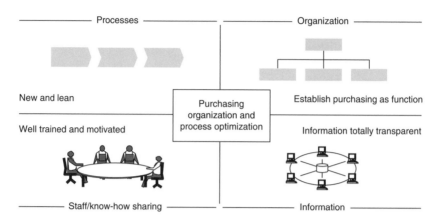

**Figure 7.4**  Companies need to focus on four areas to lower process costs –
processes, organization, information, and know-how sharing

defining the roles and competencies of lead buyers and decentralized buyers,
companies benefit from more efficient strategic and operative purchasing.
Companies will also notice that when the innovation process is reorganized,
purchasing is involved early on and has a say on costs. This is a far cry from
business environments in which purchasing works reactively.

It is not enough to reshape processes; the purchasing organization as a
whole needs to be remodeled. Developing an optimal purchasing organization takes time and should be tackled in a clearly structured manner. First, the
purchasing organization should be analyzed by commodity. While the
criteria for analyzing commodities are handpicked to suit specific customers,
common criteria include global sourcing, organizational structure, buyer
skills, and performance measurement. The next step is to draw up
organizational options, keeping individual commodity requirements in
mind. The individual commodity options are used as the basis for finding the
optimal purchasing organization. Finally, an implementation plan needs to be
hammered out, then coordinated, and followed through.

Specific actions to improve how purchasing is organized bring instant
results. By introducing new group-wide lead buyers and clearly defining
their role within the organization, purchasing becomes more transparent,
and is capable of combining decentralized competencies and centralized
coordination. It also assists companies to fill purchasing and other
positions. Synergies are optimized in purchasing when the level of coordination per commodity is made transparent. To improve its organizational structure, one of the world's largest automotive groups redesigned
its entire procurement department to make sure that all of its brands have
identical structures and reporting lines.

Purchasing needs to keep abreast of technological and IT changes to ensure that processes and the organization are well-managed and efficient. Costs can explode if purchasing uses outdated or inappropriate information systems. A common information platform integrates all market, supplier commodity, sourcing, and controlling information in one source. Purchasing departments lacking a group-wide IT platform or cross-business unit procurement information system do themselves a disservice. Manually identifying cross-business unit synergies for commodities is extremely arduous work and is error prone. No transparency exists for optimizing the supply base across business units. Today, purchasing has numerous IT systems from which to choose. An effective e-procurement platform connects authorized buyers, internal databases, and suitable suppliers.

It is essential for companies to introduce consistent commodity codes and a supplier code structure across business units that are integrated in the chosen IT system or systems. These must be designed in such a way that new commodities can be easily integrated into the system. These standardized structures enable companies to report purchasing activities and track performance results more efficiently. Without these codes and structures, a lack of data transparency ensues and identifying bundling opportunities for common suppliers is almost impossible because the manual effort required for data aggregation is significant and demotivates staff. It is not enough to introduce these standardized codes and structures; with the help of these instruments, companies need to control purchasing throughout the entire group.

As the role of purchasing within companies evolves, the demands on purchasing employees increase and change shape. Action to train staff and retain know-how will become increasingly important. Simple factors, such as increasing globalization, mean that sourcing is now done on an international playing field. Unfortunately, members of purchasing staff are often insufficiently qualified to complete their tasks adequately. A lack of language skills is a considerable handicap that robs purchasing staff of their ability to close the best deals. Companies such as IBM, Siemens or Home Depot have reacted by setting up international purchasing offices (IPOs). The main task of these IPOs is to give market research input, helping them to find and select the appropriate suppliers in target regions and manage the supplier base with locals.

Best-practice companies have endeavored, over the past years, to make improvements in all four areas. Achieving sustainable lower process costs is the reward of that proactive stance. Some characteristics are common to almost all companies that have globally aligned procurement processes and systems. They have common procurement processes, systems across business units and regions, and they have aligned procurement organizations globally where suitable. Keen to learn from the best – whether internal or external – these companies also adopt best-in-class processes and systems across business units and regions.

Then there are companies that have not only achieved this, but have also aligned processes and systems with engineering and other global functions. These companies have common interfaces between procurement, engineering, and R&D, as well as with other supply chain management functions. These sorts of companies enjoy a minimized process throughput time and cost. They, too, adopt good practices throughout their entire organization, irrespective of region or business unit.

Renault and Nissan, following their hook-up, fall into this latter category. A great deal could be achieved by moving away from the specific platforms, procurement processes, and commodity structures that had been successful at both car manufacturers to create a global, standardized structure for their joint procurement organization. Together, they chose global commodity classifications, global procurement processes, a global supplier information pool, and aligned procurement interfaces.

## Managing the supply base

The final step on the path to create best-practice purchasing is managing the supplier base. Companies embark on this path with the aim of making quantitative and qualitative improvements to the supply chain. Some might wish to improve their time to market, or become more agile; or they might want greater technology input or customer satisfaction; or they might want to reduce lifecycle and process costs, and the amount of tied capital and total cost of ownership.

The activities that a company should pursue to manage the supplier base in such a way as to improve the entire supply chain depend on what it has already achieved. Companies that have yet to deal with this issue should aim to manage the supplier base more effectively. Managing the supplier base is a continuous process of assessing and selecting suppliers. Changes in the procurement market and in a company's procurement portfolio duly affect how companies should select their suppliers.

Once companies have started to manage their supplier base successfully, they can think about developing their suppliers and supplier base. To develop suppliers, companies need to decide what their aims are, and assess the feasibility of reaching those aims with their supplier base. Developing suppliers depends heavily on a supplier's current level of performance, and the strategic corporate goals of both the supplier and the company. Strategic corporate goals are likely to be shaped by customers' and stakeholders' expectations, market requirement, and core competencies. Performance levels can be measured using quality standards, technical abilities, economic efficiency, and operative performance. Once goals have been set for suppliers, they must be communicated and monitored. Companies that do this successfully are blessed with the ideal supplier fit.

The long-term goal is to integrate suppliers and share supply risk with them. How suppliers are integrated, and the duration of that integration, depends on their development responsibilities. Suppliers need to become part of the development process and be integrated into ongoing business processes. Ideally, they will play an active role in the management of the change.

Roland Berger recently completed an international study that surveyed 1,900 companies active in 14 industries. The study showed that, although supplier management is highly important in strategic terms, it is not used as much as it should be. Hardly any companies have created long-term contracts with fixed cost-reduction scales. Few companies have designed long-term purchasing plans or systematic demand consolidation. This is a shame, especially since best-practice businesses in supplier management have better financial and earnings ratios.

Based on the study results, and drawing on experience from working on more than 200 procurement projects with medium-sized and large multinational companies over the past five years, five development stages can be identified in supplier management: 'best practice', 'runner-up', 'base', 'starter', and 'low performer'. In the study, 9 percent of companies were ranked as best practice, which means that they showed a consistently high level in all three areas: managing supplier base, developing suppliers, and integrating suppliers. Moreover, supplier integration was considered increasingly important and was used by these companies. Runner-up companies accounted for 25 percent – managing the supplier base was given priority and its importance is expanding, but developing suppliers was viewed as less important. Some 18 percent of all companies were ranked as base, meaning that they reached a consistently moderate level in all three areas. Companies that were ranked as starters – these accounted for 34 percent of all companies surveyed – showed progress in managing the supplier base and developing suppliers, but integrating suppliers remained underdeveloped. The low performers (14 percent) achieved a low level in all activities.

Clearly, many companies have only just started out on this journey. Companies that are new to the supplier management path have started to define a strategy, research the procurement market, find and audit suppliers, accredit suppliers and products, and update the database. These activities are laudable, but they need to be based on a thought-through strategy and be well coordinated. When companies manage the supplier base in an uncoordinated fashion, they have a supplier base that lacks strategic or volume-based prioritization, and they suffer from uncoordinated supplier management functions. The opposite is true of companies that manage the supply base well. To ensure that the supplier base is coordinated and managed with finesse, these companies have introduced and use supplier management, a supplier assessment system, basic tools, and supplier communications. The success factors for each of these phases are shown in Figure 7.5.

Companies that move beyond this phase start to develop suppliers in addition to managing them. This calls for deriving individual performance targets, conducting a GAP analysis, defining development action, assisting in implementing action and controlling activities. Key instruments required to develop suppliers are formal performance gap analysis, basic tools, *ad hoc* performance gap analysis, and personnel and capital transfer. A supplier development roadmap is useful for managing supplier performance.

Companies with an integrated supplier management blur the lines between company and supplier. These companies form long-term product

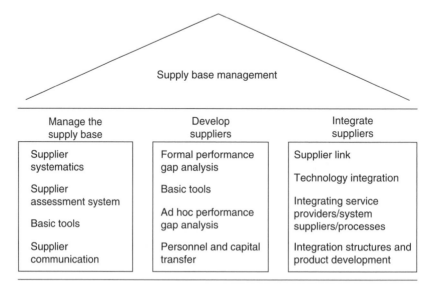

**Figure 7.5**   Success factors have been identified in three areas of supply base management

development and manufacturing processes in which their suppliers are heavily integrated from the very beginning. To pull this off, supplier strategies are needed that contain performance review and evaluation procedures, as well as procurement volume goals. Instruments to attain this goal include supplier link, technology integration, combining service providers and system suppliers, linking structures, integrating product development, and creating processes in tandem. Companies that develop strategic vendors and partnerships have fully optimized their supplier base. In these cases, vendor development and integration occurs within product development and manufacturing processes. When this level is reached, companies enjoy optimum supply leverage. Purchasing in these companies fully uses and exploits supplier capabilities. It also optimizes and combines own and supplier value chains.

## Best-in-class on a global scale

Intensified global competition forces companies to make their procurement organization as global as possible. But leading industrial manufacturers face a number of challenges as they attempt to leverage their global volumes and supply base to maximize benefits. The strategies the best-in-class companies have chosen to combat these challenges are instructive for all companies that wish to improve the performance of purchasing.

### Communication

The first challenge is how to align communication. Best-in-class companies achieve this by establishing common commodity coding, introducing a common IT/information platform to support global interaction between business units, and harmonizing worldwide organizational structures and responsibilities to leverage synergies. These are flexible enough to allow for the addition of new commodities.

### e-Procurement

The second challenge is how to reap the benefits of e-Procurement. Here, leading companies establish e-Procurement platforms to optimize interaction with key suppliers. They also unite selected alliance hubs and exchanges to reduce commodity procurement process cost, and introduce web-based procurement processes to reduce throughput time and cost. Best-in-class manufacturers utilize e-procurement efficiencies on three levels by:

- They unite hubs and exchanges. They achieve this by choosing exchanges for immediate access to a large supplier base with a focus on raw materials and maintenance, repair and overhaul (MRO). They also join alliance hubs for industry-specific commodities and joint product development.
- They implement a captive e-procurement platform. This enables them to integrate sourcing from request for quotation (RFQ) to order execution and to integrate all procurement data with Enterprise Resource Planning ERP and other back-office functions.
- They introduce and globally align web-based procurement processes. Here, they predefine procurement requirements and search preselected online supplier catalogs, automate order execution and receive products at point of use, and automate billing and controlling functions. Despite the benefits, Internet and B-2-B solutions are only being introduced slowly.

### Synergies

The third challenge is how to realize synergies. To achieve this companies have introduced global lead functions for commodities or commodity groups across all business units or divisions. They have clearly defined locally and globally purchased products and have implemented a step-by-step system. These actions help them to monitor and control savings. Here, too, there are various levels of synergies that can be attained through global commodity leadership:

- The bottom level of the rung is business autonomy with a periodic coordination via commodity strategies
- The next level is global commodity leadership across all business units for all commodities
- The final level is a globalization level that is individually designed per commodity or commodity group.

At the world's largest maker of earth-moving equipment, synergies are realized by combining division specific and company-wide commodity leadership. Europe's biggest engineering company, on the other hand, realizes commodity synergies through different levels of global commodity leadership across business units or regions.

## Lean global decision-making processes

The fourth challenge is how to create global decision-making processes that remain lean. This can be especially tricky as local procurement struggles with central procurement. To ensure effective decision-making processes, companies have installed global procurement committees on the executive level. Executives from business units and different functions – such as R&D and manufacturing – are integrated into those committees. The lens is focused on strategic and high-level operational tasks. At one of the world's leading computer software companies, decision-making is handled by a procurement council, which is chaired by a global procurement vice president. Since the role of the procurement executive council is clearly defined, a sense of fairness is established. They regularly review commodity strategies developed by global commodity councils, and they aggregate information from supplier strategies and technology roadmaps developed by their support teams. Importantly, they take decisions on sourcing and other procurement issues based on the recommendations of commodity councils.

## Aligning internal processes

The fifth major challenge is how to align processes internally and with internal customers to ensure consistency during the entire lifecycle and harmonized structures. The best companies introduce and implement common procurement processes that achieve global coordination and transparency. Additionally, they align procurement process interfaces with various functions – such as engineering – to minimize throughput time and cost. This is especially important when companies merge.

## Global management of suppliers

The sixth challenge is how to manage suppliers globally. Although most people in the business believe that global sourcing is 'old hat', the lion's share of all purchases is still made in the country where the company is based, even in large companies. The massive savings potential offered by global purchasing markets is tapped to a very limited extent. Global sourcing is full of pitfalls and companies need to take care. The recent spate of quality problems arising from suppliers from China shows how important it is to manage suppliers, not only to ensure continued high brand perception, but also to make sure that a company's pool of suppliers is large enough in emergency situations. Companies with ideal strategic supplier management select a preferred supplier base and initiate vendor development and integration programs. They manage key suppliers globally and optimize local interfaces, and they standardize supplier management evaluation processes across business units and regions.

## Outlook

As the dynamic of international business continues to increase, and global networks are formed and expanded at breath-taking speed, purchasing is left with no choice but to keep improving. Companies that adopted purchasing early have long since mastered the basics and are now seeking advanced instruments to achieve more long-lasting goals. Followers slowly noticed the benefits and now attempt to find sourcing solutions for their organizations. Irrespective of what a purchasing department might have already achieved, it must constantly challenge the existing supplier base and continually seek out innovative purchasing levers that help improve results. Skilled workers are needed that are business savvy and who have a deep understanding of engineering or other functional aspects. They must also feel comfortable doing business in a global market.

Procurement departments have made huge strides. But they should not rest on their laurels. Purchasing managers need to prove continually that they are able to implement strategic approaches that are pro-active, innovative, and cost-effective.

## Further reading

Roland Berger Strategy Consultants (2008) 'Purchasing Excellence – International Benchmarking Study'. Stuttgart.

Schwientek, Roland and Franke, Tobias (2008) 'Purchasing Excellence: International Study of Performance Diversity in Purchasing and Procurement'. Stuttgart: Roland Berger Strategy Consultants.

# CHAPTER 8

# Organizations drive strategy and performance: insights from two successful lead buying models

*Tobias Franke*

## Introduction

Procurement fads come and go. However, any thoughts that global sourcing is just the latest in that growing string of purchasing fads are misplaced. Within a short span of time, global sourcing has gained worldwide acceptance and is now firmly implemented in most large-scale corporations. Global sourcing is a direct response to the competitive pressure experienced by companies today. It is developing into the favored option for companies that need to reduce costs and to improve the quality and responsiveness of their procurement. Buyers send their largest suppliers to low-cost countries or set up small sourcing offices in these regions, in the hope of gaining better access to material and labor resources or to tap the potential of a more economical market.

While this concept sounds simple in theory, putting it into practice has often been hard. Global sourcing has placed enormous pressure on all organizations. Companies with local and rigid hierarchical structures have felt that pressure especially acutely. The biggest challenge for many companies was, and remains, how to align the organizational structure of their procurement division with the requirements of a globalized world. In such an interconnected world, each subsidiary or business unit needs to tap into many markets without building up redundancies along the way.

This tests the mettle of companies. Skilled and motivated employees are not enough to accomplish this task. An appropriate leadership concept is needed too. Companies increasingly introduce lead buying frameworks that combine these two factors, in order to tap these markets in a cost-efficient manner.

This chapter will start briefly by discussing centralized and decentralized procurement organizations, the two most popular organizational structures for many years. Following that, I discuss how lead buying systems work. I will then discuss two companies, from different industries, that combined the advantages of both centralized and decentralized structures to create a lead buying organization. Insights gained by these companies – and our project team – during the project are shared here to assist companies that might be contemplating changing their organizational structure. Project experience has shown, time and again, that this framework puts companies in good stead in an increasingly global business environment.

## Different sorts of procurement organizations

Three basic models are used in procurement organizations: centralized buying organizations, decentralized buying organizations, and lead buying organizations. The differences between the three models are outlined in Figure 8.1. There are merits to all three organizational structures and each has a role to play. All procurement departments are unique. Companies need to consider various factors to determine which organizational form best fits their needs. These factors include geographical location, the size of company, the number of employees, the industry, and the corporate philosophy. The three different procurement organizational structures can be individualized to suit the specific needs of each company.

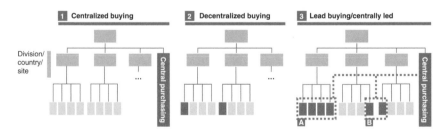

**Figure 8.1**   Three basic models are used in procurement organizations

## Centralized buying organizations

Centralized buying is the natural choice for every small company just starting out, especially if it comprises only one business unit, division or site. Some larger corporations might also have a centralized purchasing function that is responsible for driving synergies. However, this function is generally detached from day-to-day business on an operational level. Putting exceptions aside, it is usually only small and medium-sized companies that operate using this organizational model. These companies generally centralize their purchasing in the hope of achieving synergies, in terms of economies of scale but also with respect to improved administrative efficiency and the optimized use of resources. Sometimes companies choose this model because they purchase only a few commodities or categories of goods that seldom change.

Typically, operative tasks such as the processing of purchase requisition and strategic tasks – such as developing systematic category strategies or managing supplier relationships – are performed by one purchasing unit without further specialization. As business units are mostly responsible for budgets, the decision-making authority of centralized buying organizations is somewhat limited.

## Decentralized buying organizations

When a company's business units, divisions or sites at home or abroad grow in number, many take the natural next step and switch from being a centralized buying organization to becoming a decentralized one. Decentralized buying organizations can typically be found in financial holding companies with a low integration factor. This structure can facilitate the purchasing or selling off of legal units. Other companies with this structure tend to have distributed (global) sites/divisions whose purchasing functions are at a low development stage. Here, the rationale for switching structures is to gain full authority and independence in the corporate units.

Decentralized buying organizations do not support decisions being coordinated across divisions, countries or sites. This is why these sorts of organizations often build up redundant functions. Although these purchasing organizations often construct lean, relationship-driven, local purchasing departments that put them close to internal customers, they remain compartmentalized within divisions or business units. They also do not come close to gaining the negotiation power enjoyed by centralized companies. They lack scale and a unified strategy, when it comes to product and supplier selection, and negotiations.

## Lead buying

Another organizational structure that is swiftly gaining in popularity is lead buying. The basic lead buying concept has been developed for corporations that need to coordinate spend categories, supplier strategy, and markets without sacrificing the proximity to local requirements. For many companies, lead buying combines the best of the centralized and decentralized buying organizations. Typically, this organizational model is found in companies that operate in different markets worldwide, with different business units and many sites. When large-scale organizations introduce the lead buying organizational framework, they are able to strengthen their international procurement coordination and can negotiate better prices. Instead of commodities being purchased by different people within the company, in a lead buying organization one buyer – the lead buyer – is designated for a defined category or commodity.

The lead buyer has the authority to conduct negotiations and to sign contracts with suppliers. He has control over volumes that are bought from different local suppliers. Such a buyer might be in charge of purchasing raw materials company-wide, for instance, or for a certain product. This sort of set-up makes it easier for suppliers too; because they have one point of contact, they deal with one person who has clear negotiating powers. With leadership comes accountability. The lead buyer also carries responsibility for ensuring that he has selected the best purchasing strategy available.

## Transformation teething problems

Companies might face several barriers when they decide to make the transition from a centralized or decentralized organization to that of lead buying. In all transitional phases, employees experience feelings of uncertainty, are quick to put leadership into question, and tend to harbor uneasy feelings about how responsibility and accountability will be redistributed. Companies can easily assuage employees' concern by compiling a list of questions that employees are likely to be concerned about and directly answer them in a ready-to-distribute information sheet. This should contain answers to the most frequently asked questions.

Employees in decentralized organizations are accustomed to focusing on developments at plant level, and might be dismissive of best practices gained from other organizations. These companies should not be surprised if their employees are not enthusiastic about introducing lead buying, and are openly hostile to the idea of capturing cross-business synergies. In these situations, companies need to use examples of early success to boost acceptance of the new system, and win the support of influential team members. To drive continuous support, compliance, and adoption of the lead buying concept, companies should constantly communicate their strategies, goals, and performance to the various business lines and regions. Setting targets also indicates to employees that the change is non-negotiable. Awarding strong performance can also be a strong motivator.

There are most definitely obstacles when setting up a lead buying organization. However, the perseverance is well worth the effort. To show how lead buying can help companies perform better and gain noticeable bottom-line results, I will discuss two very different client success stories.

## Lead buying in the automotive industry

The first success story stems from the automotive sector, which was one of the first industries to adopt the lead buying concept. In the automotive industry, original equipment manufacturers (OEMs) and their suppliers are globalization pace setters – and they have to be. Customers in the automotive industry are well informed, have high expectations, and can be quite challenging: features seen in top of the range cars are also expected to be found in entry level cars at entry level prices within one development cycle. Finding ways to make cars both desirable and affordable is this industry's Holy Grail. Purchasing, in collaboration with R&D, plays a major part in meeting this challenge.

### Example: Leading buying in the automotive industry

One of the world's largest automotive players wanted to optimize its organizational framework and processes, and adopt a fully integrated organizational model. The Roland Berger team helped the company set up a lead buying purchasing organization, step-by-step, starting with simple harmonization and increasing this gradually until purchasing as an entire entity had been transformed.

A close look at the procurement organization and processes at the end of the 1990s revealed that synergies were not being realized between business units, brands, and countries. Procurement was distributed throughout the organization and no overarching strategy existed. Sites were bought without considering the scope or require-ments of other sites, and no alignment existed between various regions. The steps leading to an integrated procurement strategy are depicted in Figure 8.2.

Over time, and with increasingly more integration, the project team was convinced that global leverage, higher savings, efficiency and standardization could be increased at this automotive heavyweight. But how could the company best achieve these goals? The project team decided that two things had to change immediately if the company was to achieve its goals.

The company could no longer avoid setting up and implementing a standardized commodity code – basically, a common language for different commodities. This company, one of the world's largest automotive players, had no consistent code structure in place across its multiple business units for either commodities or suppliers. It suffered from a lack of data transparency, which made it almost

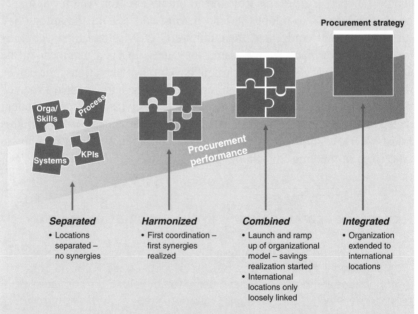

**Figure 8.2**  Only an integrated approach to procurement ensures optimum impact on a company's competitiveness

impossible for purchasing staff to identify bundling opportunities or, even, to recognize common suppliers. The manual effort required to aggregate the data was significant and unnecessarily used up resources.

Introducing a governance model was also essential. Only by doing this could the purchasing function assign tasks and responsibilities on a commodity level. This is a necessary first step on the path to becoming a fully –integrated organizational set-up.

Establishing a common commodity code and introducing a governance model are steps that are relatively easy to accomplish. There are a number of standardized solutions for creating commodity codes and a commodity code architecture. UNSPSC and eCl@ss are just two of the many solutions on the market. Since all of these standardization systems have their own set of advantages and drawbacks, the project team needed to evaluate them based on their own individual merits and fit with the company's specific needs as an automotive player. The system the project team chose to create a common language is capable of defining a reference system and code suppliers as well as spend data. It is therefore sufficiently flexible to be used as the company continues to develop. This should always be a prerequisite when selecting such a solution.

Launching the governance model involved some preparatory work, but was relatively simple to introduce once the model was clearly laid out. First, three levels of leadership and three regions were defined for the model, after considerable discussion with various key staff members. This matrix is depicted in Figure 8.3. The highest level of leadership and

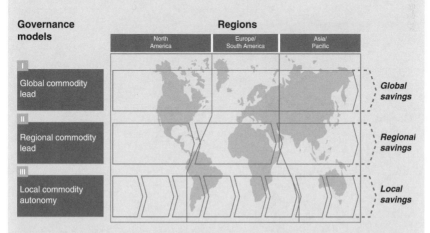

**Figure 8.3** Global lead buying consists of three governance models, ensuring global and regional savings

coordination is the global commodity lead. The commodities that fall under the global commodity lead include robots and the IT of cutting tools. Other commodities were assigned to a regional commodity lead – including, for example, motor test benches, elevators, and escalators. Regional commodity leads were created for the areas North America, Europe/South America, and Asia/Pacific. All commodities not assigned to either a global or regional commodity lead were assigned to 'local commodity autonomy'; these include such commodities as gardening and waste disposal.

The responsibilities for the key purchasing processes in each governance model were clearly defined. Moreover, it was essential that the roles of the global commodity leader (GCL), regional commodity leader (RCL) and local buyer (LB) were clearly allocated. Also, the manner in which they should interact with one another and the individual responsibilities of each leader or buyer was strictly defined. Sourcing decisions for commodities with global/regional potential are made on a global/regional basis, and approval from the GCL/RCL is required, for instance. Local buyers are responsible for managing the interface to the internal customer and operative transactions. The responsibilities of the leaders and buyer are shown in Figure 8.4.

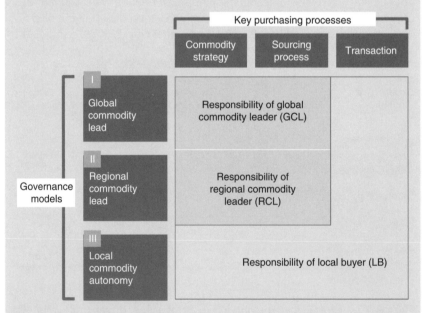

**Figure 8.4**    The newly defined governance models add the regional focus

Furthermore, the tasks and main responsibilities for the commodity leader/coordinator and local buyer were defined. In the governance model 'global commodity lead', for example, the leaders are responsible for developing, reviewing, and implementing global commodity strategies. They are also responsible for approving all major sourcing decisions, and are held accountable for commodity results. In the governance model designed for the automotive company, the local buyers are responsible for contributing to global commodity strategies, and negotiating and finalizing contracts. They are also responsible for obtaining the approval of the commodity leader, if required, and to manage the customer interface.

## Lead buying in the utilities industry

The introduction of a lead buying concept can prove beneficial for utility companies because stiff competition and strict regulatory requirements force them to find new ways to drive down operational expenditure (OPEX).

The second success story involves a utilities company. Utilities are not generally thought of as companies that use lead buying to improve purchasing departments. This is part of the reason for highlighting this particular case.

### Example: Lead buying in the utilities industry

Although all of the utility company's business units and sites were located in one country, it suffered from similar problems to the automotive company in the previous example. Despite geographical proximity, business units and sites worked independently and – more troubling still – bought independently. Potential synergies were being squandered.

A slightly different approach to lead buying was necessary here. The primary focus of the project was to streamline structures and optimize processes. To do that, the project team first had to differentiate between utility specific and non-utility specific purchasing. In a next step, purchasing segments or centers were defined, and four clusters emerged. These clusters comprised project/complex purchasing, utility purchasing, standard purchasing, and catalog procurement. They are shown in Figure 8.5.

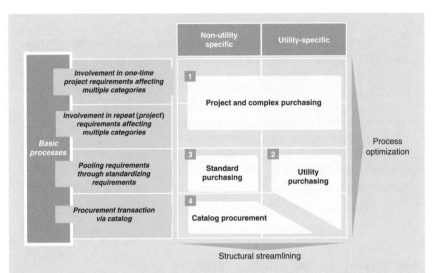

**Figure 8.5**   Purchasing is reorganized into four new purchasing segments

The company was in need of criteria that would help it splice and segment processes and purchasing structures into one of these four different purchasing clusters. A series of characteristics had to be fulfilled before a purchasing item was distributed into a cluster. A purchasing item that was designated to project purchasing, for instance, had to have either complex and innovative one-time processes (project purchasing) or repeat processes (complex purchasing), have extensive interaction with customers on a highly technical level, and clearly identifiable customers. The construction of a combined cycle gas turbine (CCGT) plant is an example of project purchasing. Project purchasing has no direct category allocation.

All other purchasing segments were allocated a clear category. Processes and structures that have utility specific requirements that cannot easily standardize materials/services belong to the category 'utility purchasing'. Another characteristic of utility purchasing is that there is low to average order frequency, and cataloging does not make good business sense. Standardized purchasing encompasses all categories that have identical requirements across companies, easily standardized materials/services, and low order frequency. Here, too, cataloging is not appropriate. Catalog purchasing was introduced for items that possess several characteristics, including considerable ability to standardize materials/services, are easy to describe, have a high order frequency, and with no direct or active interaction with the customer being necessary.

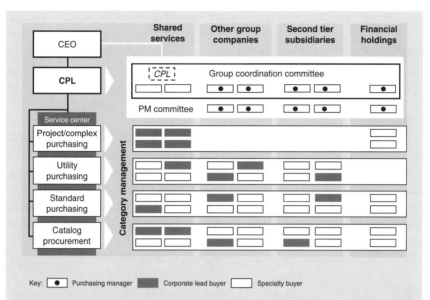

**Figure 8.6** Corporate lead buyers are responsible for group-wide coordination of purchasing activities

Based on this information, categories were allocated to specific purchasing service centers. A lead buyer was placed in charge of each of these centers. These corporate lead buyers are now responsible for group-wide coordination of purchasing activities. This encompasses shared services, other group companies, second-tier subsidiaries, and financial holdings. This is illustrated in Figure 8.6.

Project/complex purchasing was assigned to a shared services unit, while all the other categories were assigned to the most appropriate organizational unit. Appropriateness is defined by the most common use and direct knowledge. The category for high voltage cables, for instance, is assigned to the distribution company even though some cables are used in generation too.

## Overall conclusion and outlook

To reap the benefits of a lead buying organization considerable effort is generally required. An overall vision for the transformation process is essential. This enables companies to set, accomplish, and monitor targets that are relevant from a management perspective. Such a vision also needs to be communicated to all employees, irrespective of hierarchy. When employees understand why the changes are necessary, the changes will be easier to introduce. This is especially true of operational changes, such as introducing a common coding language. It also encourages employees to feel comfortable working in an organizational model in which solid lines and category leadership can deviate.

It is not only the leadership concept that is critical for successful lead buying – the right people are needed too. Lead buyers take on considerable responsibility. Companies need to assign these positions with care, ensuring that the people selected are respected throughout their divisions and various regions. Lead buyers must also be capable of nurturing relationships with suppliers. If they lack these soft skills, they put the whole model in jeopardy.

# PART III

# Manufacturing

# Introduction

# Manufacturing in a global context
*Ralf Augustin*

When the South-east Asian 'tiger' states entered the international economic arena two decades ago, there was a fundamental change to the global manufacturing footprint of whole industries: western manufacturers were challenged by fierce competitors who had created favorable cost structures and who were both eager and able to learn quickly. As a result, European hi-fi and motorcycle manufacturers – to name only two examples – were almost completely squeezed out of the market. The rules of global competition are shifting once again, with the entrance of Central and Eastern Europe, China, and India into the global economy. The impact will be much broader this time, rippling through more industries and putting greater pressure on many more companies.

Considering the magnitude of the risks that follow in globalization's wake, it is understandable that companies concentrate only on the threats. New global manufacturing entrants, characterized by their low-cost base and lower labor and environmental standards, are easy targets for distrust. These manufacturing upstarts threaten the jobs of people in the Triad region who carry out work that does not require high-value skills, shifting these jobs to emerging markets. As more players collaborate to create and improve products and services at increasing speeds, competitive pressure on companies in Japan, western Europe, and North America will continue to increase. That pressure is already too great for some companies, and insolvencies are on the rise.

The risks of globalization are real, but its advantages far outweigh the perils. Consumers in North America, western Europe and Japan benefit tremendously from the reduced cost of products manufactured in lower cost regions. Everything – from computer chips to clothes, from toasters to tires – has become less expensive since manufacturing was relocated to cheaper locations.

Companies benefit twice over: not only can they produce goods more cheaply for their Triad customers, they also enjoy the emergence of new markets bursting with an unfathomable number of consumers who crave high-quality products and brands made by 'old world' manufacturers. German and Japanese machinery manufacturers in particular benefit from the interest of manufacturers in these emerging regions, keen to obtain sophisticated, well-designed equipment.

When discussing the potential that is simmering in this region, the numbers speak for themselves. India has 300 million middle-class people (or 55 million households) and more than 60,000 millionaires measured in US$. GNP in China and India is expected to grow by at least 5 percent each year until 2020. Within the next decade, China will become the second most important consumer goods market worldwide and India will rank third. No company can afford to ignore this burgeoning market segment.

## Not only a shifting landscape, but also a different world

While, in the past, Triad companies succeeded in their global expansion primarily through exports, today matters are different. Locally made goods can be better tailored to local requirements because production is often more flexible and less costly. In addition, a number of external factors support globalization: lower barriers to international capital transfer mean global production networks are easier to build, large pools of engineers and managers are available in countries such India and China to run local operations, modern logistics and continuously decreasing tariffs lower the cost of global transport, and IT systems permit global engineering collaboration and supply chain transparency.

Companies in Japan, North America and western European have the opportunity to capitalize from this global transformation and use the low costs to their advantage. However, they need to build global manufacturing networks to reap the rewards. No aspect of global collaboration can be left to chance: every aspect must be well defined and clearly communicated. Moreover, these networks must be monitored and reviewed at regular periods to ensure that they are still valid and that they remain sufficiently flexible to respond to sudden business changes.

Triad companies need to focus sharply on manufacturing high-tech products: there is no sense in them concentrating on anything else. They cannot compete with low-tech, low-cost products manufactured by companies in newly emerged and emerging regions.

Developing, testing and ramping up innovative production technologies is the only way forward, if companies in western markets want to develop and manage a global supply base. Only highly skilled, adaptable employees who are willing to keep on improving their knowledge will thrive in this globally oriented environment. Operations in emerging markets can serve as manufacturing hubs for labor-intensive products. They can also form a local base for fabricating 'near-the-customer' goods to be sold in these markets. Operational excellence is a must in this scenario.

The traditional competitive advantages once enjoyed by Triad countries – such as a highly educated workforce, excellent infrastructure, and political and financial stability – are becoming relatively less important as developing countries improve on these fronts. This is not to suggest that Triad countries can afford to become complacent and let their high standards slip: it means that these are no longer competitive advantages but, rather, the base line that every country needs to meet. Operational excellence thus becomes an even more important factor of differentiation.

Manufacturers have focused on improving the quality of their processes as a means to achieve operational excellence for at least the past twenty years. The process is ongoing. Wave after wave of new breakthroughs keep companies busy as they learn to adapt and keep ahead. Lean manufacturing, which radically changed manufacturing practices, is helping companies remain competitive. Adopting such practices is critical as the pressure increases to be increasingly more flexible, faster and cost effective without jeopardizing traditionally high product quality.

Part III is dedicated to showing companies how they can meet the challenges of manufacturing in today's increasingly globally oriented world. For Triad countries, the nature of competition in manufacturing has changed. High quality and highly customized goods are in unprecedented demand. Global manufacturing networks are required to deliver these goods. In Chapter 9, Marco Zurru describes the successful building and continuous improvement of global manufacturing networks. Volker Heidtmann and Stephen Weisenstein, in Chapter 10, show companies how to achieve operational excellence with global manufacturing networks. Then, in Chapter 11, Dr Thomas Kwasniok and Walter Pfeiffer explain how to enable lean manufacturing through best-in-class management and by setting up support functions.

# CHAPTER 9

# How companies can optimize their global manufacturing footprint

*Marco Zurru*

## Introduction

Companies surfed the first wave of globalization largely to exploit opportunities in low-cost countries. They wanted to find suppliers and manufacturing locations that could help them decrease overall production costs as they competed in traditional western markets. The current competitive environment pushes them out into more challenging water, but the spoils of riding the swell are greater. Companies these days are searching for low-cost locations and suppliers, and they want to gain access to the large markets that are opening up rapidly in emerging economies. They also need to develop strategies to tackle the emergence of an increasing number of players from emerging countries that are quickly building capabilities to serve international clients.

To attend emerging markets, companies need to develop a new business model that provides them with the ability to manufacture customized products that are suitable for local needs. The business model also must be flexible enough to let companies closely integrate local manufacturing capacity with sales and distribution networks. That is critical if companies are going to be able to compete with new players from emerging countries that do battle on the same international markets but have lower costs. Prompt action is required in terms of cost structure and innovation capabilities, especially as increasingly more players from low-cost countries swiftly reduce the technological gap, partly by acquiring western players.

In this evolving contest, companies will gain the upper hand by designing a flexible manufacturing footprint that considers how increasing global competition affects and impacts their strategic objectives. In this chapter, I examine how companies can best design – or redesign – their global manufacturing network. First, I look at the differences in networks from industry to industry. Next, I show a handful of factors that are critical for optimizing a manufacturing footprint, irrespective of industry. These factors form the foundation of an approach that Roland Berger Strategy Consultants successfully uses when helping companies lower their manufacturing costs and develop sustainable strategies to thrive in a globalized environment. And finally, with the help of a case study, I show how following this step-by-step approach can help companies address manufacturing network design issues on a global scale.

## Footprints differ in size and imprint

Various footprint models exist, depending on the reasons behind the global manufacturing presence and industry specific concerns. Automotive players aim to reach a global customer base, and their business is driven by economies of scale. It is not surprising, then, that their footprint is already fully global. Automotive suppliers – who mostly embark on an international manufacturing journey to support their customers (automotive original equipment manufacturers OEMs) – have a footprint reflecting their clients' global presence. The multinational footprint of aerospace and defense companies, in contrast, is mostly driven by international agreements and by offset requirements. Other companies have a multi-local footprint but can leverage economies of scale for very specific parts of their value chain – consider, for example, raw material procurement or engineering.

The business environment is developing rapidly. What works for one industry at a particular time is unlikely to yield good results for others, and will probably require redesigning at a different point. No single predefined solution exists for an optimally designed global manufacturing footprint.

Each company has to design its own unique footprint. However, the design should not be set in stone. It must be sufficiently flexible to adapt to changes in the business environment. In my experience, a systematic approach is needed to accomplish this. The design should be based on a top-down understanding of the strategic drivers that force a company to expand its manufacturing footprint globally. Also, it should assess the feasibility of expanding the manufacturing network at the operational level, paying close attention to cost structure and risks. The six-step approach outlined in the next section of this chapter provides a compass for decision makers. It should alert their attention to the tricky terrain that

| STEP | Focus |
|---|---|
| • Understand strategic drivers and implications | • Priorities: cost versus market penetration<br>• Target markets and external constraints |
| • Derive the global manufacturing footprint model | • Industry cost structure and economies of scale<br>• Alternative manufacturing processes<br>• Logistics network structure and costs |
| • Segment product structure and define delocalization scenarios | • Product structure and relevant manufacturing activities<br>• Business case for delocalization of activities<br>• Risk evaluation |
| • Select target regions and countries | • Selection of potential countries<br>• Short list of activity-specific target countries |
| • Fine-tune the model and finalize the footprint | • Manufacturing scenario analysis and sensitivity<br>• Make/buy decisions |
| • Select site, suppliers and partners | • Partner/supplier identification and screening<br>• Partner/supplier selection and final make/buy decision |

**Figure 9.1**  Approach steps and focus

needs to be traversed when shaping, optimizing, and managing an evolving global manufacturing footprint. The approach and focus points at each step are illustrated in Figure 9.1.

## Step 1: Understand the strategic drivers for your global manufacturing footprint

Each industry is shaped by different factors that determine its need for a global manufacturing footprint. The same is true for individual companies. Before any company can optimize its manufacturing footprint, it must analyze the reasons why it is necessary to expand its global network and the implications of these factors.

There are two overriding reasons why companies delocalize their manufacturing activities: either they are lured by the attractiveness of potential markets, or they want to lower costs. Companies should keep these goals in mind when creating guidelines for their company's globalization strategy. The reasons for addressing manufacturing network design issues, and the challenges to reach the two manufacturing goals, are shown in Figure 9.2.

Improving cost performance is a common strategic imperative in most industries. The business case for optimizing cost is straightforward and is based on total cost of ownership. It leads to the offshoring of components and manufacturing activities that have high labor content, and are

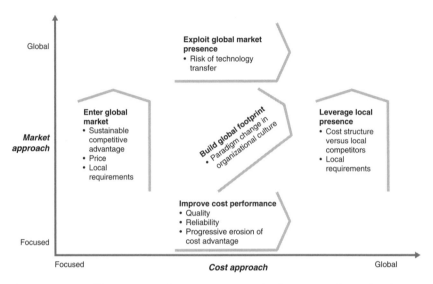

**Figure 9.2**  Different manufacturing network design goals and relevant challenges

characterized by relatively low technology and criticality. Local manufacturing operations provide labor-intensive work, simple technology, and low plant investments. While product design is not affected by the decision to delocalize production, ensuring good quality and reliable delivery are two pressing concerns once manufacturing is relocated for cost optimizing reasons. No major risk of technology transfer exists because the delocalized technology is relatively low. Companies that offshore to reduce costs need to remember that their cost competitiveness will erode over time, due to the progressive increase in local costs and cost alignment from competition.

When companies build a global manufacturing footprint in order to increase the customer base, the challenge is more complex, especially if the focus is on fast growing emerging markets: complexity enters the game as products need to be redesigned to fit the requirements of potentially millions of local but highly heterogeneous customers. At the same time, companies need to keep as many components and interfaces standard in order to leverage economies of scale. Operations are required locally, including final product assembly lines and test operations. In addition, the risk of technology transfer is greater, as suppliers and the local workforce gain access to more sophisticated technological processes. A change of paradigm in the organizational culture is required when moving to a completely global footprint. The rapid growth of local competitors is a threat that should be considered when building the business case. In comparison with foreign players, local companies require no (or limited) R&D investment, their management structure is cheaper, and they face lower compliance costs.

In some cases, companies will need to delocalize their operations in order to enter closed or regulated markets. This is true for companies in the aerospace and defense market, for instance. The aim here is not strictly to benefit from market proximity, or lower transportation and labor costs. Delocalization, in these cases, is simply a precondition for gaining local market share. Companies will need to adopt a different strategy, as business activities will need to be redesigned to meet industrial agreements. In the aerospace and defense industry, for example, extremely complex industrial footprints are designed to comply with the sector's pre-negotiated work-sharing agreements, and technological fallout requirements. In my experience, optimizing such a complex – and counter-intuitive – manufacturing footprint works only if partner companies are closely integrated on an organizational level and already have excellent manufacturing operations. The situation of component suppliers for the automotive industry is slightly different. Suppliers require a local presence to match the internationalization priorities of their OEMs. Here, the focus is on minimizing risk exposure through long-term contracts with the OEM and ensuring high quality and reliability of local operations.

Another reason for building a global manufacturing footprint is to create a defense against low-cost competition stemming from new economies. Competing purely on cost is not a sustainable strategy for any western manufacturer. A different sort of business model is required. In this situation, a company's global manufacturing footprint strategy needs to be totally integrated and aligned with that company's overall business strategy. Companies can reinforce their protective defense against low-cost competitors only by creating a sustainable competitive advantage. This can be achieved through clever product positioning or research and development, or both. Globalizing without a sound diversification strategy could prove useless.

## Step 2: Derive the global manufacturing footprint model

Once companies have a clear understanding of the reasons for developing a global manufacturing footprint, they can start defining the guidelines that should shape that presence. General aspects companies need to consider include the markets they wish to serve, local content, and cost priorities. More specific aspects that should be considered are labor content, economies of scale in each phase of the manufacturing process, alternative manufacturing processes, and transport costs. It is important to keep the company's manufacturing cost structure firmly in mind when examining these aspects.

Centralized final manufacturing operations with offshoring of components and sub-assemblies are typical in industries that demand large investments and stringent quality requirements, and in which labor content and simpler operations characterize the manufacture of components and sub-assembly. Lower labor content is required for the final phases of the assembly process. Complex mechanical systems in the aerospace and automotive industries are exemplary here. They can leverage the low cost of forgings and castings derived from emerging economies, as well as low labor costs for other simple-to-manufacture parts against downstream activities that must be centrally executed. These downstream activities require large investments for metal cutting machines and surface treatments. High quality control standards and advanced labor skills in final assembly operations are needed too.

Other industries, in contrast, are characterized by large economies of scale in upstream operations and low value-added, and limited economies of scale in final manufacturing operations, which are also burdened by high transportation costs. This is true of the aluminum industry, in which a typical global manufacturing configuration is based on a number of similar small size local plants (for example, extrusion) that are served by regional smelters, mostly located in countries where the cost of electric power is relatively low; these, in turn, are served by proprietary aluminum ore mines.

In the construction material sector, transportation costs and local requirements limit the market that could potentially be served by a single plant. Large international players leverage technical competencies and support services in order to ensure internal benchmarks, cross fertilization, and best practices. Globally shared services provide low cost support for the entire group.

The automotive industry has pushed the global manufacturing footprint to an extreme because it can profit from large economies of scale in engineering, manufacturing and procurement, leveraging the size of global markets. An international network of in-house plants and suppliers serves a global footprint of final assembly plants to produce diversified and localized models based on standardized and modularized platforms and modules. Engineering activity is shifting to decentralized centers of excellence to react more quickly and attentively to local requirements and locally designed components. For automotive suppliers, the one reason for relocating business is better to serve OEMs.

The aerospace and defense sector provides another model for a global manufacturing footprint. International agreements and offsets, and defense constraints and embargos are factors that need to be considered when defining the footprint's contour. An international military program could comprise a complex set of work packages that include four different assembly lines in four different countries, two sites for manufacturing composite wings (one country produces the right wing for all partners, another country produces the left wing), for instance. It is likely to work with various other relatively inefficient solutions that ensure that know-how and technology ownership is balanced between players and countries.

To configure the best manufacturing footprint, companies need to consider their own strategy, as well as industry and product characteristics such as economies of scale and cost structure. Cost components such as labor, transportation and energy should not be left out of the equation. At this stage, companies are also well advised to consider the availability of a skilled and reliable workforce, as well as partners and external constraints.

## Step 3: Segment product structure and define relocation scenarios

After a company has selected its overall manufacturing model based on strategic drivers and a thorough understanding of operational factors, it needs to conduct a detailed analysis to ensure that value chain activities are allocated optimally. Product structure and manufacturing operations should be analyzed in depth in order to identify the most suitable components and activities for relocation. Two dimensions are important here: economics and risk.

Economical variables are required to define the overall payback of delocalizing a specific manufacturing process. The main areas of investigation are:

- Manufacturing options (automation investments versus more labor intensive manufacturing, traditional assembly plant versus CKD)
- Required investments for each manufacturing option
- Overall cost structure (labor, materials, depreciation, energy, transportation, services)
- Expected lifecycle and cost structure evolution.

A business case is then built to provide the expected payback for each component and manufacturing activity analyzed.

Risk is then defined based on variables such as technological complexity, component criticality (the importance of reliability of delivery), quality requirements, required labor skills, and technology transfer. A risk indicator provides an assessment of the variance of the expected payback over a certain period of time if the manufacturing activity is delocalized. An illustration of a payback and risk analysis is given in Figure 9.3.

Based on risk and payback, companies should test different manufacturing scenarios. These should calculate total cost of ownership and the relevant risk for each configuration. A sensitivity analysis simulates the effect of changes in cost drivers to the total cost of ownership for each scenario analyzed.

Before advancing to the next step, companies should have a thorough understanding of the conditions necessary to relocate each manufacturing phase in the most advantageous way possible. A checklist can help companies ensure that they have considered the factor costs required to meet the specific cost structure, labor skills, specific technological capabilities, and shape of the competitive environment.

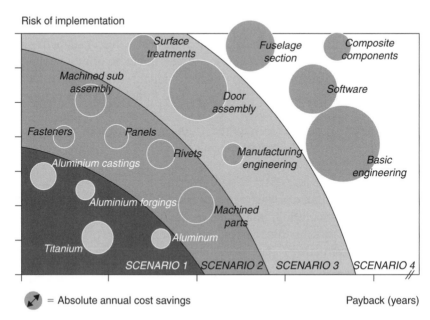

**Figure 9.3**   Payback and risk analysis

## Step 4: Select target countries

There are a number of different ways companies can select target reloca-tion countries, and these will depend on the global manufacturing foot-print strategy the company wants to pursue. In some cases, the number of countries considered will be restricted because the company knows it wants to enter a specific market that has its own unique offsets or local content requirements. In other cases, the list of countries is short because a company is relocating to serve a specific client – for example, OEM proximity for automotive suppliers, or because of very specific local content requirements. Sometimes, there will be no preliminary restrictions on potential countries that may belong to the manufacturing footprint.

The process of selecting countries for setting up manufacturing operations should be addressed in two different ways. If shortlisted countries are chosen because of strategic imperatives, companies need to consider what activities and modules can best be produced locally, considering the size of the target market and the amount of local content required. These companies also need to screen potential supplier networks and assess local technological capabilities to filter the components or activities that are most suited for local production.

In the specific case of automotive component manufacturers, OEMs' requirements and trends are a major part of the strategic decision and should be investigated in depth.

Companies must understand clients' expectations in relation to the following dimensions:

- Restrictions on sub-suppliers and/or certification requirements for second tier suppliers – aerospace and defense second tier suppliers need to pass a strict certification process
- Local content requirements – OEMs sometimes require local content from first tier suppliers to meet requirements in specific countries
- Outsourcing – OEMs often require first tier suppliers to dominate the technology, or they require specific assemblies to be in full control of the first tier supplier
- Constraints based on lifecycle phases and specific activities – OEMs sometimes restrict low-cost country sourcing until the product reaches maturity. They do this to reduce the risk of problems with first series. Afterwards, they will turn to local engineering for support and technical expertise
- General sourcing preferences – components versus modules, specific regions for low-cost sourcing.

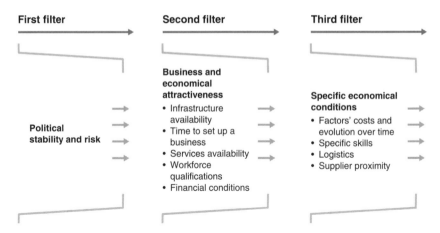

**Figure 9.4**   Selection of target countries

If cost optimization is the main reason for creating a global manufacturing footprint, the approach is the opposite. A systematic screening of potential locations has to be performed based on priority modules and activities. The process of selecting a country starts with a long list of potential countries that is gradually shortened as countries fail to meet progressively stringent criteria. Lack of political stability and risk are two of the first criteria that cause elimination, combined with external constraints such as embargos and final client vetoes.

A second filter aims at investigating the overall business situation and economical attractiveness of the potential candidate countries. Companies should check the availability and quality of infrastructure (transportation, electricity, gas, water, and real estate), the legislative environment and bureaucracy (time required to set up a business; availability of legal, accounting, recruiting, and logistics services), financial conditions (corporate tax, incentives) and manpower (skills, unemployment, wages, and attitude).

A third filter is then used to determine the impact a specific delocalized activity or component would have on the company's overall business model. The sorts of aspects examined here include specific technological skills, the existence of a relevant supplier base, the presence of competitors, logistics capacity, and cost of labor over time.

## Step 5: Fine-tune the model and finalize the footprint

Once a company has selected a shortlist of potential locations for a specific manufacturing activity, it is time to simulate the impact of that delocalized manufacturing activity at each of the short-listed locations. This quantitative simulation provides companies with a handful of potential scenarios for the selected manufacturing footprint model. The scenarios reflect each manufacturing activity to be relocated in target countries.

Three main performance indicators are put under scrutiny for each scenario: first, the expected value over the entire lifecycle; second, overall risk; and third, flexibility (the ability to cope when environmental factors change unexpectedly).

A simulation model is built to compare the economic performance of each scenario, based on the expected evolution of external variables over time in each country (sales volumes, costs, for example). The model provides the required investment and expected return for each scenario. Companies perform a 'what if' analysis to understand the best- and worst-case scenarios for variables. Sales volumes, implementation timing, and costs are some of variables that are included in the model. Risks such as currency movements, supply interruption, political instability, and transportation delays should be included in this analysis. The most attractive configurations are selected for a final examination that measures the flexibility of each selected scenario.

The worst-case scenarios are also analyzed in order to understand and calculate the potential cost of reconfiguring the footprint. A recovery plan is built for selected scenarios, which are compared. Make-or-buy and investments decisions are made to minimize risk and maximize flexibility.

## Step 6: Select site, suppliers and partners

Selecting sites, suppliers, and partners is one of the most important tasks companies need to undertake to ensure that strategic guidelines provide tangible results. The selection of site, supplier, and partner should be based on a structured process that starts from the identification of a long list of potential suppliers and/or partner companies. These are then screened to reach the best solution.

To select the most appropriate site, companies need to investigate four areas: investment, infrastructure, legal environment, and HR availability and skills. Figure 9.5 illustrates how different locations can be compared.

When choosing a supplier and partner, it makes sense, first, to undertake desk analysis. During this phase, a long list of potential candidates will be chosen based on the selection criteria: technology, size, manufacturing capabilities, and client base. Desk research should be complemented by interviews with industry experts to ensure completeness and to iron out any misunderstandings or false assumptions.

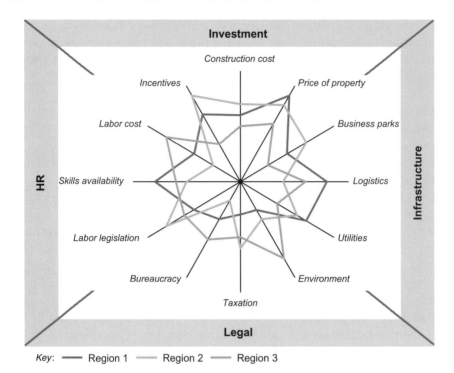

**Figure 9.5**　Site selection

Depending on the size of the long list, telephone interviews or questionnaires should be used to screen possible suppliers and partners. Here, companies can detect whether the long list candidates are interested in collaborating. It also gives companies the opportunity to complete and cross-check information regarding technical capabilities, size, and client base.

Once a shortlist is defined, an on-site assessment with a team comprising technical and financial experts is necessary to provide comprehensive information about the quality of the management team and employees, technical tools and capability, process quality, delivery reliability, financial stability, and cost structure. A request for quotations on pilot components and a business case should conclude the selection process and launch the negotiation phase.

## Global manufacturing footprint – a process without close

Companies need to monitor their manufacturing footprint periodically, checking to see whether it is still relevant and to determine whether external factors make adjustments wise. What made economic sense a few years ago might, in the meantime, have become a competitive disadvantage in the quickly evolving world of manufacturing. This is especially true when it comes to footprints that are heavily reliant on technology or low-cost country manufacturing. Technology, thanks to its very nature, is programmed to become obsolete. The only uncertainty is how quickly it will have to be replaced. Similarly, low-cost countries are developing so fast that some lose their competitiveness within a few short years and are superseded by other countries that are possibly located on the opposite side of the globe. This is why it is so important for companies to consider future trends and avoid focusing on existing conditions when designing a global manufacturing footprint or redesigning an existing one.

## Case study: How the approach works in real life

Our client, a multi-national industrial engineering company, pursues a strategy to increase its global presence with the aim of leveraging potential new markets and to defend itself against the increasing onslaught of competitors from low-cost countries.

Its presence in emerging markets to date has been based on partnerships with local players. Direct industrial activity has been limited. While this activity has led to significant sales in some business areas, it has come at a heavy cost: namely, large technology transfer. Previous partners are now able to offer similar solutions not only in their home country, but also abroad, with an extremely competitive cost structure.

The project team was asked to define a new footprint model to maximize the increasing volumes that can be captured in the Far East market and to make a dramatic reduction in the current cost structure. The footprint model had to include a strong industrial and procurement presence in emerging countries to guarantee market access and cost competitive *vis-à-vis* local players.

A detailed cost simulation revealed that the company could gain large cost advantages by serving global clients from China. To leverage the global footprint fully, a new procurement organization was designed and implemented that shifts local procurement to a single global procurement responsibility for each business segment. The project team segmented the product structure in detail and mapped the advantages and disadvantages of local capabilities compared with a global capability. As a result of this mapping exercise, activities were identified that can be relocated and sourced globally – including, for instance, all steelworks, as well as basic and detailed engineering.

China was selected as the target country for extending the industrial presence, based on consolidated presence, size of the market, and overall industrial structure, including the supplier base. A detailed screening of target companies was performed (starting from a long list of more than 300 state-owned and private companies, and design institutes, covering all the relevant business areas) that identified potential players and targets for acquisition. The project team whittled down this long list until the 20 most attractive and appropriate companies remained. Out of this shortlist of 20 candidates, one company was targeted for acquisition mainly due to its technical capabilities, size, and ownership structure. Our client was successful in its goal and, following the acquisition, a new manufacturing model was introduced.

The new company now acts as the main manufacturing and engineering location to serve all of the Far East for a specific technology. Other selective regions will also be covered by this location in the future. It provides engineering services to a specific business area/technology, and the parent company aims to gradually extend its engineering support to other technologies. It should act as the service hub for low-cost procurement in the region, within the scope of the new global procurement model.

Taking this step represents a considerable change in the overall footprint of the company. However, management considers it to be just an initial step, one that needs to be taken to cope with rapid market and technological change. The company is well aware that its manufacturing model and footprint will need to adapt continuously in order to remain competitive. A systematic approach that analyzes strategic options and defines concrete implementation solutions has proven to be the key for this company, enabling it to continue doing business successfully in the global market.

## Outlook

The manufacturing models and footprints of global companies will be placed under increased pressure in the future. The speed of evolution in newly emerging markets, the rate at which low-cost players are catching up in terms of technological competence, and the rapid development of cost components mean that companies need constantly to reassess their footprints.

To compete in the future, companies will need to master three skills. First, they must show flexibility and be willing to adjust their footprint to align with anticipated market changes. Manufacturing footprints have to be sufficiently malleable to follow the continuous evolution of international markets. An optimal balance of internal and outsourced activities, and a flexible supplier base and modular products are required to adapt quickly, minimize investments and risk, and optimize results.

Second, they must be able to keep their core competencies while outsourcing low-value skills. Finding the balance between in- and outsourcing takes time and careful consideration. Companies are wise to proceed here with caution. Greater education levels among the workforce in emerging countries, weak copyright protection legislation, and the increased ease with which information can be duplicated expose global players to a great risk. Companies face a real threat of losing their technological competitive advantage.

Third, companies must be capable of managing complex organizational structures with multiple reporting lines in different geographical areas. A new generation of managers with dexterous management skills that permit them to cope with organizational complexity is a must as global footprints increase in size and become more complicated. Managing multiple reporting lines, dealing with conflicting objectives, and coping with an increased need for strategic control, while delegating most operational decision making, will be some of the skills required for managers in the future.

## Further reading

Falb, R. (2006) 'Global Footprint Design – Die Spielregeln in der internationalen Wertschöpfung beherrschen'. Roland Berger Strategy Consultants. Stuttgart.

# CHAPTER 10

# Leveraging manufacturing excellence in global production networks

*Volker Heidtmann and Stephen Weisenstein*

## Introduction

Manufacturing excellence – lean manufacturing – the Toyota production systems – regardless of the name that is applied, the elements that make up a strong and efficient manufacturing system and process are well known. Principles such as 'just-in-time production and logistics', 'built in quality', and 'continuous improvement' are applicable across manufacturing industries and are applied in many ways. Business people have toured the best plants and read the many books on the subject as they strive to eliminate waste from their processes and achieve the greatest possible cost and quality performance.

When managers question the competitiveness of a plant or operational process, they try to conduct benchmarks to confirm or quash their doubts. Benchmarking the industry leader has its advantages, and adopting selected ideas from competitor plants definitely provides a great many benefits: however, the two tasks are not always easy to undertake. In their hurry to turn to the competition for ideas, many companies ignore the obvious first step: share and leverage best practices within your own organization and between your plants.

We frequently find varying levels of success in implementing world-class manufacturing systems and processes, even within manufacturing networks belonging to the same company. Why can one plant be so successful and a sister plant be so poor? This chapter answers that question, and provides direction to managers seeking to introduce manufacturing excellence throughout all their operations. After outlining the steps that are necessary to leverage manufacturing excellence in global production networks, we show how this approach worked in a real-life business setting, drawing on a project we completed in the automotive industry.

## Be your own benchmark

The benefits of turning a company's gaze inwards are tremendous. First, the benchmarking process is significantly easier because of improved access to information and greater transparency. Similar products and corporate culture make it easier to transfer best practices when they are unearthed. This increases standardization between plants, which not only drives efficiency but also flexibility.

Our approach to launching a manufacturing excellence effort starts with a project structure and then transfers the task into the line organization. In our experience, a four-step process ensures that the project challenge is tackled pragmatically and with a clear structure, which is critical for successful completion. Companies that follow this process work with project teams to gain a deep understanding of the current status of their processes and particular operation, develop an overall vision for the focus area, become involved in making improvement plans that are feasible, and ensure that implementation efforts are taken seriously. They achieve this last step in part by communicating the reasons for change and highlighting quick wins, which has the additional benefit of motivating staff. The process is illustrated in Figure 10.1.

## Preparation

To realize the benefits from optimizing a plant network, good preparation is essential. Selecting the right plants for comparison and getting the right people on board is important in order to find the most relevant management practices and transfer them to other plants. It is also crucial for acceptance of the necessary changes in all locations.

In most cases, a plant network cannot be analyzed entirely. Even in networks with barely more than ten plants, looking into each plant thoroughly is a formidable task. The endeavor would most probably be doomed from the first day because freeing up the resources necessary to conduct the project would be almost impossible.

A more practical approach is the so-called T-shaped project design, which is shown in Figure 10.2.

During the T-shaped project approach, all plants are analyzed using a standardized quick scan. This gives the project team a high-level overview of processes, practices, and procedures. In-depth analysis (comprising plant visits, interviews, and detailed data gathering) is started afterwards, and focuses on a small number (typically, four to eight) of the most

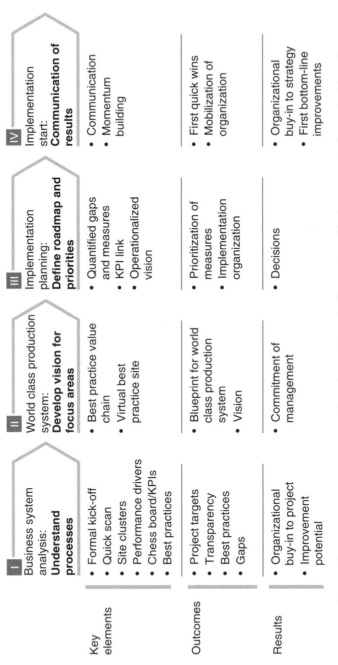

| | I | II | III | IV |
|---|---|---|---|---|
| | Business system analysis: **Understand processes** | World class production system: **Develop vision for focus areas** | Implementation planning: **Define roadmap and priorities** | Implementation start: **Communication of results** |
| Key elements | • Formal kick-off<br>• Quick scan<br>• Site clusters<br>• Performance drivers<br>• Chess board/KPIs<br>• Best practices | • Best practice value chain<br>• Virtual best practice site | • Quantified gaps and measures<br>• KPI link<br>• Operationalized vision | • Communication<br>• Momentum building |
| Outcomes | • Project targets<br>• Transparency<br>• Best practices<br>• Gaps | • Blueprint for world class production system<br>• Vision | • Prioritization of measures<br>• Implementation organization | • First quick wins<br>• Mobilization of organization |
| Results | • Organizational buy-in to project<br>• Improvement potential | • Commitment of management | • Decisions | • Organizational buy-in to strategy<br>• First bottom-line improvements |

**Figure 10.1**  Proven four-step process ensures that the project challenge is tackled pragmatically and with a clear structure

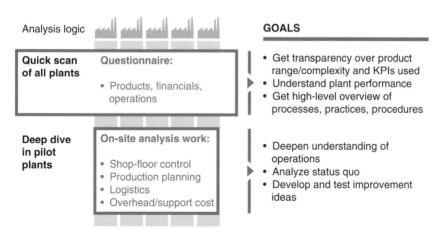

Analysis logic                                **GOALS**

| Quick scan of all plants | Questionnaire:<br><br>• Products, financials, operations | • Get transparency over product range/complexity and KPIs used<br>• Understand plant performance<br>• Get high-level overview of processes, practices, procedures |

| Deep dive in pilot plants | On-site analysis work:<br><br>• Shop-floor control<br>• Production planning<br>• Logistics<br>• Overhead/support cost | • Deepen understanding of operations<br>• Analyze status quo<br>• Develop and test improvement ideas |

**Figure 10.2**   A T-shaped logic ensures breadth and depth of the analyses

relevant plants. Plant selection depends on a plant's technological and economic profile. Plants should be selected in such a way that the core technologies and production processes of the company are reflected. At the same time, all economic conditions should be reflected as well. To gain a good cross-section and a fair indication of economic conditions, both high labor cost and low labor cost sites should be included. Similarly, small and large plants should be examined, as should plants showing good and less favorable economic results. Best practices are then identified within the focus plants and are subsequently rolled out to the entire plant network.

To arrive at project results that are meaningful, and also implementable, it is crucial to have the right people on board. In our experience, a combination of local plant experts and global production staff has proven to be particularly successful. In this arrangement, local experts can contribute their detailed knowledge about production and logistics processes. This results in very specific actions being developed, which factor in possible implementation problems already in the concept phase. Global production staff functions can provide overall methodological guidance and continuously align the project with the greater production environment and, hence, prepare the subsequent rollout.

Implementation tends to run more smoothly when project members who enjoy broad professional acceptance are selected. Ideally, they should be opinion leaders in their field of expertise. This can mean the power to make formal decisions in the case of divisional managers, but also professional standing when well-respected functional experts are involved. With this mixture of highly respected people, employees at individual plants will find it easier to accept concepts already developed and implemented at other sites.


## Benchmarking

The actual project should begin with a quantitative analysis of all plants in the network. Typically, common reporting figures are not sufficient. Depending on the project focus, additional information will be necessary. For this purpose, we recommend the development of a standardized questionnaire. Its content should typically include basic profit and loss data; manufacturing-specific cost details such as labor cost breakdowns, depreciation and maintenance costs; and asset data for machinery, equipment, and inventories. Non-financial information such as headcount, quality data, and logistics performance should also be collected in the questionnaire. Whatever information is gathered, all parties involved must have a common understanding of the data if it is to be interpreted in a meaningful way. To this end, a detailed description of the data is necessary. In our experience, offering a central support to clarify open questions during the gathering of data also supports consistency.

The results of the quick scan allow the project team to assess each plant using quantitative information. The quick scan enables the project team to distinguish strong from weak performers, both financially and operation-ally. It lets the team identify specific performance profiles, too. One plant may show poor financial performance, for example, but could have excellent quality figures. Another plant may score highly on both criteria. Based on these insights, the team can select the focus plants to be analyzed in depth during the project. At the same time, the analysis already provides a first indication of good and bad practices.

Identifying best manufacturing practices requires a much closer look at a plant. This can be gained through a several-day 'deep dive' plant visit. Typically, these visits will involve an investigation of product planning, examination of forecasting, studying the information systems (IS platform) and key performance indicators, as well as an analysis of the shop floor. During the shop floor analysis, the teams will look at control systems and batch sizes in addition to inventory management and inventory levels. Once these aspects have been considered, the teams tend to move on to logistics, examining the plant's subcontractor management, inter-company logistics and material management. The types of activities that might take place during a five-day pilot plan visit are shown in Figure 10.3.

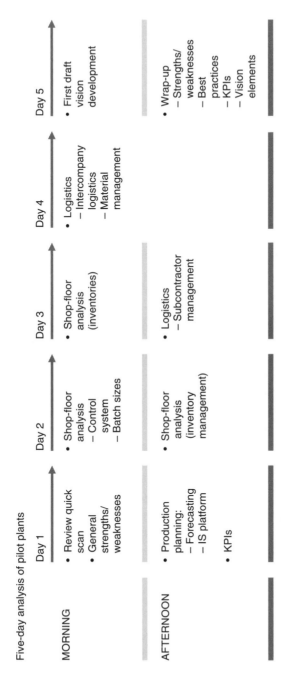

**Figure 10.3** A structured approach is used to analyze current processes and define new operations strategies

On-site discussions between the project team and plant experts provide a detailed picture of a plant's performance. The discussions serve to identify approaches, methods, and systems that have been applied successfully and which can be transferred to other places. As all relevant data is available on-site, the findings can immediately be supported with quantitative information.

## Concept development

Developing a common manufacturing concept is the most difficult part of the project. In this phase, the findings of the analysis phase have to be combined. This often means finding solutions that reflect very different plant environments. This phase is also tricky because of the human element involved. The personal convictions of team members, which may be reasonable when viewed from an individual perspective, often have to be resolved as they are no longer sufficient if considered from a global viewpoint. Open discussions and tact are paramount in this context.

As a vehicle to reach these results, workshop-style, full-day events have proven to be particularly successful in our experience. They allow the project team to step out of their daily business and focus fully on the project tasks.

To encourage target-oriented discussions, individual topics should be prepared in advance in specialized sub-teams. Here, both local and global experts should have extensive discussions on detailed approaches and possible solutions. A basic agreement should be reached at this level, and local plant requirements and experiences should be duly considered.

The results from the expert teams are eventually combined during the global workshops. Here, agreement has to be reached among all responsible decision makers. A project lives or dies by the ability to gain consensus at this stage. Without it, the project is doomed to fail because people involved in the implementation phase but who are unconvinced tend to sabotage efforts or slow down progress. Ultimately, the concept has to be endorsed by the entire leadership team of the company.

## Roll-out

While identifying best practices and developing a common manufacturing concept is the core of the improvement effort from a content point of view, the implementation phase is the most critical phase when it comes to achieving measurable results.

Companies that do not gain the firm commitment and support of all plants in the network will face difficulty when trying to implement a common manufacturing concept. The responsible plant managers should agree upon the developed concepts before the actual implementation begins. Including manufacturing heavy-weights in the concept phase pays off at this stage, because they will be able to defend the project results against potential criticism from outside the team more easily than others. At the same time, top management should express its support as well to ensure the plants' commitment lasts.

Once agreement on the new manufacturing concept has been reached, the concept has to be individualized for each site. General rules have to be translated into specific actions with dates and improvement targets. People have to be assigned responsibility too. This, again, is a task that should take place on-site, in discussion with local experts.

## Making the transformation stick

One might think that clear action plans should be enough to guarantee a successful implementation, but habits developed over many years are hard to change. Implementing a new way of organizing manufacturing is prone to fail if left unattended, so strong is the resistance to change. Only central monitoring of the implementation process and regular reviews of the implementation process by top management can ensure that the good intentions and first positive steps are not lost. Individual plants should receive central coaching support; it is not always unwillingness that prevents change but sometimes simply the difficulties of putting change into practice on-site.

With the start of the implementation phase, the responsibility for the success of the implementation should be transferred to the line organization. Plant managers and division heads are the personnel to drive implementation. Otherwise, a lack of hierarchical support is likely to smother implementation efforts in the face of operational needs.

Figure 10.4 shows an example of a real implementation structure in which content team leaders adopt the coaching role while the line organization, consisting of plant managers and operations directors, ensures hierarchical support. The plant process owner has an ongoing dialogue with the plant manager and a content team member, at least at the beginning of the implementation phase, and input about implementation content and progress from plant experts is exchanged. In the case shown here, a content team member and the plant manager discussed results with

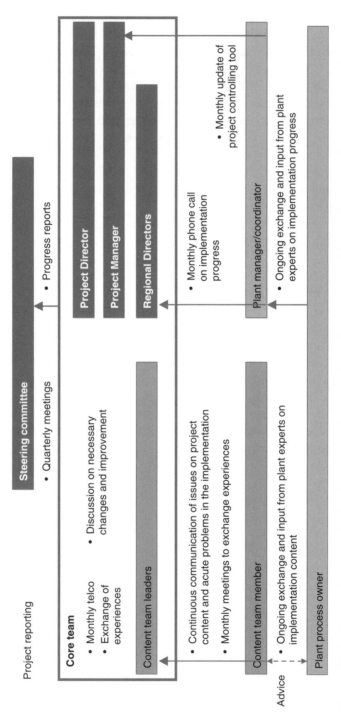

**Figure 10.4** The project organization is set up to keep track on the progress of the project – regular communication is key

Best practice sharing process

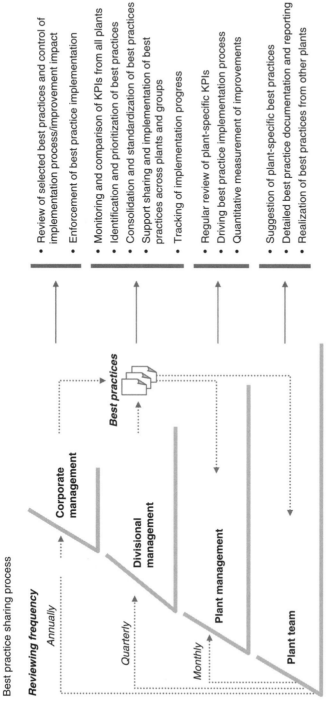

**Figure 10.5** A regular communication process drives the sharing of internal best practices

content team leaders, regional directors, and project managers on a monthly basis.

The final step in implementing a common manufacturing system is to ensure that sharing best practices does not remain a one-off effort but, rather, becomes part of a company's day-to-day reality. In short, identifying and sharing best practices has to be institutionalized. A multi-level process that includes all parts of the manufacturing organization can provide an effective structure for this. Each level has a role to play in identifying internal best practices and ensuring that they are adopted. An example of this type of structure is given in Figure 10.5.

Ideas are generated on a plant level through joint teams of operators and functional experts. Practices that are relevant for sharing between plants are communicated to a central operations excellence function, which owns the common manufacturing system and develops it further. The function also coordinates the sharing of ideas and practices across plants through formal reports and personal meetings. Involving operators and functional experts who have participated in the development of best practices on the plant level can improve the acceptance of ideas and provide a motivational boost to plant level activities. Involving top management at the same time signals to the plants how important these efforts are.

So, how does this approach work in real life? We applied it at one of our clients from the automotive supply industry.

## Case study: Leveraging manufacturing excellence

The company is a global manufacturer of engine components with production sites spread around the globe. Each site had considerable freedom in designing its production and business processes – a common practice when managing spread-out production networks. The consequence was equally as typical: each of the plants had, over time, developed a very specific set of production processes with very different levels of operational performance. Specifically, inventory levels were a problem. To align the operational performance of all plants on a higher level, a project was initiated to develop and introduce a common approach to production logistics.

After the collection of key plant data from all sites, six were selected as focus plants for closer analysis. During plant visits and through the analysis of detailed performance data, six areas for action were identified: production planning, shop floor control, global logistics, production key performance indicators, production IT systems, and indirect functions. Each area was addressed by a team of experts gathered from various sites around the globe. The results of each team were then refined in two global workshops. These two events were the core of the project, the moments when all experts and key decision-makers met to approve the new concept.

To ensure a smooth and consistent implementation, detailed action plans were worked out together with each plant's management team on-site. Responsibility for implementation was dedicated to one clear responsible team member per plant, who supervised all local activities of the project. Local activities were accompanied by regular reviews by the company's top management.

Overall, the implementation of the new production system aimed at a 50 percent reduction in inventory over five years. In addition, a reduction in manufacturing cost of 8 percent was expected. The effects were distributed over time, coming both from short-term actions, such as the optimization of planning algorithms, and long-term actions, such as changes in plant layout or reorganization of indirect functions.

## Outlook

In the future, manufacturing excellence will be less about understanding the 'what' of lean principles and efficiency techniques and, instead, will be focused on the 'how'. Understanding manufacturing excellence and being able to lead an organization in achieving it are two very different competencies. Techniques such as those we have outlined in this chapter will be critical as companies fight to improve their competitiveness. Continually improving manufacturing performance throughout their global networks is central to that struggle.

# CHAPTER 11

# From maintenance to quality control: effective support functions leverage manufacturing performance

*Thomas Kwasniok and Walter Pfeiffer*

## Introduction

'We recently redesigned our factory layout and material flow, optimized shop floor processes and implemented lean manufacturing principles in production. However, the impact on overall manufacturing performance is below expectations, because we keep suffering from frequent short-term changes of our production schedule,' a production site manager at a modern and highly automated pharmaceutical plant in Germany confessed. Erratic sales forecast figures were the reason he gave for the plant's poor supply performance.

Over the previous twelve months, market demand had grown by 50 percent in some of the company's major markets. The average number of items out of stock had risen from around 150 to more than 400 during that period. International sales affiliates wanted shorter lead times to capitalize on short-term opportunities in their respective national markets. In spite of its manufacturing best practices, the German plant got the blame for the company's inability to keep up with market growth.

A detailed analysis of the situation revealed that the root cause was not outside, but inside the plant. Lead times for quality control had increased dramatically due to resource bottlenecks – the number of staff authorized to release batches was not scaled up along with recent volume growth – and poor planning in the quality control department. There was an information disconnect from export order processing, and even from production scheduling. Long and unpredictable lead times to affiliates resulted in an extraordinarily high share of rush orders, making it almost impossible for the plant to optimize production sequences. Capacity was lost on changeovers, and key performance indicators on delivery performance were not met. Operational equipment efficiency – the percentage of theoretical capacity of packaging lines that is actually used for productive work – suffered, too.

'We had focused on our main process: bulk manufacturing and packaging of pharmaceutical products. We did not realize that at some point the efficiency of our main process was limited by the effectiveness of a support function – quality control, in our case,' the site manager concluded.

What the site manager discovered about the quality control support function in his plant holds true for most manufacturing support functions. Whether equipment maintenance, factory logistics, utilities supply or wastewater treatment, if the support function is not effective it cannot leverage manufacturing performance. When the support function fails, costs can balloon.

This chapter investigates how a support function can be designed, mostly by using manufacturing equipment maintenance as an example. While some of the details are specific to that case, the general approach to tailoring an effective and efficient support function to meet the needs of the manufacturing process can be transferred to other support functions, too. This is noticeable at the end of the chapter, when we discuss the steps a refinery took to outsource support functions. In addition to detailing the building blocks for managing maintenance comprehensively, the article also shows how Roland Berger teams execute maintenance excellence programs. Further project examples are provided to show how the steps can be applied in real life in various settings, and the benefits the approach brings.

## Impact of support functions on manufacturing performance

Effectively managing support functions does not come cheaply: failure is a costly alternative. Companies need to keep these two factors in balance. A service level setting for a support function should aim at the lowest total cost. When it comes to equipment maintenance, short inspection intervals and comprehensive maintenance activities – such as analyzing the deep root cause of malfunctions – reduce failure costs.

A high level of equipment reliability is usually expensive because of personnel and training costs, and administrative overheads. However, it translates into short downtime and few quality defects. Minimum maintenance – 'run to failure', in the extreme case – can save maintenance costs, but results in unscheduled downtime and production delays. Lost

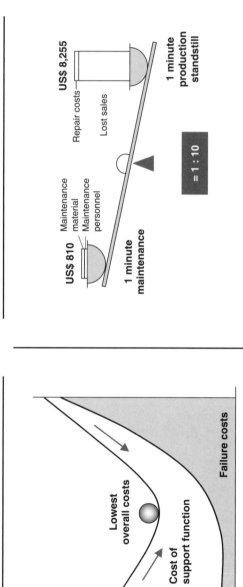

**Figure 11.1**  Costs of support functions and failure costs work in opposite directions and have to be balanced

orders are only one result of that failure. In addition, equipment defects tend to be more severe than with regular maintenance, as there is a risk of collateral damage to other units. When the cost of overly cautious maintenance is weighed against the steep cost involved in negligent maintenance, cautious maintenance is the cheaper option.

To illustrate that point, the average cost of equipment maintenance – personnel plus material cost – at automotive suppliers is approximately US$810 per hour. When production comes to a standstill, this causes damages of US$8,255 in lost sales and equipment repair costs per minute.

Setting costs aside for the moment, effective support functions also bring other benefits: product and service quality tend to increase, the more effective a support function. Product quality defects become less frequent when equipment maintenance is well managed. Service quality improves as the availability of products becomes better. Production planning is more reliable and customer lead times are shorter because fewer time buffers are required.

## Tailoring a supportive function: manufacturing equipment maintenance

A support function is designed, ideally, to meet the needs of the specific manufacturing process using as little capital and at the lowest cost possible. To achieve this, companies first need to understand the bare minimum requirements necessary to ensure efficient maintenance. For most companies, maintenance is efficient when equipment is available at a level that is acceptable from a manufacturing point of view. Companies also need to pay careful attention when designing processes, the organization, and tool support.

The ideal balance between maintenance cost and equipment availability differs vastly between industries, but also between different production lines and technologies. The amount of equipment that can be purchased on a specific maintenance budget also varies tremendously, depending on whether best practices are applied.

A recent benchmarking study of engineered products, automotive suppliers, and chemical companies conducted by Roland Berger Strategy Consultants suggests that automotive suppliers – on industry average – have the worst cost-to-availability ratio of all three sectors. The spread between low performers and best practice is especially wide in the chemical industry.

The importance of the cost of failure is also pronounced to varying degrees in different industries. In a workshop production environment, an

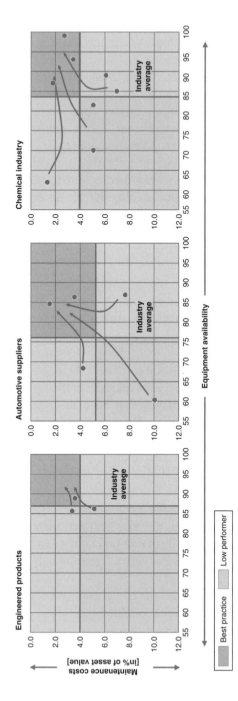

**Figure 11.2** A benchmarking study of maintenance costs and equipment availability shows the improvement potential for different industries
*Source:* Empirical study by Martin Weiss.

equipment failure affects only one production stage. Work-in-process buffers the implication between stages. An assembly line is hit much harder, because the entire line stands still if any single stage fails to operate properly. In the process industries, the cost of failure might even be a product loss, which is extremely costly because of rework or complete disposal. One cross-industry trend is clear: as the share of equipment cost to total production cost increases, the greater the impact of maintenance management on overall production cost.

A comprehensive approach to managing equipment maintenance – and manufacturing support functions – comprises six building blocks: strategy, process, organization, personnel, IT systems, and control. Managing spare parts is a special topic that appears in all six dimensions. It is a support function to the support function of equipment maintenance.

## Building block 1: Strategy

Companies can pursue three different maintenance strategies: breakdown, predictive, and preventive. Breakdown maintenance ('run to failure') aims at maximizing the useful life of all parts. Equipment is not serviced regularly, but only when a failure occurs. Breakdowns cannot be predicted, and this has implications for production planning. Predictive maintenance is based on frequent checking and a proper understanding of equipment wear and tear. Maintenance is performed when a certain level of wear and tear has been reached. Preventive maintenance uses regular service intervals. Parts get serviced and changed on a fixed schedule. Servicing times, as well as cost and capacity, can be planned in advance.

Companies should choose what strategy to follow based on the probability and impact of possible equipment failures. Roland Berger uses a risk-based method to classify possible failures and to determine the most appropriate maintenance strategy and parameters. This method is based on a failure mode and effect analysis (FMEA). It assesses all the failure modes that can be observed with a specific piece of equipment, and then describes all possible causes for those failures. Statistical data is evaluated to estimate the probability of each individual cause. The severity of each failure mode represents the associated failure costs.

The ability to detect a failure mode or failure cause in advance is another factor that should influence the choice of maintenance strategy. Probability, severity and detection effectiveness can be aggregated into a risk priority number. All three are used separately to determine what strategy is best for dealing with each failure mode. A service plan can then be worked out for

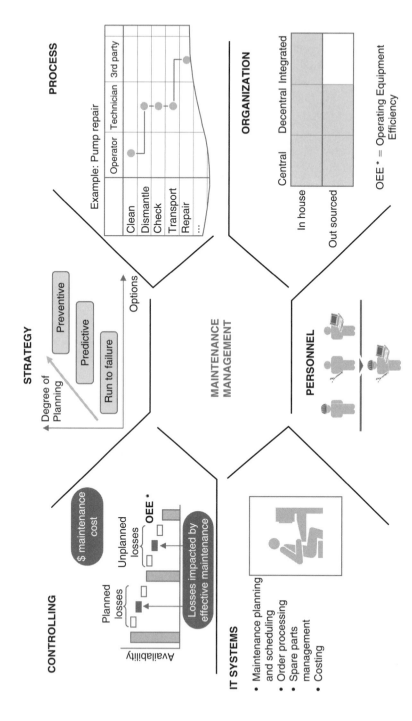

**Figure 11.3** Comprehensive maintenance management consists of six building blocks

each piece of equipment. Through the risk-based method, the selected maintenance strategy is clearly influenced by the equipment lifecycle. After a new piece of equipment is installed, early breakdowns are likely to occur because of poor component quality, assembly errors or design faults. Thereafter, breakdowns are seldom observed. When they occur, operator errors, dirt or maintenance mistakes are generally responsible. Later in the lifecycle, attrition breakdowns dominate. Since these are caused by component wear and material fatigue, they can be predicted.

## Building block 2: Process

Executing the selected maintenance strategy involves three levels of planning.

- Strategic parameters have to be set. Parameters – such as fixed maintenance intervals, number of operating hours, and level of wear and tear – that trigger maintenance are defined per equipment type and maintenance activity. These parameters help companies find a balance between maintenance and failure cost.
- A detailed work plan per activity is required. This allows companies to determine standard times and the spare parts and tools that will be needed for operational planning purposes – in most cases, the technical content of maintenance activities is specified by the equipment supplier. However, companies might find it worthwhile to review the activities with in-house technical experts and suppliers in order to detect potential for improvement.
- Companies need to make plans regarding employees and outsourcing partners. Production employees need to be involved in the coordination of production planning, especially during downtimes caused by maintenance.

## Building block 3: Organization

Based on experience, on average, only 20 percent of maintenance jobs actually require maintenance experts. Equipment operators can complete many simple maintenance activities – such as cleaning, set-up, and lubrication – after some training. This reduces costs and processing time because no maintenance personnel have to be called in, and operators are not idling time. Expert assistance would probably have to be brought in for more sophisticated tasks such as regular servicing or fixing minor breakdowns. Heavy maintenance, general overhaul, and refurbishment should remain the domain of dedicated maintenance personnel.

Integrated maintenance improves maintenance efficiency by minimizing the number of interfaces and handovers between single activities comprising a maintenance task. Companies also enjoy greater responsiveness and highly motivated employees when first level maintenance is integrated into production. However, investing in initial training and ongoing coaching of operators, and encouraging knowledge sharing between production lines and across sites is expensive. It is also difficult to adjust capacity for maintenance when the operating crew of each line is solely in charge of the majority of maintenance tasks.

Companies might also choose to have a dedicated pool of resources for maintenance, either on plant (decentralized) or company (centralized) level. With the decentralized option, companies profit from good knowledge of the plant and short distances. The opposite side of the coin is the need for greater resources, because a decentralized maintenance team's workload fluctuates. A centralized organization benefits from the sharing of knowledge, and a more balanced workload; however, it also faces long distances, lack of local knowledge, and difficulties motivating employees.

There is a promise of efficiency gains when companies share resources and balance workloads with maintenance, especially when engineering is done in-house and machines are built on site. Both functions typically struggle with workload fluctuations due to their limited internal customer base. A well-rounded mix of all three concepts – centralized, decentralized, and integrated – is essential to setting up an effective and efficient maintenance program.

Companies that choose decentralized or central maintenance units also need to decide between make-or-buy, in-house or outsourcing. It is now common practice for virtually all services related to equipment maintenance to be offered by equipment suppliers and third party service providers. Specialized suppliers, which are often located close or even on-site, are offering more and more production support services. The scope of outsourcing can vary from selected operational maintenance tasks to complete maintenance planning and execution. From a utilization point of view, an internal team should be used to carry the base workload, while demand peaks should be covered by scalable external resources. When considering a plant's ability to operate independently from external providers, companies might wish to ensure that an internal team is at least capable of maintaining the emergency mode operations of their production equipment. They should also be able to perform critical maintenance tasks without external support.

The advantages of outsourcing are clear. Fixed maintenance costs become variable, thus reducing utilization risk and bridging capacity shortages. It creates more efficient cost control, eventually lowers maintenance cost, and ensures better quality service. As well as gaining access to the external competencies of specialized suppliers, the internal service shop also gains free capacity for projects dependent on know-how. The disadvantages are clear, too. Companies risk losing internal skills, and the ability of internal resources to repair defects and operate product equipment self-reliantly is undermined. Long process times, quality issues, and delivery risks are also potential problems. Companies that outsource maintenance tasks need to have rules in place to resolve process issues. To control external maintenance providers, a clear description of process interfaces and service levels is essential.

## Building block 4: Personnel

When operators take on maintenance tasks, they must be trained and coached appropriately. Depending on the type of maintenance job, technical skills might be required. Operators must be equipped with analysis and problem-solving techniques, and guidelines that enable them to diagnose breakdowns efficiently and make decisions quickly.

## Building block 5: IT systems

Computerized maintenance management systems (CMMSs) provide support for equipment maintenance in four areas.

- Maintenance planning advises companies when maintenance work is required according to parameters set for each piece of equipment. It also helps companies to schedule capacity planning and to staff maintenance tasks.
- Maintenance order processing creates work orders, facilitates communication between internal functions and external service providers, and reserves and cancels spare parts and tools. It also triggers further Enterprise Resource Planning (ERP) functions, provides traceable documentation of machine history, and tracks relevant information such as the cause of a problem, downtime involved and recommendations for future action.

- Spare parts management is responsible for controlling spare parts inventories and procurement.
- The monitoring and reporting area is responsible for reporting maintenance costs and service levels.

While work order processing and basic reporting are covered by modern ERP systems, advanced planning can be improved by employing specialized software solutions. Most of these are designed to work as add-on solutions that link with ERP systems such as SAP R/3. Some CMMS products focus on particular industry sectors – for example, the maintenance of vehicle fleets or healthcare facilities. Others aim to be more general.

## Building block 6: Control

The purpose of maintenance control is to deliver information necessary for steering maintenance activities. Maintenance control needs to measure both maintenance and failure costs. A CMMS can assist companies to book all maintenance activities to the right cost centers so as to distinguish cost incurred to one production line from another, and to distinguish between regular inspections and servicing, preventive repair work, and defect repair. This becomes more challenging in an integrated maintenance organization, where operators spend part of their time on maintenance tasks.

Avoiding failure costs is the real value that effective maintenance provides. Since avoided failures do not show up in accounts, equipment downtime is widely used as a proxy to measure the effectiveness of equipment maintenance. A measurement of operating equipment effectiveness identifies planned and unplanned losses of equipment availability. Planned losses are times when planned maintenance jobs take place; it also covers times when no orders are planned or operators are unavailable. Unplanned losses are caused by equipment breakdowns, and variances in set-up and cleaning times. Quality loss and operator breaks and speed are found in this category too. An accurate assessment of maintenance effectiveness distinguishes losses by their root cause.

The target for equipment downtime should be based on the availability level defined for each piece or type of equipment in the strategy phase. The target also reflects the probability and impact of failure drawn from historical data stemming from the FMEA.

## A support for the support function

Although equipment maintenance is a supportive function, it also draws on another level of support: spare parts management. Spare part logistics is responsible for ensuring that spares are available at the right place when they are needed. They are also in charge of keeping logistics cost and capital employed under control. To set up spare parts management, the same six dimensions (the building blocks) need to be considered.

Strategies for spare parts supply vary from locally held stock (which is the most expensive but is always available), to central stock and call-off on demand from one or multiple supplier(s). Parameters such as target inventories have to be set in order to control the process of spare parts procurement. The organizational set-up is likely to reflect the centralized or decentralized strategy of stock keeping and reordering. Employees have to be trained and be supported by an IT system that provides inventory transparency, and triggers purchase orders according to the respective replenishment strategy and parameters. Maintenance control monitors the cost and capital employed in the spare parts inventory, and compares it with availability and the lead time experienced by the internal customer, the equipment maintenance function.

## Executing a maintenance excellence program

When executing a maintenance excellence program, our project teams adhere to an approach that comprises three phases: positioning, concept, and implementation. While each phase has its specific objectives and deliverables, in every step the consultants pay attention to each of the building blocks previously outlined.

Before the first project phase begins, there is a preparatory phase during which targets are set for the program. Companies might want to improve maintenance in a variety of areas. Common targets are lowering maintenance cost, reducing failure cost, improving product quality, and raising service quality levels. Target setting needs to reflect the expectations of internal customers and consider interdependencies with other functional areas.

The equipment availability target of maintenance – and cost incurred – is, to a large degree, determined by decisions made elsewhere in the organization. These decisions also affect the equipment availability necessary to satisfy external customers. For instance, manufacturing technology chosen by R&D determines what manufacturing equipment is purchased. This impacts the options and requirements for maintenance. Easily maintained machinery, for which spare parts are easily available at low procurement costs, makes the job of equipment maintenance easier. The job is also made easier with the use standard machinery that comes with maintenance services from the equipment supplier or can be completed by a range of third-party providers. More elaborate equipment developed by an in-house machine building function requires advanced internal maintenance skills.

Decisions on production planning and scheduling narrow down the options for corrective, predictive or preventive maintenance. The delivery service levels promised to external customers by sales and supply chain management functions significantly impact maintenance management by setting standards for product availability and buffer inventories. Our project approach to tailoring a support function emphasized intense involvement among the respective functional interfaces in the client organization.

Once the expectations are specified and agreements have been reached between the equipment maintenance function, internal customers and other stakeholders, the project is conducted in three steps: positioning, concept, and implementation.

## Positioning

In an exercise spanning two to four weeks (depending on the size and complexity of production equipment being examined), consultants gather and analyze production data from the shop floor and ERP systems. Benchmarking maintenance costs and equipment availability with industry peers provides an assessment of the initial situation. Depending on the quality of data available, an FMEA is conducted to evaluate the capability for probability, severity, and detection for typical equipment defects.

## Concept

Based on the findings of the positioning phase, the most adequate maintenance strategy is chosen by equipment type through Roland Berger's risk driven approach based on FMEA results. Further concept detailing deals with process design (including maintenance parameter setting), make-or-buy decisions, organizational set-up, skills and

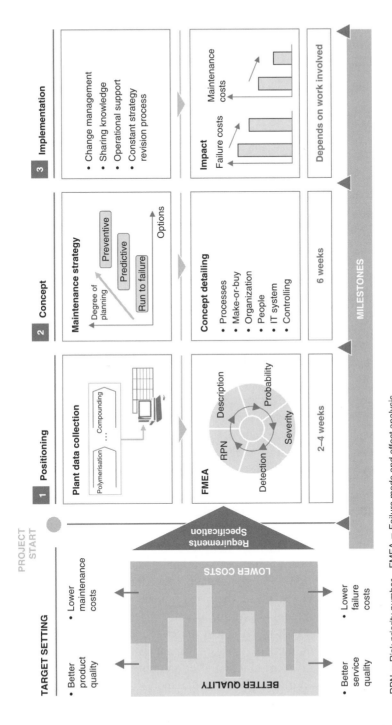

**Figure 11.4** A Maintenance excellence program needs clear target setting and is structured in three project phases

RPN = Risk priority number   FMEA = Failure mode and effect analysis

qualifications requirements, IT system selection, and a comprehensive and consistent control system. This project phase typically takes six weeks. At the end of the concept phase, an implementation plan has been generated and is ready to be executed.


## Implementation

Successful implementation involves more than simply installing the new structures, processes and systems. Key success factors are change management, and communication and knowledge sharing between external consultants and client employees on all levels of the client organization. Pragmatic operational support on the planning – and even shop floor – level is frequently required during the initial phase, especially when a company is transitioning towards an integrated maintenance organization.

After initial implementation, the selected maintenance strategies need to be constantly revised and improved, based on the findings from maintenance control and in adjustment to a changing production environment. From our experience, three principles need to be adhered to if a project is to be successful:

- There needs to be close cooperation with the maintenance organization
- Teams need to develop a workable concept that all parties, including interface functions, have agreed on
- Companies need to choose pragmatic solutions.


## Maintenance in Europe's chemical industry

Two examples from the chemical industry will elucidate what companies have to gain by properly managing their maintenance support function. Before embarking on a maintenance excellence program, many companies first have to place their maintenance building blocks in order. Because equipment downtime usually affects a whole series of production steps, the cost of failure in the chemical industry is high. In addition to lost output, there is also a significant risk of material loss. This has to be reworked or even scrapped after an equipment breakdown.

Our first client is a global player in the specialty chemicals industry, and our project focused on selected major sites in Europe.

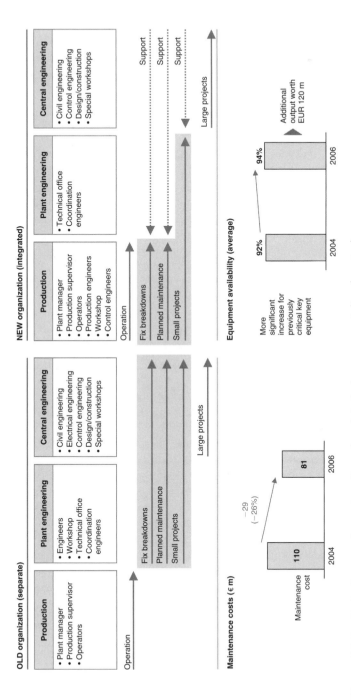

**Figure 11.5** Project example: major sites of a global player – specialty chemicals

## Example: Availability of critical production lines

Equipment maintenance was organized on two organizational levels: plant engineering and central engineering. Despite increasing efforts to improve maintenance, the client felt that the availability of some critical production lines was insufficient, resulting in loss of sales.

The project team's analysis revealed that the company had no defined maintenance strategy. Maintenance control was budget-oriented only. Employees in the plant engineering departments were, on average, highly qualified, but their workload and utilization fluctuated due to their high level of specialization. Operators hardly participated in maintenance activities, which led to significant idle periods as they waited for experts from plant engineering to arrive to perform tasks that were often simple. The participation rate of operators was 8 percent. Plant engineering performed 35 percent of all maintenance jobs, 57 percent was contributed by central engineering, of which only 15 percent was undertaken by centrally coordinated third parties. The overall share of planned maintenance was at a low 28 percent of all maintenance jobs.

The project team developed differentiated maintenance strategies for the client. An evaluation of the technical content of maintenance tasks led the team to conclude that operators could handle the majority of tasks. The decision was made to move towards a decentralized maintenance organization that was integrated with production. The plant engineering team was drastically reduced to a technical office with a number of coordination engineers. The workshop – formerly run as part of plant engineering – was transferred into production. The production function now deals with most planned maintenance jobs and small breakdowns, raising their share of maintenance work from 8 percent to 28 percent. The number of interfaces and handovers between subsequent work steps of maintenance tasks has fallen significantly. Processing times have also decreased.

Plant engineering and central engineering provide assistance on small projects, while large projects requiring specialized skills and tools are still run by central maintenance. In order to increase utilization of central maintenance staff and to gain access to external expertise, the outsourced portion of maintenance hours was almost doubled, from 15 to 27 percent. The headcount in central engineering was reduced by 38 percent of its original size.

The investment in an extensive training program for operators and the installation of a medium-range CMMS tool paid off after eight months of project work at a pilot plant and subsequent roll-out to all

European sites. Annual maintenance costs were reduced by 26 percent from €110 million to €81 million. Equipment availability increased from 92 percent to 94 percent, which represents additional output worth €120 million in sales revenues.

Besides compelling financial figures resulting from the project, another figure illustrates how much difference the program has made. The portion of planned maintenance grew from 28 percent to 70 percent. Equipment maintenance, which used to be a fire-fighting exercise performed by a poorly motivated and underutilized team with little attachment to production goals, has been turned into a well-planned activity. As a bonus, the majority of operators perceive the work as enriching their jobs.

## Shared support functions in the chemical industry

The second example demonstrating what can be gained by properly managing the maintenance support function shows how outsourcing production support functions can save costs – provided that the third-party provider operates on a more favorable cost basis. Outsourcing opportunities have grown substantially over the past years in Europe's chemical industry. The restructuring of all but one of the big conglomerates during the 1990s – BASF is the exception – has transformed former mono-sites into open industrial parks.

### Example: Outsourcing production support functions

The sizeable support functions of the parent companies had lost major parts of their customer base. Splitting up the support functions between the new production companies and business segments would have destroyed synergies, even within major chemical sites of companies such as Bayer (split into Bayer and Lanxess) and Hoechst (partitioned from 1994 until the merger with Rhône-Poulenc in 1999). The solution was to split real estate, site infrastructure, and services from the production companies. Bayer Industry Services was founded to look after Bayer's sites – the former Hoechst sites in Frankfurt; Infraserv service three other major locations.

The restructuring not only fragmented large companies, it also forced capacity adjustment. Some European production units were downsized or closed. Industrial areas and service capacities became available to third parties interested in starting up business in the new chemical parks. The result of this development is a wide range of supportive services advertised to chemical production companies: from general and location specific (such as real estate and basic infrastructure, site security and utilities) to production related and location independent (such as engineering and equipment maintenance). Today, there are more than 40 chemical parks in Germany alone.

## New developments in refining organizations

It is not only the chemicals industry that has seen benefits when support functions are redesigned to meet the needs of the manufacturing process, as our next project example shows. The case we draw on involves a refinery.

Refineries currently enjoy favorable conditions. High overall economic growth translates into healthy margins, and the demand outlook for the near future is quite promising. But the oil business is subject to global geopolitical forces and is strongly influenced by local catastrophes. Following Hurricane Katrina – which had a devastating effect on oil production and refining centers in the Gulf of Mexico, Louisiana and Texas – refining margins reached a peak. Since the business is cyclical, it is only a matter of time until the next major downturn hits.

Strong demand has led to new requirements. A workforce that has experienced repeated waves of job reductions and has been taught to follow a 'break–fix' maintenance philosophy struggles to run a plant at 100 percent over extended periods. Additionally, as refiners were reluctant for many years to hire enough employees, workforce gaps are common in this sector. Since it takes several years to train new personnel so that they are able to contribute fully to successful operations, this gap cannot be closed quickly. All too often this leads to management stretch. Too many initiatives in too many areas – ranging from operations over capital projects to service function management – have to be started at once. What changes to the refinery organization can managers make to ensure that their refineries are able to cope with the new challenges?

In our experience, a few key elements help prepare a refinery organization to meet the requirements of today's business landscape and to secure long-term viability. One element is a site fitness program (SFP)

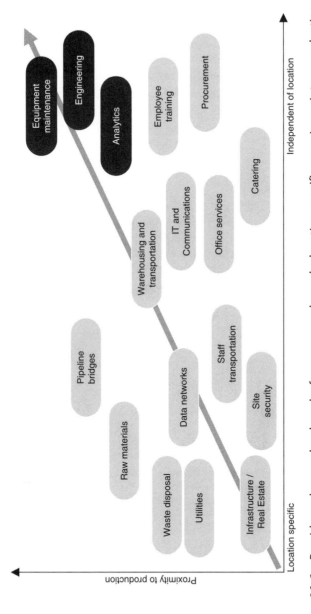

**Figure 11.6** Providers have developed from general and location-specific services into production support functions independent of location

for organizing the site. The goal of any SFP is to increase a refinery's flexibility. This program enables the refinery to undertake careful review and documentation of all functions, after which core business functions can be separated from support service functions. Core functions that are strategically relevant for the site because of their impact on the business and critical know-how include functions such as operations and operations planning. Key functions, by contrast, are crucial to the site but have no unique critical aspects. These functions are required by the core functions and, in some cases, are enforced by legal regulations. Examples of such functions are maintenance, fire services or HSSEQ. Materials management and facility management are typical examples of support functions.

## Example: Flexibility

In one project, we helped a German refining site transform itself into a flexible refinery by following a SFP. First, the refinery – with our help – reviewed its functions and identified the different groups of functions that needed to be optimized. The core functions were optimized for maximum performance. Next, the support functions were reviewed, with close attention paid to opportunities to optimize site services that could improve processes and release cash. These functions were viewed as candidates that could either be pooled together in a service center with other sites or outsourced to specialized third-party service providers. The refinery decided to outsource its materials management.

A second element was the identification of value-added service partners for non-core activities. An outline of these two elements is provided in Figure 11.7.

| Total site fitness Program for organization (SFP) | • Site fitness program: review of all functions in a refinery<br>• Identify core business activities<br>• Identify organizational alternatives for all other functions inside or outside the organization |
| --- | --- |
| Identification of value-added service partners | • Identify non-core activities that can be provided by service partners<br>• Key: qualified partners consider the relevant function as core business<br>• This can include services, supplies, etc.<br>• Should also include financing of capital employed |

**Figure 11.7** Two elements needed to create a high performance refinery organization

In the implementation phase of the project, the management of the refinery decided to outsource one of its support functions – the materials management of the refinery – to a value-added service partner. Some clear criteria separate a value-added service partner from a classic vendor. A value-added partner operates activities as a core business, continuously strives to optimize the joint partnership, is careful to stay in a neutral position, and complements the service offering with other value-added partners to form a value network. The role of vendors, in contrast, is typically restricted to selling parts and distinct services.

Although the refinery had a clear idea of what it wanted to achieve, finding a partner turned out to be a challenge. The large list of candidates quickly dwindled once the requirements of materials services for a refinery were explained in detail. The new partner had little time to get on board and handle regular operations because the refinery had scheduled its next turnaround one year hence. A turnaround is a major undertaking in this business. The whole refinery is shut down and equipment is checked for functionality and remaining lifetime, and replaced as appropriate. This has major implications for the supply of spare parts and materials. Several hundred purchasing requests must be processed within a short time frame.

Eventually, an appropriate partner was found and the whole materials management function was transferred to this partner. In agreement with the refinery, the new partner built a new warehouse immediately outside the refinery and optimized all material flows. This also allowed the refinery to offer the services to other prospective sites in the region once the turnaround had taken place. The transfer was executed successfully. Getting the partner on board brought significant improvements. Management and the key refinery team can now focus on core business activities.

Overall, the SFP and the outsourcing of the refinery's materials management resulted in a successful turnaround. Because of these two steps, labor costs were reduced by around 20 percent and material costs by 2–3 percent over a period of three years. Specific key performance indicators for the refinery were improved. These included total employees/refinery production, maintenance cost/refinery output, and return on capital employed. Finally, the headcount and cost base has become more flexible, giving the management room to maneuver in response to shifts in the business climate.

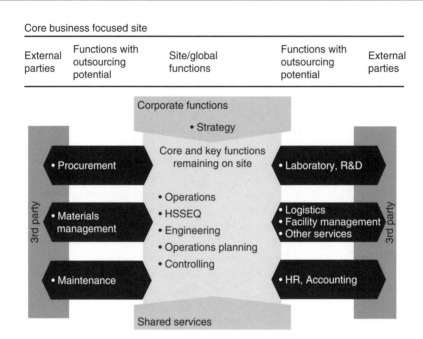

**Figure 11.8** A German refining site transforms itself into a flexible refinery

## Outlook

The reasons for a production company to share support services with other customers are synergy creation and a favorable cost base resulting from economies of scale. As a future trend, chemical parks and location-independent providers will extend the range of their service offerings along the value chain of the chemical industry, from pure support functions to closer to the production process. The same pattern is discernible in other sectors too. While services become more sophisticated and customer-specific, interdependencies between service providers and customers increase. A key success factor will be a seamless and efficient integration of all providers into the customer's business process. This helps maintain flexibility and variability of cost, which is the main reason why organizations outsource respective functions and services.

## Further reading

Roland Berger Strategy Consultants (2004) 'Global Footprint Design'. Stuttgart.

# PART IV

# Supply Chain Management

# Introduction

# Supply chain management – more than just logistics

*Robert Ohmayer and Steffen Kilimann*

Supply chain management is not a fancy consulting term for familiar functions such as logistics, transportation or warehousing. As the contours of the business world have shifted radically during the past decades, the demands on the supply chain have expanded. An integrating role, responsible for linking major business functions and processes into a cohesive and high-performing business model, has become necessary for business success. In many companies, supply chain management has taken on this central corporate role. The focus is no longer on how to move goods from A to B or how to organize a warehouse. Supply chain management sidesteps the function-based corporate organization and, instead, integrates the core functions that create value in an end-to-end process.

## Why is supply chain management so important?

Emerging economies provide new market opportunities and are shifting the center of gravity for sales and operations. Western European markets have become more mature and are highly competitive, which places the customer in a strong position. Whether markets are mature or developing, satisfaction and loyalty are essential to processes that serve the customer, including the supply chain. To meet demand, companies need to focus sharply on solutions and services. Relying on products is no longer enough. The supply chain has to expand and be able to serve a multitude of offerings.

The outsourcing of manufactured components is leading to increasingly complex business processes that require special attention and close monitoring. The scope of the supply chain is extending to manage this growing variety of interrelations. Productivity is taking on a new meaning: it refers not only to cost efficiency, but also to asset and service efficiency. Successful companies today strive for highest performance and lowest costs in equal measure.

The importance of supply chain management in corporate strategy, especially its direct impact on return on capital employed (ROCE), is clear. Supply chain decisions directly influence the value drivers of asset turnover and operating profit margin. Optimizing inventories throughout the logistics chain boosts asset turnover, for example, as does streamlining production and logistics networks. Reducing the complexity of both product ranges and processes in the logistics chain lifts the operating profit margin.

That is why supply chain management that aims to boost ROCE must be closely aligned to upstream corporate decisions. But a 'one-supply-chain-fits-all' mindset is not the right strategy. Successful companies tend to align their supply chain to the requirements of the relevant business segment or business unit. Customer and market requirements should be at the forefront of all supply chain decisions. Finding the right segmentation is definitely the key here. In highly competitive commodity markets, a cost-efficient supply chain with short lead times is critical. By contrast, in markets with more strongly customized products, a flexible and responsive supply chain is paramount.

Supply chain structures should be rigorously adapted to fit the relevant market requirements. This must be reflected in all structures, from supply chain organization to monitoring systems, and from production and logistics networks to processes and systems.

How can companies achieve supply chain excellence? Drawing on insights and experience gained advising clients, Roland Berger Strategy Consultants has created a framework for establishing end-to-end supply chain management. It covers all areas of supply chain strategy, from performance through to supply chain enablers.

In Part IV, we showcase our end-to-end framework, which is also illustrated in Figure IV.1. We describe the various methods and procedures for optimizing the supply chain at the level of strategy, performance and enablers, and employ examples from past projects and survey results to demonstrate the practical value of these methods and procedures. Dr Steffen Kilimann and Robert Ohmayer, in Chapter 12, use a case study from the electronic components industry to explain how companies can align their supply chain to the demands of a global market. In Chapter 13, Alexander Belderok and Thomas Hollmann show what impact can be achieved when complexity is correctly identified and

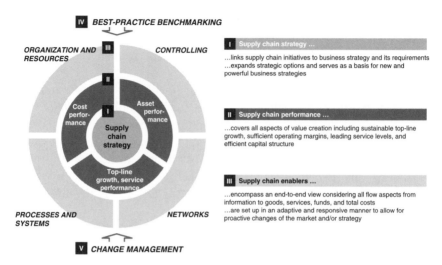

**Figure IV.1**    Our framework for end-to-end supply chain management

effectively managed. Using the results of a project from a healthcare company, they highlight the key levers for reducing complexity. In Chapter 14, drawing on a survey and case study examples, Roland Schwientek and Christian Deckert demonstrate how companies can boost their supply chain performance by achieving excellence in working capital and, in Chapter 15, Ingo Schröter and Stephan M. Wagner present best practices in establishing supply chain organizations.

# CHAPTER 12

# Global supply chain management: a success factor for global players

*Robert Ohmayer and Steffen Kilimann*

## Introduction

Supply chain management (SCM) is the nervous system of today's global economy. It has grown beyond its operational roots, when it was a way of controlling the flow of goods and services, to take on a more strategic role. As well as encompassing all operative core processes, it is now responsible for managing costs, and also reducing complexity and redesigning value chain structures. SCM directly influences the success of a company's key financials, such as return on capital employed (ROCE). Logistic functions such as inventory management, transport and warehousing were once purely functional and managed on a country-by-country basis only. These days they are bundled together and managed by an SCM manager who steers inventory and production capacity for an entire region or on a global scale.

However, SCM is a highly complex undertaking. New trends are emerging and, with them, a series of challenges. These have to be addressed if companies are to have supply chain excellence. In our view, companies require a strategic approach to master this complexity and to move through these obstacles. For this purpose, we have developed an end-to-end global supply chain management framework.

To illustrate how our approach works – and to highlight its tangible benefits for companies – we discuss a real project in which we helped a global producer of electronic components to achieve leaner production, distribution, and customer service structures. Before discussing our approach, we examine the trends and challenges in supply chains today. We pay particular attention to the increasing importance of global value chains; the division of labor in networked value chains; the growing complexity of product portfolios; and the demand for higher levels of service, reliability and flexibility. Following this, we discuss how companies can manage global supply chains.

## Trends and challenges in supply chains

Supply chains are becoming more complex in terms of geographical spread, functionality, and product portfolio. This is altering the way supply chains need to be managed. One of the greatest challenges companies face today is ensuring that the savings they realize by manufacturing and sourcing in low-cost countries are not negated by higher coordination and management costs.

Today's companies are increasingly globalizing their value chains. They do so mainly to secure cheaper supplies of products and services, and to open up new markets. The volume of foreign direct investment (FDI) is a clear indication of the extent to which value chains have become globalized. Over the past 20 years, FDI has risen continuously by an average of 10 percent per annum. No signs indicate that this trend will slow down or reverse in the near future, as can be seen in Figure 12.1.

As companies assume a more global footprint, their supply chains become more intricate, sometimes spanning several continents. Adidas, for instance, manages only design, marketing and customer service from its headquarters in Germany. Production has been almost completely relocated to low-cost countries, while distribution and sales are organized on a global level. This, in itself, presents new challenges in terms of building up and managing supply chains. Suppliers, production networks, and logistics networks located in different parts of the world must all pull together.

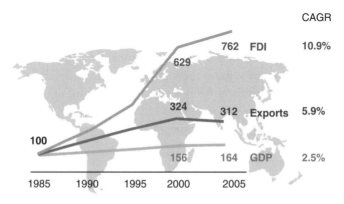

**Figure 12.1** World GDP, world exports, world FDI

Supply chains are also becoming more complex as the division of labor in networked value chains changes shape. With the Internet as their backbone, modern information and communication technologies cut transaction costs. This helps companies to specialize and facilitates effective networking. These technologies empower companies to reduce vertical integration by outsourcing more materials and services. The automotive industry has been a forerunner of this trend. According to a study of the automotive supplier market that our company conducted in 2007, the share of value creation of original equipment manufacturers (OEMs) will shrink to 25–30 percent by 2010. This means that suppliers will take on even more responsibility for developing and producing cars, leading to even more complex networks of product and information flows between suppliers and OEMs.

The division of labor is also becoming more pronounced as the management of supply chains transcends corporate borders. Both the automotive and retail industries, for instance, are very advanced in integrating logistics to ensure smooth product flows and to satisfy required service levels. In addition, the more specialized services offered by logistics providers allow many companies to outsource parts of their supply chain. Smoothly integrating these providers is one of the key challenges facing the discipline of supply chain management today.

The complexity of the supply chain is also turned up a notch as companies vary their product portfolios to an ever-greater degree. Central European companies, in particular, are trying to compensate for rising costs at home by focusing on product innovation. They are offering a broader range of customized, high-quality products accompanied by excellent service. At the same time, they are seeking to diversify into new market segments. Product differentiation has risen particularly dramatically in the automotive sector, and premium OEMs and mass manufacturers alike are embracing this trend. To counter increased competition, automotive manufacturers are placing new product variants on the market and launching model offensives at an unprecedented rate. By taking this action, they aim to increase the total number of units sold – or, at least, to keep this level stable. The number of models of cars and light commercial vehicles in Germany rose from 140 to 335 between 1985 and 2005. If OEMs' plans pan out, the number will increase to more than 365 model types in 2010. The number of models per brand mass manufacturers have offered rose from three-and-a-half in the 1980s to more than eight today. Similarly, the variety of car configurations has also swelled. For its Mini brand alone, BMW offers customers the choice between 418 different paint and color combinations.

As a result of these changes, supply chain management is forced to meet ever more intricate and involved requirements. The complexity of development, finishing, and assembly processes increases. Different market segments expect different service levels and are exposed to varying levels of cost pressure. Companies must master a tricky balancing act: They must keep a cap on their supply chain costs while still delivering high-quality, made-to-measure customer services and broad product portfolios.

As supply chains become more complex in terms of geographical reach, functionality, and product offerings, the people who manage them have to do more to ensure high service levels, rapid responsiveness, and flexibility. The trade-off between product costs and supply chain costs needs to be weighed up carefully. The more customized products and services are, and the faster companies have to respond to market trends, the more difficult it is to globalize production and sourcing policies.

Companies moving in this direction must modularize their products as far as they can while introducing new variants as late as possible. They must also keep stocks low and operate fast supply chain processes. One way to do this is to implement cross-docking and merge-in-transit procedures that allow customer-specific products and product ranges to be merged and assembled from different sources without any need for warehousing.

Supply chain processes must become extremely reliable, too – especially in sectors with short product lifecycles, such as the PC, mobile phone and fashion industries. Best practices developed in these industries can be transferred to other sectors. If companies in these sectors fail to learn, the costs can be horrendous. Companies in the retail sector, for instance, have endeavored to improve their supply chain processes over the past few years in order to increase their product availability. Since the average out-of-stock rate of European retailers is between 7–10 percent, retailers have a strong incentive to achieve high service levels and create supply chains that function perfectly. Surveys show that if a product is not available for customers, then 9 percent of them will not be tempted to purchase an alternative product. This amounts to €4 billion in lost sales in Europe alone.

## Optimizing global supply chains – a success story

Aligning the supply chain with global requirements is a strategic management challenge. Optimizing individual functions in the chain tends to be counterproductive, as these typically pursue conflicting goals. For example, establishing alternative sources of supply in low-wage countries and/or relocating production facilities inevitably leads to higher shipping costs, longer replenishment cycles, and higher working capital. It is therefore necessary to take an overview and optimize all aspects in a considered and coordinated manner.

Drawing on the extensive experience we have gained in building and optimizing global supply chain management strategies for companies in a wide range of industries, we have developed an end-to-end global supply chain management framework. We wish to show how useful and practical this framework is, and will draw on a project to do so. The project team developed a holistic supply chain strategy for the region Europe, Middle East and Africa (EMEA) for a global producer of electronic components. The project was set up and implemented in several phases and subsequently rolled out globally.

## The globalized company suffered from severe supply chain deficits

Our client is a fast-growing producer of electronic components; a manufacturer of electronic connectors, switches and fiber optic products. Its global revenues exceed €5 billion, one third of which is generated in the EMEA region. The product portfolio is highly complex, spanning over 500,000 different products and variants. Furthermore, the company serves a broad range of industries, from automotive, engineering and aerospace through to consumer products and communications. Each of these industries places widely differing demands on the company in terms of product specifications and service levels. The company serves 90,000 customers in 57 countries from 174 manufacturing and warehouse locations.

### Example: Global supply chain management framework

In EMEA, the company was having a very hard time meeting required service levels. The inevitable result: dissatisfied customers, lost revenues, and high costs for emergency shipments. The 'ship-to-request' service level averaged just 79 percent. In other words, approximately every fifth order was not delivered on time or was completed inaccurately, despite the company's steep supply chain costs.

Historical development was part of the reason for the company's unfortunate predicament. The company's supply chains had evolved over time. Sales growth had led the company to follow its customers and gradually expand in all core European markets. Warehouses and production facilities were set up piecemeal in the various countries. In some cases, local manufacturers were acquired to penetrate these markets. As the production network grew across Europe, complex inter-company supplier relationships involving multi-step ordering and delivery processes emerged between different countries. In one country, for example, on average 30 percent of all products sold were manufactured in a different country.

Another driver of complexity in the supply chain was the outsourcing of parts of production to external vendors, some of them in countries with low labor costs. Outsourcing had been engaged in to improve flexibility and reduce labor costs. Yet, information was far from transparent on a global level because of the many and varied supplier relationships the company had. Exacerbating the problem, IT systems were only networked across borders to a limited extent.

The broad product and customer portfolio caused even greater complexity, leading to a large number of unprofitable, low-volume products and customers. In addition, responsibility was fragmented within the supply chain. There was no one person responsible for supply chain management at a national or enterprise-wide level. Efforts to optimize existing systems were limited to individual functions and countries.

## Holistic supply chain optimization is the key

To improve service levels and reduce supply chain management complexity, the project team designed and implemented a holistic strategic approach. The approach draws heavily on the Roland Berger supply chain excellence framework.

It is our conviction that supply chain strategy, performance, and enablers must fit together seamlessly and dovetail perfectly with a company's specific goals if success is to be achieved. How strategy, performance, and enablers work together is shown in Figure 12.2. The supply chain strategy lays the strategic foundation for transforming the supply chain, empowering the company to shift its focus away from a country-by-country perspective in order to develop a global value chain. In the example of the global electronic components manufacturer, core logistical functions were bundled in business units that served multiple

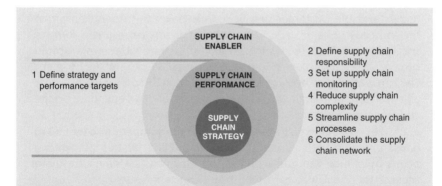

**Figure 12.2** Supply chain strategy, performance and enablers fit seamlessly together

countries. At the same time, corporate functions such as warehousing were reorganized as shared service centers. These now serve all business units.

Supply chain performance links strategic company objectives to specific supply chain targets. One example is to vary cost and service level targets for different customer and product segments. Reconfiguring the supply chain is one of the most powerful levers to optimize the ROCE. It can influence profitability by improving cost structures and service levels, and an optimized network will have a significant impact on capital turnover.

Supply chain enablers refer to the conditions that must be put in place to achieve defined performance goals. They include organizational and resource sizing issues, monitoring and control, key performance indicators (KPIs), processes, system requirements, network structures, and material flows, for example.

**Defining the strategy and target gets companies off to a good start**
There will never be a one-size-fits-all supply chain. The requirements that different customers and markets place on availability, delivery times, and costs vary too widely for that to be possible. Each supply chain must be examined on its own merits and segmented in line with specific market demands. For our client, defining different cost and service level targets for its various business units was the necessary first step. While the automotive industry insisted on service levels upward of 99 percent, other sectors were happy with lower service levels. Considering the exorbitant expense involved when a car assembly line grinds to a halt, the difference in service level expectation was

understandable. Customer-specific segments were also identified within the business units. In this way, preferential service – in the form of special logistical processes such as direct shipment, for example – could be given to strategic key accounts as opposed, say, to small customers. The aim was to raise average service levels from 79 to 95 percent across all business units, albeit with considerable variations depending on the customer and industry.

Besides improving delivery performance, the company also wished to boost earnings before interest and taxes (EBIT) by five percentage points by reducing logistical and supply chain costs. One main way to achieve this goal was to establish a consistent, cross-border supply chain management system within business units, and to link this new system to a robust supply chain monitoring unit. Shipping and warehousing functions across the business units were bundled to form shared service units and thereby tap further synergies. To ease the vast complexity of the product and customer portfolio, a distributor channel was set up to serve small customers. This move alone streamlined the product portfolio. Consolidating responsibility for the supply chain at business unit level also created leaner processes by eliminating complex inter-company handling processes that had been made obsolete. The company's traditional warehousing structures and production constellation no longer lined up with market requirements and were consolidated throughout Europe. Figure 12.3 outlines the main elements of the company's initial situation and targets.

**Delegating supply chain responsibility ensures account ownership**
Previous over-emphasis on country organizations and functions had prevented the company from optimizing the supply chain as a whole. For example, functions such as customer service and materials management, whose processes are closely intertwined, were kept separate within the organization. Customer service was attached to marketing/sales, while materials management belonged to production. Accordingly, it was impossible to assign responsibility for order fulfillment from start to finish.

Typical target conflicts made matters worse. Production was largely measured in terms of capacity utilization and, naturally, preferred large production batches. By contrast, materials management needed greater flexibility to accommodate made-to-order parts. Each function was trying to optimize its own activities, but there no one who was overseeing and taking responsibility for the supply chain as a whole. This had a negative impact on service levels and costs. To solve these problems, the company established one unit that was responsible for

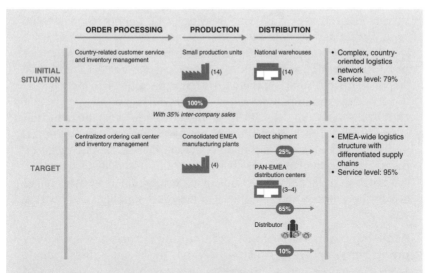

**Figure 12.3**   Initial situation and targets

the entire supply chain in all countries within a given business unit. All the necessary core functions – including forecasting, customer service, materials management, and production and operational procurement – were subsumed under these supply chain management units.

Stronger customer orientation and process ownership are two of the main advantages of such integration. Understanding precisely what customers need and want makes it easier to plan capacity and inventories. With this knowledge, the supply chain manager could strike a better balance between forecasts and current demand on the one hand, and machine and tool capacity – both internal and outsourced – on the other.

All non-core supply chain functions – such as warehousing, shipping and strategic procurement – were bundled in shared service organizations that serve all business units. These functions can be grouped together on a horizontal level because they have nothing to do with consistent order management within the business units. One crucial benefit of this strategy is that synergies can be tapped across multiple business units. It is also easier to charge business units accurately and fairly for services rendered.

**Monitoring the supply chain creates global transparency**   To maintain an unobscured view over the entire logistical chain, and to manage it effectively in the long run, supply chain managers need a consistent, hierarchically structured system of KPIs. These must link specific enterprise- or business unit-wide ROCE targets to operational supply chain performance targets.

KPIs provide support for the two main drivers of ROCE: profitability (the return on sales) and asset turnover. For instance, the KPI 'Emergency Shipment Cost to Total Shipment Cost' tracks the long-term reduction of unnecessary extra shipping charges. This has a direct positive impact on EBIT. At the same time, the KPI 'Inventory Coverage' plots the reduction in inventories, which in turn has a positive effect on asset turnover. A direct and consistent cause-and-effect correlation exists between a number of operational supply chain KPIs and top-level ROCE targets.

At the electronic component manufacturer, the KPI tree was modeled across the entire enterprise and also included suppliers and outside vendors.

**Reducing complexity and streamlining processes improves profitability**  Inherited structures had left the manufacturer's supply chain extremely complex. Complexity was driven by large numbers of small customers and by items with low production volumes. To some extent, fixed handling costs for order acceptance, and picking and shipment processes are independent of the size of an order. This means that small customers who order low volumes create disproportionately high process costs relative to the value of their orders. The result is a negative contribution to EBIT. This problem initially did not show up in costing calculations at our client because the same mark-up for order handling costs was used for every order and for every customer. In effect, large customers were subsidizing their smaller counterparts. In contrast to their larger competitors, small customers were able to buy at lower costs, thus creating a situation that was actually increasing the number of unprofitable customers.

To rid the company of this situation, the project team encouraged it to set up a different distribution network. A distributor, however, can bundle orders on a completely different level. Distributors specialize in a particular industry segment and can supply customers with products from a wide range of vendors in a single consignment. This drives up the value of orders. Moreover, distributors can also bundle the demand expressed by multiple customers, which has the effect of consolidating orders. Distributors also specialize in the efficient handling of small orders, such as parcel handling. Introducing a distributor streamlines processes and thereby improves profitability. On the sales side, two potentially contradictory effects can occur, however. As a rule, distributors can boost sales because they provide better care to small customers. On the other hand, their specialized skills also enable them to deliver rival products, which can detract from sales.

The transition from country-focused to business unit-focused supply chain management also let the company streamline the order handling, inventory management, and production planning processes. Segmenting the supply chain by customer groups within each business unit further simplified the company's processes. For example, customer service units in each country had hitherto looked after order handling issues for large automotive customers. Following realignment, EMEA customer service units were set up as 'single points of contact'. These units can now track order status and product availability throughout Europe, and large customers see their orders fulfilled faster and more flexibly. If an important product is not in stock at the usual regional warehouse, customer service staff can have it shipped directly from another regional warehouse. In extreme situations, the same staff can even authorize direct shipment. Now that order handling has been centralized for large accounts, both demand management and forecasting are more efficient. Customer demand data flows into a single unit that caters to multiple countries.

Smaller customers that mainly operate on a 'general business' level tend to want a local point of contact: creating 'virtual' customer service units satisfied this requirement. Though physical units still exist in various countries, they are linked together by a single, central system.

Inventory management and production planning activities have likewise been centralized at EMEA level within the supply chain management function in each business unit. As a result, all production capacity and parts inventories for a given business unit are now managed by a single central unit. Similarly, the new materials management unit within the supply chain management organization plans both inventories and the production capacity needed to replenish them for the whole of Europe. Inter-company ordering processes between countries used to be very complicated. Since all that has been eliminated, processes have been accelerated and are completed more reliably, which can be seen in Figure 12.4. Throughout the entire EMEA region, production capacity and inventories can now be planned better on the basis of demand data that is collated centrally by a single customer service unit. Capacity utilization has improved and inventories have been reduced.

Centralizing the inventory and production planning processes also enabled the product portfolio to be reclassified into make-to-forecast, make-to-stock and make-to-order products. In the past, the detailed criteria for these definitions had never been standardized at pan-European level. Nor did any uniform planning philosophy exist. The practice of harmonizing planning parameters and defining appropriate

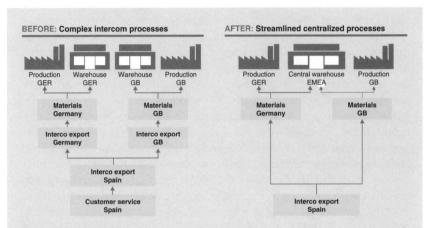

**Figure 12.4** Elimination of inter-company flows through direct ordering

production strategies further lowered inventory levels while, again, improving deliverability.

These changes naturally placed new demands on the company's IT systems. The IT systems used previously in different countries were scarcely harmonized. Network links were rudimentary at best. Order data was the main item that was exchanged between systems. To centralize inventory and production planning, the various national systems had to be linked using an enterprise application integration (EAI) platform. Once this had been done, transactions could be handled in real time across all the networked systems. In the long term, the company plans to integrate all sites and functions in a given business unit into a single enterprise resource planning (ERP) system.

**Consolidating production and distribution network saves time and money** Legacy production and distribution structures reflected an inherited bias towards individual countries. Production capacity was therefore comparatively small in most countries. Since there was no clear assignment of production capacity at a given plant to a particular business unit, different business units often accessed the same machines. This inevitably created conflicts over the use of capacity, added uncertainty to the planning equation, and ultimately caused delays in delivery.

Owing to the traditional country focus at the company, plants in many countries handled every step in the production process single-handed. Cross-border production networks existed only to a very limited extent – between Germany, the Czech Republic and Switzerland, for example. The company was prevented from exploiting economies of scale and specialization in the EMEA region because of this largely 'autonomous' production strategy. Utilization at some plants was below capacity. Also, too little use was also made of the labor cost advantages of off-shoring labor-intensive steps in the production process to low-wage countries.

Realignment of the production network in Europe centered on radically consolidating production capacity. The number of the company's plants was reduced from 14 to four main plants and two specialty plants. Two plants in Central Europe were expanded to form a networked facility for technology-intensive production. Two plants in Eastern Europe were similarly networked to handle assembly-intensive steps in the production process. In addition, two smaller plants that manufacture special purpose parts were retained. At each plant, production capacity was assigned to the business units and adjusted on the basis of strategic capacity planning. For each business unit, consolidation achieved the critical mass that was needed to enable appropriate specialization. Planning and production became far more reliable.

With production planning and control handled by the supply chain management unit at each business unit, the plants provide production and associated infrastructure on a shared service basis.

As with the production structure, distribution also had a heavily decentralized structure in the past too. Each country had its own production facility and/or distribution point, which drove up infra-structure and inventory costs for the entire group. The same products – including slow-moving items, in some cases – were kept in stock at several warehouses around Europe. Little was known about what was in stock where at any given time.

Radical consolidation was the key to realigning this distribution structure. The 14 existing warehouses were condensed into four regional warehouses. C products were all stored at one specific regional warehouse. Each warehouse maintained the product range that was needed in its region. The warehouses also became organized as shared service units that could be used by all the business units. Products now arrive here straight from the production plants – an arrangement that keeps local ex-works distribution to a minimum. As a result, production facilities themselves now only operate as a buffer function for direct shipments. This function serves only for products with high to very high consignment volumes that justify direct ex-works shipment to customers.

Warehouse consolidation created a single-step storage constellation. In the past, inter-company shipments had accounted for a large proportion of shipments, and always involved two steps: consignments were first dispatched from the warehouse in the country of origin to the warehouse in the target country, and then to the customer. These two steps extended delivery times, doubled the amount of handling and increased inventory costs. The combination of one-step storage and direct shipments has sharply reduced inventories while improving the service level.

The regional warehouses needed to meet tight delivery deadlines demanded by customers. To enable them to do so, transport providers were recruited who could exploit significant bundling synergies while guaranteeing short delivery times in their catchment area. At the same time, consignment stocks were set up on customers' premises to handle extremely critical parts with extremely short delivery deadlines and strict availability requirements.

## The results speak for themselves

Realigning supply chain management created much leaner production, distribution, and customer service structures in the EMEA region at this particular manufacturer of electronic components. Multi-step inter-company processes were eliminated. Supply chain management was established as a central organizational unit in each business unit. An end-to-end cross-border supply chain management was introduced throughout the company.

This enabled the company to meet its target and raise service levels from 79 to 95 percent in all business units. Indeed, the automotive business unit now comes close to a service level of 100 percent. Since processes and planning are now substantially more reliable, the huge expense of emergency shipments has declined significantly. Besides improving service levels, the new leaner structures also cut costs sharply, leading to a 5 percentage points increase in the EBIT margin.

## Success factors in global SCM implementation

Seen in its global context, supply chain management is far more than a way of controlling the flow of goods and services. It is a pivotal tool in reducing complexity and redesigning value chain structures. It is equally vital in the drive to improve cost structures and service levels. Many enterprises, however, still fail to grasp the significance of this discipline.

To a large degree, they remain focused on individual functions and countries. Such companies tend to see supply chain management as a minor corporate function that concerns itself only with materials management and shipping. One change is crucial if global supply chain management is to be implemented successfully: companies must cultivate an understanding for the need for transformation, for changing existing structures and processes. The extent of the necessary changes and the inherent potential must be spelled out.

Moves to establish global supply chain management must be initiated by top management. Broad-based support must then be solicited in the business units and country organizations. All supply chain functions in the existing country organizations must be actively involved from the earliest stages of conceptual development. It is no secret that internal power plays are a significant and detrimental factor in many change processes. This can be reduced when key activities are bundled in a business unit-wide supply chain management function. A supply chain leader should be appointed to drive the process of redesign and transformation. Ideally, this should be the person who will subsequently spearhead the supply chain management function. All parties involved must help design the strategic roadmap and define unambiguous targets for the supply chain. Everyone has to know exactly where the company is heading. Once this strategic foundation has been laid, the work of realignment can commence.

To minimize the complexity of realignment, it is advisable to begin by setting up a pilot supply chain management unit for just a few countries in one region (such as EMEA). Global rollout can then take place in phase two. Whatever the geographic scope, it is imperative to adopt a holistic approach to realignment. No aspect should be left out. Distribution and production structures, order handling, inventory and production planning, organizational issues, and process definitions must all be remodeled in the change process. Only then will a lean, agile supply chain structure emerge.

Moreover, a detailed implementation roadmap must be drawn up that clearly plots the individual steps in the transformation process. Change obviously has to take place while the company continues to go about its normal business. Accordingly, it makes sense to model every step of the transformation in a master plan and identify those actions that are critical. For example, closing a warehouse in a particular country must not pose a threat to compliance with defined service levels. As a rule, pilot projects should be used to test and fine-tune the defined changes. Rollout can then take place when new processes have proven their practicality.

# CHAPTER 13

# Complexity management: the starting point for improving performance

## Alexander Belderok and Thomas Hollmann

### Introduction

Supply chains are becoming increasingly complex and more difficult to manage. While globalization shoulders a large share of responsibility for this rise in complexity, almost all aspects of the supply chain contribute to this development. Whether extending operations to new regions, launching new products and services, forming partnerships and alliances or outsourcing functions, each of these activities can create value. If they create value, these complexity-adding activities also create what we refer to as 'good and necessary' complexity.

Negative or unnecessary complexity, on the other hand, adds no or little value to either the consumer or the company. Companies' unshakeable belief in innovation being the answer to customers' growing power and unpredictability – and, therefore, the remedy for staying ahead of the competition – is behind much of the unnecessary complexity found at companies today. While innovative products with every sort of bell and whistle imaginable might please buyers, they sometimes unnecessarily complicate a company's operations and lead to higher costs.

Learning to recognize when complexity is justified is vital for sustainable, long-term growth. Clearly, driving negative complexity out of a company's operations can bring strategic benefits; there are, however, times when managing complexity would bring greater advantages.

In this chapter, we will delve more deeply into complexity, and look at how negative complexity affects businesses and organizations today. Next, we examine the most common drivers of complexity. Following this, we discuss the importance of managing complexity. Finally, we turn our attention to a case study that illustrates the benefits of managing and reducing complexity in the healthcare sector.

## What is complexity?

Complexity tends to sneak into organizational structures as companies market a progressively larger portfolio of products, services, features, and options. Encouraged by innovation and sales targets, plus an eagerness to satisfy customers' every need, companies unwittingly welcome complexity into their operations. Production, engineering, and logistics often further complicate existing operations as companies attempt to manufacture every product in every batch size in every throughput time.

With customer preference in constant flux, many businesses continue to expand their portfolio, placing more goods or services on the market. Responding in this manner can bring positive change to companies and add value to customers. When a company's portfolio of goods and services is misaligned with market needs, however, the number of price points, line extensions, and other goods and services stop creating value for customers. They become barriers not benefits. This is complexity in what we refer to as its 'bad' or 'negative' form.

Unless a company uses a mechanism to manage its entire portfolio, complexity will become part and parcel of its processes and costs will rise. Over time, the cost of complexity infiltrates all products. This is known as a 'complexity tax'. In the name of relentlessly pursuing customer demand, company growth eventually suffocates under this burden. Managing complexity can help companies break that pattern. By tackling the complexity issue, companies are better positioned to weigh up the additional costs required to add value, and to develop innovations more efficiently. But identifying complexity is not always easy. In a product-based company, the results of complexity can be highly visible. Think, for example, of a large warehouse with many different parts or finished goods. Complexity can be much harder to identify in a service environment, where products are not physically present.

In our view, there are seven main complexity drivers: organizational, process, suppliers, engineering, manufacturing, brand and channel, and customer. These are shown in Figure 13.1. Some complexity drivers will affect some companies more than others. Identifying what complexity drivers are at play in your business is the first step to managing them.

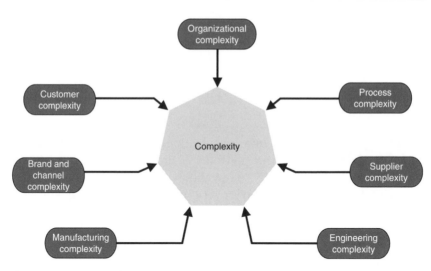

**Figure 13.1**   Complexity drivers

## Why is complexity management important?

Complexity management is important because it dramatically affects a company's bottom line. In one project case, an industrial products company built up a very complex product portfolio. Owing to the company's non-transparent processes and systems, it was unable to determine the true profitability of its products. When the Roland Berger project team analyzed the figures, it became clear that complexity-related costs were consuming more than 7 percent of total revenues. This makes no business sense – and, unfortunately, the cost can also be much higher. On a different project with a manufacturing company, the project team calculated that a complexity burden of 22 percent was added to total production costs. Typical costs are shown in Figure 13.2. Complexity's tax on resources, processes, and systems is threefold:

- It adds costs that cannot be offset in the marketplace
- It distracts management
- It ties up resources that could otherwise be directed towards growth opportunities.

By gaining transparency as to the sources of complexity, companies can identify real cost-to-serve and, in a next step, allocate resources more appropriately. As a consequence, a company can then increase the added value of its products on the marketplace, which will help spur growth. The impact of complexity differs from industry to industry, as is shown in Figure 13.3. The extent of the impact is determined by the

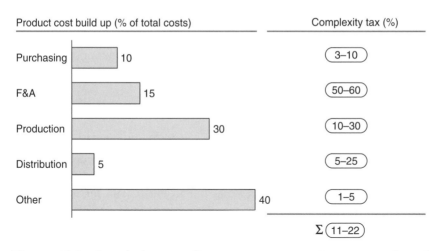

Figure 13.2   Complexity tax often amounts to 11–22 percent of total
product costs

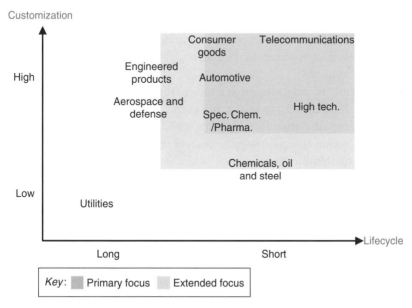

**Figure 13.3**   Complexity's impact differs from industry to industry

degree of customization needed to meet individual customer demands, and the length of the subsequent product and technology lifecycles. The number of brands, models, and distribution channels can also ramp up the level of complexity's impact.

## Complexity is cross-functional

Companies that can truly distinguish between customer demand and necessary growth opportunities are in a much better position to deal with complexity than those companies that fail to understand this distinction. Evaluating the trade-off between the cost and value of complexity is not simple. This is not surprising, considering that complexity pays no heed to functional, business, and geographical barriers. It spreads through them, making it intrinsically difficult to manage. Companies that encourage strong interaction between sales, product development, and operations tend to manage complexity well. Indeed, the degree of interaction among various functions is a telltale sign of how well a company will manage its complexity.

At far too many companies, however, information flows are insufficient and are rarely connected across the different functions. In the flavor industry, for instance, sales departments are generally willing to accept less than ideal supply conditions if it means they will close a deal. The product development function is focused on composing 'totally new' flavors rather than using a 'modular' approach, which is believed to limit creativity. Both these tendencies add cost across the value chain in this particular industry.

Complexity is cross-functional in nature. This is why managing complexity requires strong leadership at the senior business level. All too often, however, the attention of senior management is caught elsewhere. Without someone at top management level who oversees complexity, it is almost impossible for companies to evaluate the additional costs incurred by the complexity to operations, and to weigh these against the actual benefits for the product and the end-consumer.

Learning to manage complexity trade-offs effectively can be a slow process. Most companies are under relentless pressure to deliver tangible quick wins, which is why traditional efforts at complexity management often concentrate on reducing the cost of complexity (for example, through stock keeping unit (SKU) rationalization) rather than highlighting its strategic value. By recognizing that complexity might be a good thing in some circumstances, managers can decide when to reduce or add complexity. The right level of complexity increases the competitive offer.

---

## Textbox 13.1
## Stock keeping unit (SKU) rationalization

Although appealing in its simplicity, typical SKU reduction efforts seldom guarantee lowered complexity costs. The roots of complexity must be recognized. These generally include the complexity drivers of products, the hidden cost of SKU proliferation, and the costs that ultimately represent hidden taxes on customers or consumers who end up paying more for a variety of products that they neither need nor want. This is especially true for 'innovative supply industries', in which a large part of the portfolio is renewed each year. These are characterized by short product lifecycles and numerous product introductions. More and more industries understand the problems with this approach and are increasingly addressing complexity across all businesses and functional areas in the company. In order to make complexity manageable they switch to a 'modular' approach, which lowers overall supply costs and boosts innovation.

---

### How is complexity addressed?

Complexity is best addressed using an approach that takes both the value and cost sides into account from the start. The insights gleaned from this approach enable companies to reduce complexity and to prioritize, scope, and prepare optimization efforts properly while providing the foundation for managing complexity effectively and in a sustained fashion. Figure 13.4 outlines the overall approach and shows how different opportunities can be quantified against each other.

Addressing complexity in its entirety creates more benefits and, perhaps more importantly, will make savings more sustainable. It also gives companies greater control over new product development. Challenges in the flavor industry can be instructive in this context, too. In the flavor industry, almost half of a company's portfolio is renewed each year. Most product additions add little or negative profitability. More is not necessarily better. A holistic approach to portfolio development and a better understanding of which additional product adds costs and which adds value through transparent allocation of complexity costs would give companies long-term growth without compromising their products.

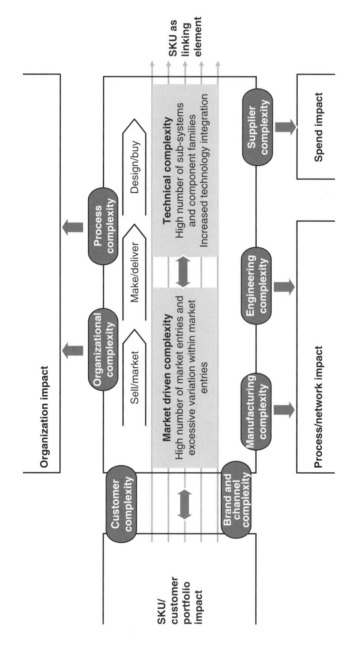

**Figure 13.4** The overall approach aims to quantify and prioritize different opportunities against each other

In complexity management, it is important to distinguish between complexity that is visible to the customer and complexity that is not. Visible complexity is product and packaging standardization that rationalizes product offering or changes customer-discernable attributes. Invisible complexity encompasses the raw material: component and packaging standardization that specifically targets efficiency improvement without discernable customer changes. Typically, the invisible complexity is easier to address, as it does not directly impact customer satisfaction. With visible complexity, the gains are usually higher; however, they are more difficult to reap as the impact of the changes needs to be communicated to the customer. Often, the customer will demand a share in the benefits.

A typical project aimed at making complexity more transparent follows a three-step approach, which is outlined in Figure 13.5.

The important first step in complexity management is to develop a thorough understanding of the complexity of a business, its value chain, and the costs and values that are associated with each step of that value chain. Understanding the entire process allows a company to identify the discrepancies between production costs and incremental value to customers. Bicycle manufacturers, for example, often install different types of alarm bells on city bicycles. This results in high inventory, a complex supply chain, and assembly differences. While an alarm bell adds, perhaps, 1 percent to customer satisfaction, because it is installed during the last step of the production process it amounts to more than 1 percent in additional costs.

Creating cost transparency can be difficult and depends on the level of sophistication of the accounting systems. In most cases, detailed cost information is not readily available. An unorthodox approach is required, one which combines a bottom-up estimation of costs with a top-down assessment of the value chain. Although detailing the cost of all products is a time consuming job, it serves as the foundation for future analysis.

At this stage, it is important to gain critical insight into the demands of the market. Formed from a needs-based segmentation of the market (based on value drivers), questionnaires and interviews determine how various customer segments perceive the value of the company's products and services, and whether they are willing to pay a premium for certain added values. Customer added value can be measured with a conjoint analysis test that forces customers to select their preferred product offerings. It is important, here, to identify customer 'threshold'. The information gained from a detailed cost analysis, location in the value chain, and the type of value-added provides clarity into the elasticity of the various complexity drivers.

|  | Understand complexity | Re-design complexity | Manage and control complexity |
|---|---|---|---|
| **Objective** | Connect the cost and value of complexity | Balance the trade-off between good and bad complexity | Benefit from lower cost and re-ignite growth |
| **Actions** | • Determine scope of project (product and customer groups)<br>• Collect process and product information<br>• Baseline cost to produce product properties/features<br>• Determine added value of product properties/features (e.g. using conjoint analysis) | • Define target features and operational costs<br>• Assess costs and benefits of redesign<br>• Start proof-of-concept pilot<br>• Prioritize and plan improvements<br>• Build business case for change | • Install complexity management task force (program officer)<br>• Assign target and responsibilities for improvement initiatives<br>• Monitor and control progress |
| **Deliverables** | • Develop an overview of operational costs versus added value of product properties<br>• Bottom up estimate of total complexity costs | • Target added value map of operational costs versus added value<br>• Bottom up estimate of savings potential (feasible)<br>• Pilot improvement project<br>• Business case for change<br>• Implementation plan | • Lower cost operations with less complex production processes |

**Figure 13.5**  Detailed approach

Matching these insights with a cost transparency model informs a company about the trade-offs that must be made. Such a comparison not only locates where profit is made, but it also pinpoints where changes to price and improvement in value perception can be made. This is the second step, in which complexity is redesigned. It is critical not to focus simply on the SKU tail-end optimization, but also to identify non-value added complexity across all SKUs, materials, and customers, or even a combination of the three. To obtain the right level of transparency, it is necessary to build a detailed complexity database. Along with profitability and value-added thresholds, filters such as strategic or commercial arguments should be used to identify SKUs, raw materials, or customers for rationalization. At this point, it is recommended that a pilot project be started to test the effectiveness of the concept. Based on improvement potential, investment levels, and potential risks, improvements can be prioritized.

The final step of the project is the implementation phase. This is when complexity must be managed and controlled. Implementing complexity management is demanding and, while it affects most areas of the organization, there is little to show at the beginning for the effort. In our experience, it is best to minimize the impact of the transition by delegating improvement targets and responsibilities to lower levels in the organization. Crucial to the success of this approach is the presence of a coordination entity, usually a specially established program officer, to monitor and steer the process. In the longer term, this program officer also needs to prevent complexity from arising again.

It is important at this stage to analyze the external processes with several archetypal customers in order to build in immediate reality checks. When closely examining customer interaction, it is also essential to monitor internal processes. Based on a process gap analysis, a set of recommendations can be developed that range from process changes to governance improvements, or even organizational modifications.

It is important to anchor complexity management into a company's processes to prevent it from returning after the 'clean-up'. By examining the processes, governance, culture, incentives, and infrastructure of the organization, a company can manage complexity on an ongoing basis. Rewarding proliferating products – what many companies do, in their quest for innovation – is likely to keep churning out complexity that does not drive value creation. Finding the right balance is not a one-off event. Understanding what keeps creating complexity in organizations is necessary for striking that balance again and again. Tools should be used that effectively manage trade-offs, and connect those parts of the organization that respond negatively to complexity with those that seek it.

With such tools in place, a company can compartmentalize its processes. For instance, a snacks manufacturer can separate its scalable activities (or example, peeling, cutting, pre-cooking potatoes), which tend not to become complex, from its differentiating activities (for example, specific seasoning to comply with local taste preferences), which lean toward complexity. Other tools, such as incentive systems that foster transparency, are also vital. Managers should be willing to identify shared goals and to manage complexity across departments and corporations.

## Case study: Tackling complexity from the sourcing side

To illustrate how the approach works from beginning to end, we describe in the following segment a project we completed for a state-owned university hospital in Germany. This university hospital emerged from the merger of three state-owned university hospitals, all of which had comparable areas of expertise. Due to their similar fields of activity, the initial assumption was that synergies, especially in purchasing, could easily be realized. Yet, a quick and easy win proved difficult owing to the different methods of treatment, which required different products, individual order codes for similar order items and different IT systems. Since, historically, there had been sufficient government and third-party funding, and freedom of medical research was valued more highly than economics, there was no tight budget control and therefore no need for active management of the post-merger integration and the realization of synergies. This situation was not unique to hospitals in Germany but, rather, was a malaise affecting the healthcare sector throughout most of Europe.

Hospitals, and the healthcare sector at large, started to face major changes, however, when politicians began tackling the problem of the ailing healthcare system. They were particularly concerned about the growing imbalance between the rampant cost of healthcare and the stagnating number of payers. Funding from government was reduced significantly, and a lump sum compensation system was introduced. This meant that each hospital would receive the same amount of money for a specified medical treatment, irrespective of the cost burden at any specific hospital. As a result of this system, inefficient hospitals would no longer be rewarded for incurring additional cost and efficient hospitals would gain a windfall.

Facing those altered circumstances, the newly combined state-owned university hospital decided to put into action a project aimed at leveraging purchase power in order to unleash substantial savings.

## Identifying the main drivers of complexity

Added complexity was almost programmed in from the moment the three hospitals decided to merge. The hospitals simply lacked organizations and processes that were sufficiently integrated to benefit from synergies. Whereas, in the past, this non-value adding complexity would not be too problematic owing to a healthcare system that encouraged wastage, those days were now gone. The hospitals could no longer ignore the complexity issue.

In this case, the main complexity drivers were:

- **Organizational complexity** Although the three state-owned university hospitals shared similar areas of expertise, each had a very different history and specific culture. This sometimes resulted in rivalry between the major opinion leaders. There was little transparency, and even less motivation to integrate similar departments. What was missing was the desire to create a lean structured organization.
- **Process complexity** In many of the departments, the medical treatment process differed from hospital to hospital, mostly due to historic reasons. In most cases, these small differences meant that material and machines were used differently, creating additional complexity throughout the organization.

Although common IT systems had recently been established, it was still impossible to gain transparency, especially regarding purchasing volumes and cost. Material and supplier master data were not harmonized. These data need to be harmonized before proper analysis can be completed and actions can be defined that will help organizations to tackle complexity from the sourcing side.

- **Supplier complexity** Even though the number of sales representatives in German hospitals fell significantly in the past, the power of the medical and pharmaceutical industry is still of considerable importance. As many suppliers fund hospital research, there is often a strong bias when it comes to selecting suppliers. Other suppliers enter the hospital market by leasing machines at aggressive prices. The ramifications of this behavior are considerable: hospitals deal with a large, diverse pool of suppliers. At the merged hospital under review, more than 4,500 active vendors belonged to the supplier base. Worse still, the supplier base was extremely fragmented, with approximately 3,500 vendors allocated an annual sourcing volume of less than €20,000.

## Addressing complexity

As the aim of the project was to unleash savings in purchasing, the focus had to be on reducing supplier, organizational, and process complexity. The project team did this by optimizing the purchasing organization and purchasing processes.

The first step was to develop a thorough understanding of the complexity of the hospital business, and the cost and values associated with it. At the end of this step, it was clear where complexity was artificially high and did not increase value for either the user or the customer. The project team performed an in-depth analysis of the value and the associated cost for each medical procedure. The value of each case is the amount the hospital is given by the health care system according to the logic of diagnosis related groups (DRGs). This is a fixed amount. When comparing the cost incurred by the respective departments at each of the three hospitals, the gap between the best department and the others was significant, amounting sometimes to as much as 35 percent. To understand how much complexity in purchasing contributed to this significant divide between the best and worst performers among the departments, the project team clustered the purchasing volume into coherent commodity groups and identified major differences in purchased products across the three hospitals.

The project team also identified huge variety among the number of different products ordered by the respective departments at each of the three hospitals. The best hospital could satisfy customers' needs with fewer different products than the other two. Those hospitals that ordered a large number of different products tended constantly to add new products to their existing order portfolio. Old products kept on being ordered simply because they already existed on some order forms. In many cases, a strong relationship with the sales representative also existed. New products were added to the order forms when requested by patients, even when these very specific products only deviated slightly from standard products already on the inventory.

To identify non-value adding complexity and the products that could be removed from the inventory lists, the project team conducted interviews with industry experts and held workshops with identified key users. These users were responsible for the major share of consumption according to the quantitative analysis. The team filtered out unnecessary products that could be eliminated easily by substituting the product or by adapting processes.

After completing step one – understanding where complexity is artificially high – it was clear that standardizing purchasing throughout the merged hospital would be paramount to reducing complexity.

The first task was to standardize purchasing codes across the three hospitals in order to make equal or similar products readily visible. Accepted teams consisting of selected experts from each hospital clustered the various products into item groups with comparable functionalities. For each category, a standard 'must use' product was defined for all users in the hospitals. This enabled the hospitals to pool similar products, thus ensuring a reduction in the total number of different products purchased. Using special electronic order forms and required authorization levels, correct implementation for ordering standard and non-standard products was put in place and enforced. As a result of this action, the number of articles used was reduced substantially. Some 11 percent fewer articles were purchased in complex commodity groups for very specific treatments. In areas that could be more easily standardized, the hospitals lowered the number of articles by 33 percent.

By bundling the products, the project team also helped the merged hospital to increase its purchasing power and gain better rates. Introducing preferred suppliers per product group with standard 'must use' products for all users meant that the market share of the respective suppliers also increased. These were granted around 80 percent of the sourcing volume within a category. Substantial cost savings were realized and the average full year sourcing volume was slashed by 25 percent.

The hospital was able to optimize its purchasing processes by further standardizing the IT systems. This had the additional benefit of reducing complexity over the long term. Online internal market places were established, limiting the non-standard order portfolio. In order to reduce the number of these non-standard orders, strict authorization levels were implemented and supported by top management.

Quick wins are great, but in order to build on these and install a sustainable complexity management throughout the merged hospital, several institutional changes were necessary. In the third step of the project – manage and control complexity – four changes were made:

- A systematic commodity management program was installed in the purchasing organization. This allows the strategic sourcing organization constantly to monitor developments in internal demand and helps them to keep an eye on products purchased across all locations. It also enables them to watch how the supply markets develop.

- Standardization councils were established, comprising representatives from all relevant locations and from different hierarchical levels. Quarterly reports that are submitted to the board of directors have been defined. The gained momentum of the project work is thus maintained and complexity management becomes an integral part of all business decisions.
- A powerful controlling system based on a dashboard of key performance indicators (KPIs) was defined. Goals for the different areas were defined based on the status at the beginning and at the end of the project. These are to be monitored on a regular basis.
- Changes were made to contracts with various strategic suppliers in order to push efforts to integrate suppliers more comprehensively. Preferred suppliers – which were granted large chunks of the hospital's spending volume – agreed to submit proposals that outlined how they would further streamline their product portfolios. In addition, the power of sales representatives was substantially reduced in order to increase barriers preventing new samples and products being distributed among end-users. This was one of the main drivers of the ever-increasing product variety in the past.

As a result of the project, the state-owned university hospital saw an annual saving of €20 million, which was attributable to complexity being reduced significantly. In addition to the savings, the hospital was able to reduce the number of different products ordered, saw increased transparency, and now benefits from improved logistics processes and inventory management. To enumerate:

- Annual savings of EUR 20 million – based on relative savings compared with the annual spending of between 8 and 29 percent
- The number of SKUs was reduced by 11–33 percent in the different commodity groups
- Inventory was cut down thanks to the significant reduction in the number of SKUs. Non-standard products were defined as non-stocking items, and minimum inventory levels for standard products could be optimized
- Standardized rules concerning purchase price led to increased transparency in the purchased and used product portfolio. Cost awareness increased substantially in an area that too seldom is driven with an eye on business
- Strategic purchasing decisions were made possible thanks to the newly created transparency KPIs that tracked the relation between the value of products and cost. In some cases, a broader product portfolio could be justified because of significantly higher earnings.

## Manage complexity before it suffocates growth

As described by the project example, as well as by the conceptual framework above, complexity management techniques are strategic tools with which corporations are able to maximize the margin generated from their operations. In our experience, companies understand that complexity is something that needs to be tackled by top management using a cross-business overview. They are the people who want, and have, the skills to connect the cost and value of complexity, manage the trade-off between good and bad complexity, and reignite growth. Tackling complexity is not a low-hanging fruit, but it always pays off for our clients.

# CHAPTER 14

# Working capital excellence: how companies can tap hidden cash reserves in the supply chain

## *Roland Schwientek and Christian Deckert*

### Introduction

As supply chain management should take a holistic view not only on cost, but also on assets and cash as well, in this chapter we will present and discuss our current thinking on working capital management. Working capital reflects the money invested in supply chain processes in the form of accounts receivable, inventories, and accounts payable. Based on our experience, optimizing working capital management can achieve amazing effects on the financial performance of an enterprise and its supply chains.

There is never enough to go round: this is true of all scarce resources, and it is certainly true of money, especially in the corporate sector. Companies' thirst for cash is unquenchable. Some want to pursue growth strategies by penetrating new markets, developing innovative products or acquiring other firms. Others need to be turned around to get out of trouble. The common denominator in all cases, however, is a considerable need for funding.

Meeting this need for funding in the most efficient way possible is one of the central strategic challenges confronting top management. In this chapter, we first look at the financing tools available to companies, and illustrate just how important working capital is for supply chain excellence. Next, we show Roland Berger's approach to optimizing working capital. Finally, we look at best practices today and those of tomorrow, drawing from a working capital excellence survey we completed in 2005 and 2006. In our experience, all three working capital items display optimization potential.

## Making working capital work

Companies have an array of external and internal financing tools at hand. In the case of external funding, companies draw on capital market resources. These resources must be procured on the stock markets or from banks, in the form of equity or debt. Today's capital markets demand profitable growth and a continual increase in the value of the company. Enterprises constantly strive to qualify for external funding. They must repeatedly prove that they are able to use capital efficiently and generate adequate returns.

In the case of internal funding, financing needs are covered by cash flows generated within the company. This cash usually derives from operating income, financing activities or divestments. In other words, companies pay their way out of their own pocket. Where necessary, they increase funding by boosting sales or cutting costs. Very often, reserves can also be identified and tapped in the supply chain. Improving cash flows from the supply chain can reinforce a company's ability to meet its own financing needs.

Seen from this angle, working capital takes on singular significance. Working capital is the money that is tied up in the company's supply chain processes and which must be invested in order to generate sales revenues. It is normally defined as the sum of inventories and receivables from customers less the short-term or trade accounts payable. All the key functions in the supply chain – purchasing, production, logistics, distribution, sales, and so forth – use working capital and must be closely coordinated. Average working capital in selected European industries is shown in Figure 14.1.

Depending on the industry, working capital can account for as much as 30 percent of total assets reported on the balance sheet. This item obviously ties up a huge amount of resources. Equally obvious, however, is the realization that proactively managing working capital can free up resources that are tied up unnecessarily in the supply chain. Such working capital management essentially operates in two ways: by reducing accounts receivable and inventories while increasing accounts payable, and by reducing working capital.

## Receivables, inventories and payables

By reducing accounts receivable and inventories while increasing accounts payable, the volume of liquidity tied up on the balance sheet is immediately scaled back. Inventories are adjusted to customers' needs and service levels, receivables are collected earlier and with more

234

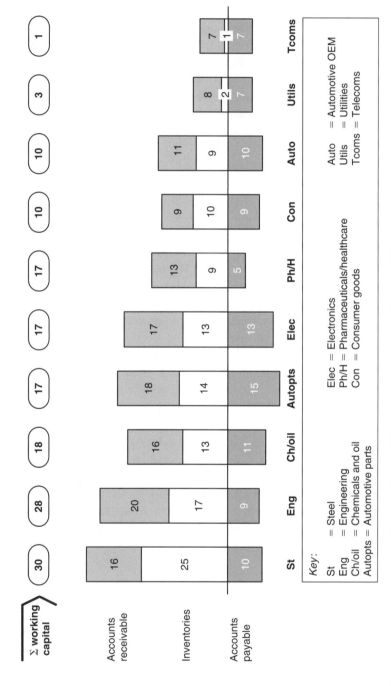

**Figure 14.1** Average working capital in different industries – total assets (%)

stringency, and accounts payable are negotiated with longer payment terms (which must be met so as not to wreck the relationship with the supplier). Freeing up cash that was tied up but can now be invested strengthens the company's position and unburdens credit lines. Indirectly, this step also impacts the income statement. Better service levels and deliverability along the supply chain leave customers more satisfied, and can drive up sales. In addition, there is less risk that inventories and receivables might have to be written off. Cash flow increases again, further improving the company's ability to pay its own way.

## Reducing working capital

Reducing working capital lowers the amount of capital tied up in the company and thereby raises profitability. In other words, the return on capital employed (ROCE) increases. Key ratios – such as ROCE or company value, which capital market stakeholders monitor closely – reflect this development. Improvements in operating earnings that can be measured in terms of performance ratios make it easier for a company to tap financial resources on the capital markets. These steps strengthen the company's external financing capabilities too. Figure 14.2 shows how managing working capital can directly and indirectly influence ROCE.

We have empirically analyzed the impact of working capital management on ROCE for Europe's top 500 companies and have found a clear positive correlation between excellent working capital management (based on working capital productivity = sales/working capital) and superior ROCE. Companies that put working capital into their management focus usually profit from better financial results.

Proactively managing working capital clearly emerges as a core element in strategic supply chain management. Using this tool, top management can tap potential that hitherto remained hidden in the supply chain. Internal funds can therefore be used more efficiently to meet the company's financing needs: financial management overall can be optimized as a result.

## Optimizing working capital – Roland Berger's approach

Our approach to optimizing working capital can be divided into two phases. After first realizing quick wins by tapping short-term cash flow potential in the supply chain, we then place these gains on a sustainable footing. This strategy helps companies to plug any immediate gaps in

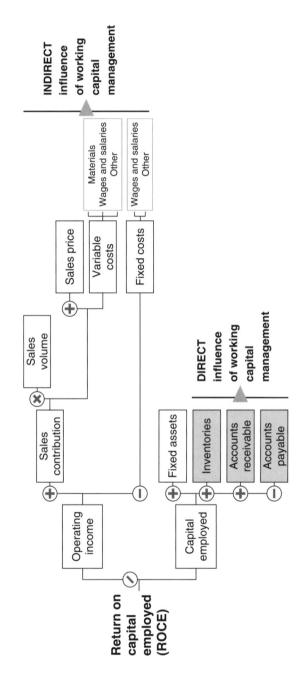

**Figure 14.2** ROCE drivers

funding quickly and then maintain a more stable financial position in the medium term.

All three structural levels of supply chain management – inventories, accounts receivable, and accounts payable – are activated to achieve these goals: the foundation is laid by defining a strategy and setting targets on the basis of a comprehensive benchmarking exercise. This exercise spans different business units and competitors, but also includes other (unrelated) industries. Once targets have been set for the company, we examine performance deficits in existing core processes (order-to-cash, purchase-to-pay and forecast-to-fulfill). On this level, in order to improve the financing situation, we identify suitable optimization levers that can reduce inventories and accounts receivable while increasing accounts payable.

We have helped many companies improve how working capital is managed within their organization. The benefits of taking on this challenge are enormous. A global manufacturer of production systems for automotive assembly, for example, wanted to reduce working capital in a sustainable manner. We analyzed inventories, accounts receivable, and accounts payable at all the company's production locations worldwide. An extensive benchmarking exercise compared companies in both this and other industries, and identified possible areas of potential. The plan of action that was then drawn up to optimize working capital allowed our client turn working capital worth more than €200 million into free cash flow.

Setting targets, examining performance deficits, and identifying optimization levers is the crux of our approach. To support implementation of the specified actions, we also define and craft enablers (such as training to help staff understand and optimize working capital, and development of appropriate control and analysis mechanisms) to ensure that positive outcomes are sustained in the long term.

Our strategy of optimizing inventories, accounts receivable and accounts payable has proven its value in many projects. It is applied in the following four steps:

## Step 1: Achieve transparency

We begin by systematically gaining an overview of all ratios and the underlying figures for the client's key working capital items worldwide. We are particularly interested in turnover ratios for inventories, receivables, and payables that can be used both to compare performance across internal business units and to benchmark the company against external competitors. The important thing here is to ensure that the data analyzed is comparable across business units and with external data. In this phase, the main challenges are usually posed by creating transparency from incompatible master data sets, which must be harmonized across different systems. Another issue is the consolidation of inter-company sales, which might deteriorate the complete picture if not dealt with appropriately. Finally, an enormous amount of data must be examined in minute detail – sometimes every receipt should be checked for accounts receivable and payable analyses. We also make inventories and analyze the three core processes in the supply chain – order-to-cash, purchase-to-pay and forecast-to-fulfill – in detail. This, of course, also includes customer, vendor, and competitor analyses. This whole exercise constructs the framework from which to assess working capital performance and define first hypotheses on key weaknesses that prevent the company from realizing its full potential.

## Step 2: Perform benchmarks and set targets

The second step is to identify other companies and industries that lend themselves to benchmark tests on the basis of the defined ratios. Benchmarking must encompass both quantitative data analysis and a qualitative assessment of existing processes. This dual approach delivers a reasonable perspective on the client's current performance and identifies key performance deficits. Fine-tuning the ratios used is a crucial success factor. It helps companies avoid comparing apples with oranges, and encourages acceptance of the findings. To fine-tune ratios, and thereby obtain comparable data, it is necessary to analyze relevant structural factors when comparing rival firms. Differences in factors such as sales channels, customer structures, vertical integration, global sourcing, and supplier/logistics structures must all be factored into the equation if the benchmarking exercise is to deliver valid, usable results. We usually also analyze the 'balance of power' from an industry and customer/vendor perspective in order to understand the rules of the underlying business models, as well as country specifics. For example, import and export regulations in Eastern Europe, the Middle East or South America can have direct implications for working capital management.

In the context of receivables and payables management, it is especially important to take account of regional variations in ratios, processes, and business practices. The way cash management is handled can sometimes vary significantly from country to country. In Southern Europe, East Asia and South America, for example, comparatively long payment targets are commonplace and meet with broad acceptance. Other regions tend to prefer shorter targets, insist on punctual payment, and also make use of cash discounts. When identifying ratios, attention must likewise be paid to the various companies' accounting policies. It is important to gain a full understanding of the relevant items on the balance sheet, and to adjust them where necessary. Once the benchmark analysis has been completed and performance deficits have been isolated, top-down targets must be defined for the identified turnover ratios and then agreed with the appropriate managers.

For example, with a large client from the consumer goods industry, we agreed to set an accounts payable target range that was based on the industrial average payment periods of the main supply markets on the lower end and adjusted competitor benchmarks from industry's best performers on the higher end. The client far exceeded the lower end goal and committed himself to a bottom-up action plan that would close the gap to his competitors as well as unleash a cash potential of more than €300 million from his balance sheet.

## Step 3: Define levers and actions

In collaboration with all project participants, the next step is to identify suitable levers and actions to plug performance gaps in the three core processes sustainably. Ambitious companies aim to set new standards in their industry through such projects. Sample levers include:

- **Inventory management**: Modifying the depth of stocks, adjusting the flow of materials (structural changes) and optimizing scheduling parameters (process changes); planning, purchasing, production, and logistics departments are mainly involved here
- **Receivables management**: Optimizing the dunning system and receivables monitoring, and renegotiating payment terms with top customers; sales and finance departments are mainly involved with this
- **Payables management**: Adjusting the payment process, renegotiating terms with top suppliers, and conducting value-based negotiations on the basis of suitable IT tools; purchasing and finance departments are mainly involved in this area.

During bottom-up workshops, detailed planning takes place with relevant managers, and commitment for the implementation is gained. We usually initiate lever discussions based on existing levers and further optimization measures that we have derived from our project experience on working capital issues, as well as our working capital studies (see results below). The identified levers are fleshed out in detail and the resulting financial effects – on cash flow, earnings before interest and taxes (EBIT) or economic value-added – are calculated. Regarding accounts receivable and payable, it is often possible to negotiate optimal payment terms while also committing to price adjustments. Realizing working capital effects without deteriorating the profit and loss statement clearly should be the goal. Here, management needs to decide whether EBIT or cash has priority, and whether improving cash may be negotiated for price adjustments (buying cash). To determine the optimum from cash and cost effects, we introduce simulation tools that show specific financial consequences from different negotiation options. These can directly support purchasing and sales in negotiations.

It is imperative for different corporate functions to work together in this phase, as the core processes in question exist on a horizontal level in most companies. The involvement of purchasing and finance staff is crucial, for instance, when discussing strategies to optimize accounts payable. Both functions are involved in the bottom-up planning phase and must closely act together in order to achieve company best performance. Conducting decentralist workshops with relevant managers from all necessary corporate functions has proved very effective, and we believe that it is a central success factor for working capital projects. For workshop moderation, we usually staff team members that bring with them a thorough understanding of the key corporate functions involved. For instance, when talking about measures to optimize accounts receivable, it is necessary to have a trained moderator with sales experience present, for reasons of acceptance and commitment. Finally, priorities are defined for the entire set of activities by calculating the anticipated effects and evaluating the ease of realization. The outcome is a prioritized package of recommended actions. At the end of this phase, we verify whether the anticipated effects will, in fact, meet the defined targets, or whether further adjustment is necessary.

In addition to concrete optimization levers for the generation of quick cash, Roland Berger project teams also deal with what are referred to as enablers. These are structural changes in the organization, processes, and systems put in place to create and maintain the management environment for successful working capital performance on a long-term basis. Usually, one of the main enablers is the target setting and monitoring process used to steer working capital performance. Work targets, which are derived from the specific project, can be set for the organization involved. These must be monitored closely to ensure realization. Targeted communication of project activities and measures to market project achievements also belong to the enabler concept. Other enablers include training and qualification measures that put people in a position to drive working capital processes in the supply chain actively and on their own.

## Step 4: Secure buy-in and implement measures

The defined activities are now condensed into a plan of action. People are given ownership of certain actions and are held responsible for implementing them within defined deadlines. The plan of action has to be communicated to, and coordinated with, both the top and operational management levels. It is vital that the project sponsors – and everyone else involved – buy into the project. Once management commitment has been secured for the project, communication takes place on a wider scale and implementation can begin. Strict monitoring accompanies the entire implementation phase to ensure that actions are taken swiftly and the targeted effects realized in full. Reviews with the responsible managers should be held regularly. During these sessions, the project status, obstacles and possible counter-actions to ensure completion of project activities in time should be discussed.

The crucial factor when improving the performance of working capital is to identify the right optimization levers and create the necessary implementation commitment from all involved managers. The following three case studies demonstrate the benefits that can be realized when companies focus on the right process and pull the correct optimization levers:

### Case study: Consumer goods industry

In this case, the client is a well-known maker of basic materials for the consumer goods industry. Highly complex products and orders had caused the company to run up above average inventories at every link in its core process chain. The project aimed to reduce inventory volumes sharply. The project team focused its attention on production planning and order scheduling. In close collaboration with the client, sustainable reductions of more than 30 percent were made to inventories by optimizing planning processes and streamlining the very broad product portfolio. At the same time, product availability improved significantly.

## Case study: Energy sector

While managing inventories was the right lever to be pulled at the consumer goods manufacturer, managing accounts receivable was the key focus of our work with a company in the energy sector. We were commissioned to find ways to optimize accounts receivable and inventories at a water utility with operations all over Germany. The client wanted to free up financial resources for capital investment purposes. The team began by systematically examining the core processes in the areas of order, performance, and receivables management. By adjusting its system of installments and advance payments, improving its dunning procedures, and introducing new IT, the client was able to recover €150 million from the balance sheet in cash.

## Case study: Media group

Managing accounts payable is the third classic lever that can be aggressively pulled. Our client, a media group, is run in accordance with value-based management principles. We used simulated calculations to show the group how better use of cash discounts could positively impact profits and company value-added. The client's purchasing guidelines were adjusted accordingly. We supplied purchasing with tools that would permit that department to evaluate the impact of the different prices, payment terms, and delivery terms offered by different suppliers while negotiations were still in progress. We also defined key values for discounts and payment targets, and standardized these worldwide. Although greater use of cash discounts initially increased the burden on working capital, it ultimately boosted profits and significantly increased the value of the company.

In our experience, plugging performance gaps in the three core working capital processes is essential for a company's long-term survival. Yet, companies have a mind-boggling array of levers and actions at their disposal. In our international study of working capital, we investigated and evaluated an extensive set of common optimization levers. The findings of this study are presented in the following section.

## Working capital excellence – learning from best practices today and tomorrow

During the period 2005–6, Roland Berger Strategy Consultants surveyed 500 large and medium-sized companies in Europe, North and South America, and Asia in order to gain a coherent overview of best practices today, and to understand what would be the motivating factors for tomorrow. The bulk of the companies surveyed are active in the engineering, consumer goods, automotive, and electronics industries. However, companies from the areas of pharmaceuticals/healthcare, basic materials, chemicals and oil, utilities, and transportation were also examined. Some 42 percent of companies had sales of less than €1 billion, 25 percent had sales ranging from €1 to 5 billion, and 33 percent reported sales of more than €5 billion.

When surveying the companies, we honed in on three topical issues. We were curious to know what was 'state of the art' and what best practices existed in working capital management. We also wanted to know what the key deficits were. We asked company representatives: what trends does the future hold and how can companies prepare to face them? We were also driven to find out the nature of success factors and how could companies close the gap with the leading lights in their industry?

We would like to share some of these results, paying particular attention to best practices, targets/strategies, organizational forms, and process issues. By sharing this knowledge, companies might be able to see how they can tap hidden cash reserves in their own supply chain.

## Best-practice companies: 15 percent of participants rank as stars

As far as the relevant balance sheet items are concerned, around 15 percent of the companies that took part in the study can be regarded as best-practice players in managing working capital. These companies achieve outstanding economic performance relative to their working capital. They apply a broad spectrum of proven and innovative management methods effectively and efficiently.

Regarding the use they make of available financial potential and the developmental status of the tools they use to manage inventories, accounts receivable, and accounts payable, all the other companies fall short of the industry leaders – in some cases, by a long way. We discovered that 60 percent of study participants have not quite reached the same excellence in financial results and management methods as best practice companies but are on the right path. By contrast, 25 percent of all participants – the stragglers – have a great deal of ground to make up.

Using a detailed benchmark analysis of the companies that took part in the study, we examined financial performance on the basis of turnover ratios for the three elements of working capital. Figure 14.3 shows an example taken from the receivables management benchmark analysis.

In this benchmarking exercise, we rated potential. Companies that fall below the 25 percent line are already excellently positioned and have little potential to improve their overall financing situation. Companies that are better than the industry average but do not belong to the best 25 percent exhibit moderate potential. By contrast, all those companies that are below average urgently need to take steps to improve.

The outcomes of the benchmarking study make it simple for companies to compare their current financial position with that of the industry as a whole. Companies can easily identify any discrepancies between their own situation, the industry average, and the best-in-class performers. They can assess the financial performance of their efforts to manage working capital, before moving on to decide what corrective action must be taken. Companies need to maximize their working capital management, the importance of which will increase in the near future. This quick benchmarking exercise is only the first step and needs to be broken down further to meet company specific situations – for example, by factoring in adjustments considering customer/vendor structures, the degree of vertical integration, or any further business model and supply chain characteristics.

## Working capital management and its importance in the near future

The companies that took part in the study themselves assessed their current use of levers to optimize working capital management and the importance these levers will have in the near future. This input enabled us to plot the developmental status in the management of inventories, accounts receivable, and accounts payable for each company. The results identified:

- 48 inventory management levers
- 22 receivables management levers
- 12 payables management levers.

Having collated the results for all participants, the following picture emerged for the three components of working capital.

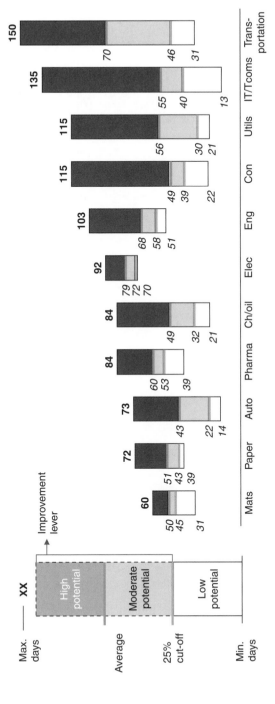

**Figure 14.3** Industry benchmark for debtor days
*Note:* Debtor days = Accounts receivable/sales×360 days

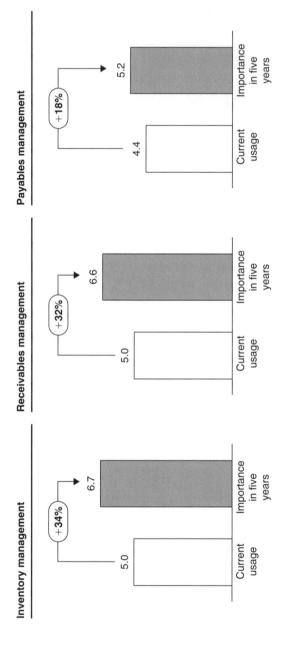

**Figure 14.4** Current and targeted future status
*Note:* 0 = not in use/not important, 10 = extensive use/very important

The study revealed that potential exists to improve the management of inventories and accounts receivable by more than 30 percent in the near future. In addition, the potential for improving the management of accounts payable is put at nearly 20 percent, on average. Clearly, the companies in the study are very keen to make significantly improvement in the way they manage accounts receivable and inventories. By contrast, the forecast for the management of accounts payable is more modest.

## Considerable optimization potential for all three working capital items

The greatest potential to improve inventory management practices exists in electronics/IT, engineering, and the steel industry. On the other hand, comparatively little potential for optimization remains in the automotive, utility, and pharmaceuticals/healthcare industries.

As far as receivables management is concerned, the need for action is greatest in pharmaceuticals/healthcare, electronics/IT, and utilities. Potential for optimization is only slight, however, in the automotive, chemicals/oil, and telecommunications industries.

Finally, the utility, pharmaceuticals/healthcare, and engineering industries have most to gain by optimizing the management of accounts payable. The telecommunications, chemicals/oil, and electronics/IT have the least to gain. The optimization potential for working capital items in different industries is illustrated in Figure 14.5.

Generally speaking, there is still considerable potential for companies to optimize the financial performance of their working capital by applying specific methods and tools. Companies are strongly advised to measure their working capital management practices systematically against industry benchmarks. The tools already in use should be reviewed and optimized on a regular basis in order to keep them effective and efficient. When appropriate, new and innovative methods should also be introduced.

It is clear from the outcomes that the practice of managing working capital has reached widely differing stages of development in different industries. None of the industries investigated was found to have little potential for optimization in all three items of working capital. In other words, every industry still has work to do. Those industries with the greatest untapped potential can learn a much from those that have reached a more advanced level. In practice, a cross-industry comparison of the tools and methods applied can be very helpful.

Let us now take a closer look at the outcomes of the study with regard to targets, strategies, organizations, and processes.

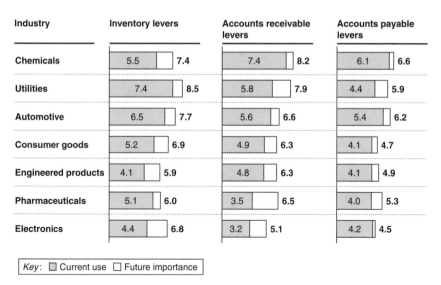

**Figure 14.5**  Current use and future importance use of working capital management levers by industry

*Note*: 0 = No usage, 10 = Comprehensive usage of all levers

## Top-down targets and strategies to manage working capital

If it is to succeed, working capital management must be lived out from the top down and throughout the company. It must filter down through every function. If this is to happen, however, top management must first recognize the importance of this practice and devote sufficient attention – and resources – to it.

Our study found that top managers actually do tend to rate working capital management as fairly to very important – and the attention this issue commands today is high. It is reasonable to assume that the importance of working capital management as an aspect of strategic management has, by and large, already been recognized. Nevertheless, top management must sharpen its focus on this key issue in order to exploit potential in the area of both internal and external financing more fully.

Consensus between companies was greatest regarding the objectives of receivables management. Of companies surveyed, 82 percent stressed a clear focus on optimizing liquidity, and 80 percent on reducing the risk of default (in response to a multiple choice questionnaire). The substantial importance attached to reducing default risks is laudable. Defaulting customers are, after all, a common reason why companies run into financial trouble.

Similar unity prevails concerning the goals of inventory management. Most customers see this as a way to comply with defined customer service levels, to optimize tied up capital, and/or to run inventories down as far as possible. The respondent companies disagree only on the purpose of efforts to manage accounts payable. The three most frequently cited reasons were: to take advantage of cash discounts, to optimize processes, and to optimize liquidity. However, these goals were advocated by far fewer companies and are inherently self-contradictory in some cases. The findings of the study confirm that companies still pay too little attention to managing accounts payable and have yet to realize how much potential lies dormant in this area. As a rule, best-practice companies accept a trade-off between the use of discounts and long payment targets. To some extent, these policies are also aligned with standard practices in different regions.

Nearly 90 percent of companies already derive the goals of their inventory management activities from corporate strategy. All identified objectives are then institutionalized in target agreements for the units affected. However, only best-practice companies tend to do this to the same extent in relation to the management of accounts receivable and accounts payable. Here again, companies still have their work cut out if they want to close the gap on the best in their respective industries.

Another important issue that needs a solution is target conflicts between working capital targets and other operational targets – for example, a high service level in inventories contradicts the working capital target of low capital binding. In such instances, top management has to present clear rules for operational managers to ensure acceptance and fulfillment of working capital targets.

Taking inventory management as our example, we would now like to explore those factors that help and hinder the practice of working capital management. Companies point to a lack of forecasting options for sales, a lack of end-to-end transparency, and inordinately high customer service levels as being the main obstacles. Conversely, they see the main success factors as extensive transparency, optimized processes, and improved sales forecasts. These factors confront companies with the need for action both internally and externally. However, most current projects to optimize inventory management focus largely on internal aspects such as optimized inventory control, more efficient systems, and sustainable reorganization. At the time of writing, only a small share of companies are making any efforts to try to improve external aspects, such as sales forecasts and interfaces to customers. A crucial weapon for companies seeking to bring their inventory management activities into line with best practices will be external management issues that transcend company boundaries. One example involves closer collaboration with customers in order to optimize demand projections and customer service levels as a team effort.

## Crafting an effective and efficient organization

Trying to find the most suitable organizational form is perhaps the most delicate challenge in the context of working capital management. Ultimately, almost every corporate function that plays a direct role in a company's value chain influences working capital. Three core process chains must be coordinated effectively and efficiently with all these functions, if optimal results are to be achieved. These three processes are:

- Forecast-to-fulfill (order management, purchasing, production, and distribution) for the management of inventories
- Order-to-cash (sales, invoicing, monitoring, and closure) for the management of accounts receivable
- Purchase-to-pay (purchasing, payment, and monitoring/closure) for the management of accounts payable.

Our findings indicate that there is significant pent-up demand for organizational change that will improve the management of working capital in today's companies.

The need for coordination is perhaps most complex in the context of inventory management. Figure 14.6 presents organizational forms that are conducive to successful inventory management.

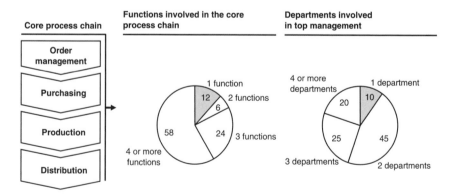

**Figure 14.6**  Organizational forms conducive to inventory management (study participants %)

At about 90 percent of companies, at least two top management departments and two operational management functions are involved in the relevant core process. At 20 percent of companies, a minimum of four top management departments are involved; and at 60 percent of companies, a minimum of four operational management functions play a part. Coordination between so many different functions and units can become extremely complex.

The number of interfaces and potential conflicts can be reduced and coordination can be simplified by bundling responsibility in the hands of a smaller number of functions and/or top decision makers. Organizations become much more efficient and processes run more smoothly as a result. At best-practice companies, it is not surprising to find that a chief operating officer (COO) is often the one board member who is responsible for coordinating the purchasing, production, and distribution functions. Ideally, the COO only has to refer back to the sales director who is in charge of order management. Other companies have set up working capital councils to bring together relevant functions discussing working capital issues.

A similar pattern emerges in the management of accounts receivable, even though only two functions – sales and finance/monitoring – generally have to be coordinated. At no fewer than 30 percent of companies, at least two top management departments share responsibility for accounts receivable. Operational management is delegated to at least two different functions at 43 percent of companies. Here, too, these different units all have to be coordinated. Since 42 percent of the respondent companies operate more than one function that interfaces with the customer, the principle of one-face-to-the-customer cannot be adhered to. Once again, responsibility should be concentrated in fewer hands, and the tasks assigned to sales and finance/monitoring should be defined more clearly to smooth the relevant process flows. At best-practice companies, sales functions tend to have the most say in shaping and driving processes. Accordingly, the activities of sales might additionally be managed by a system of incentives and bonuses based on ratios that measure receivables outstanding and/or receipt of payment.

At 94 percent of the companies in our study, the management of accounts payable was assigned at top management level to one board member only – normally the chief financial officer (CFO). On this score, responsibility is assigned unambiguously. At 48 percent of companies, at least two functions (usually purchasing and finance/monitoring) are in charge of operational management. Again, best-practice companies clearly delimit the tasks entrusted to each party. Purchasing, in particular, must possess sufficient financial expertise to know which levers (such as negotiating cash discounts in place of long payment targets) will have what impact on earnings and the value of the company. Clear procedural instructions and staff training can be very useful on this score. At finance/monitoring, it is important to ensure that process steps such as invoice verification and processing are handled quickly and reliably to meet payment agreements.

## Inventory management – a vast store of untapped process potential

In closing, let us turn our attention to the core processes in the practice of working capital management. To each of these processes we have attached specific optimization levers and methods, some of which are already common practice while others are more innovative and have not completely entered day-to-day business. We asked the participants in our study to assess the usefulness of these levers and methods today and their future importance. A summary of their responses for each core process and process step is presented in Figure 14.7.

Armed with this information, companies can now identify those process steps that will, in future, present the greatest optimization potential for each aspect of working capital.

Potential in the management of inventories is more or less evenly spread over the various process steps. Order management serves as a good example. The companies we surveyed believe that rolling sales forecasts and effective claims management will be the most important levers to optimize this aspect in future. The greatest need for action is identified in the integration of customer planning, the segmentation of orders and the reduction of complexity within product portfolios. Here again, the study highlights the interface to the customer as one key area in which inventory management can be optimized. Best-practice companies are already facing up to these future challenges.

The greatest potential to optimize the management of accounts receivable is seen to be in sales. Three specific levers were predicted to be the most important in future:

- The rules governing delivery moratoriums
- The monitoring of payment patterns
- The automated supply of customer information to sales.

The companies in our study saw the need to optimize internal sales incentive systems, segment customers on the basis of their payment patterns, and automate the supply of customer information to sales as the areas where most work still needs to be undertaken. Once again, best-practice companies are already using these levers to improve receivables management. Many of

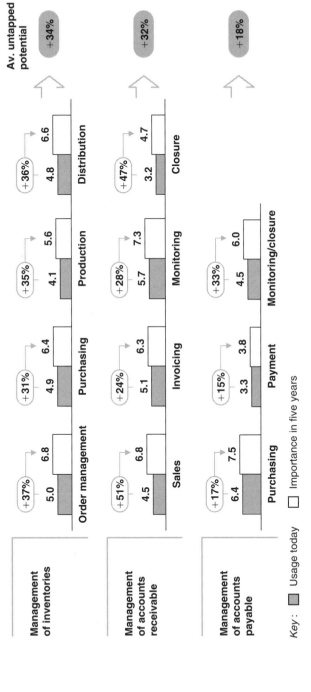

**Figure 14.7**  Untapped potential in each core process

*Note:* 0 = not in use/not important, 10 = extensive use/very important

*Key:* ▉ Usage today  ☐ Importance in five years

the other companies lag the front-runners – and would do well to apply the results of this study to close the gap.

What remains is the potential to improve the management of accounts payable. As we have seen, the study participants tend to see this aspect as less important than the other two elements of working capital. Across all three of the process steps, the companies nevertheless identified the coordination of payment terms with business planning, the standardization of payment terms, and the use of direct debit facilities as the most important levers for the future. The first of these three levers is also the one where most improvement will be needed in the years ahead. Best-practice companies draw on financial mathematics models to calculate the optimal balance between price discounts and payment term targets. This is usually done region by region, as payment term habits vary considerably. This having been done, they then standardize and negotiate payment terms accordingly.

To keep the findings of our study as applicable and practical as possible, we also analyzed which of the optimization levers named by the participants harbor the greatest potential for improvement, and how much they cost to apply. This analysis will help companies to select the methods that will best help them take the next step toward best-practice status. As an example the results for inventory management are shown in Figure 14.8.

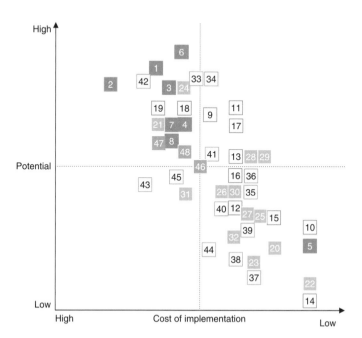

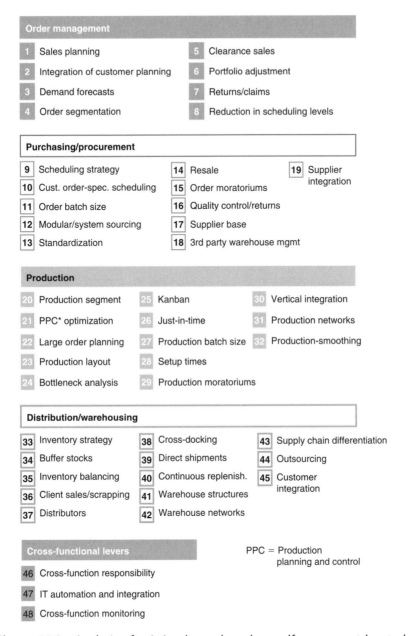

**Order management**

| 1 | Sales planning | 5 | Clearance sales |

1 Sales planning
2 Integration of customer planning
3 Demand forecasts
4 Order segmentation

5 Clearance sales
6 Portfolio adjustment
7 Returns/claims
8 Reduction in scheduling levels

**Purchasing/procurement**

9 Scheduling strategy
10 Cust. order-spec. scheduling
11 Order batch size
12 Modular/system sourcing
13 Standardization

14 Resale
15 Order moratoriums
16 Quality control/returns
17 Supplier base
18 3rd party warehouse mgmt

19 Supplier integration

**Production**

20 Production segment
21 PPC* optimization
22 Large order planning
23 Production layout
24 Bottleneck analysis

25 Kanban
26 Just-in-time
27 Production batch size
28 Setup times
29 Production moratoriums

30 Vertical integration
31 Production networks
32 Production-smoothing

**Distribution/warehousing**

33 Inventory strategy
34 Buffer stocks
35 Inventory balancing
36 Client sales/scrapping
37 Distributors

38 Cross-docking
39 Direct shipments
40 Continuous replenish.
41 Warehouse structures
42 Warehouse networks

43 Supply chain differentiation
44 Outsourcing
45 Customer integration

**Cross-functional levers**

46 Cross-function responsibility
47 IT automation and integration
48 Cross-function monitoring

PPC = Production planning and control

**Figure 14.8** Analysis of existing levers based on self-assessment by study participants

## Bottom line – untapped potential persists in all industries

The study shows that managing working capital is already an established practice in one form or another at many companies. At the same time, it also reveals the considerable potential for improvement that exists in relation to targets and strategies, organizational forms, and processes in all the industries examined. Working capital is clearly an issue that belongs on top management agendas and is one that should be reviewed and optimized on a regular basis.

So how does your company become a star? Essentially by doing two things:

- Gain a transparent understanding of the individual items of working capital
- Analyze, (re)design and apply suitable management methods on an ongoing basis.

Having benchmarked financial ratios and examined the levers of optimization already in use in a range of industries, it is clear to us where untapped potential lies. In relation to inventory management, for example, we know that there is a real need to improve the interface to the customer. However, optimization will only succeed if top management grasps the potential impact that working capital can have on strategic management. The entire enterprise must be made more sensitive to the possibilities that will arise by proactive management of working capital. Suitable knowledge can then be cultivated, allowing the company to define appropriate targets. When such an open culture exists, the practice of optimization can take root and grow throughout the organization.

### Further reading

Schwientek, Roland and Deckert, Christian (2005) *Working Capital Excellence Study I – Managing accounts receivables and payables.* Stuttgart: Roland Berger.

Schwientek, Roland and Deckert, Christian (2006) *Working Capital Excellence Study II – Managing inventories.* Stuttgart: Roland Berger.

# CHAPTER 15

# Supply chain organization: a key enabler for successful supply chain management

*Ingo Schröter and Stephan M. Wagner*

## Introduction

Well-functioning supply chains are reliable and responsive, and remain cost efficient despite being flexible. As supply chains become more global and complex, however, supply chain links become strained, and supply and delivery glitches tend to increase. Companies are often robbed of their ability to respond quickly because they are weighed down by overly complex structures that have arisen, for instance, after embarking on a quick session of mergers and takeovers. Other companies might be burdened by conflicting operating styles and processes, and a lack of standard procedures throughout the entire supply chain. This prevents them from being best-in-class, especially in today's highly competitive business environment in which a smoothly run operation is paramount.

When companies manage to embed supply chain management into their organization, use simple coordination tools such as setting goals for divisions, and coordinate their external supply chain with precision, their supply chains become extremely efficient and perform with fewer hiccups. As a result, these companies manage to notch up remarkable savings. In many ways, supply chain organization is the linchpin for making sure that supply chains are cost efficient, reliable, and responsive. These are the hallmarks of success in an increasingly competitive environment.

A study recently conducted by a joint team of Roland Berger consultants and researchers from WHU – Otto Beisheim School of Management[1] revealed that many companies realize that their supply chain organizations can still be improved. More than half of the 200 companies that were interviewed for that study said that there is significant room for improvement in their supply chain organizations. Companies recognize that while purchasing functions, for example, have made huge leaps and bounds over the past years, supply chain organization has not developed as quickly. Improvements can be made in companies working in all industries.

Globalization and increased complexity are definitely the main forces driving the necessity for enhanced supply chain organizations. Yet, specific challenges push this trend in individual industries too. In the automotive sector, there is a need for demand-driven logistics for flexible production, and for greater supply reliability. Manufacturers of engineered products must deal with continuous outsourcing and reduced lead times. Pharmaceutical products and medical device producers must integrate their distributors, and become more flexible and more efficient. Food manufacturers have to negotiate with retailers that have gained considerable clout and are increasingly demanding.

In this chapter, we describe the study findings, as they provide insights about the elements necessary for creating and maintaining an effective and efficient supply chain organization. We also demonstrate how companies can transform themselves into a best-practice organization, by examining how 'organizational talents' (that is, firms that exceed their peers in supply chain performance) manage to achieve better performance.

## Organizational talents master their supply chain organizations

In the study, the project team asked supply chain and logistics decision makers how they currently organize their supply chains. Most of the managers interviewed were responsible for the logistics or supply chain activities of their firms, while others were purchasing directors or general managers. In terms of size, we surveyed companies across the board, although our focus was on medium-size and larger players. Only 14 percent of companies examined had annual sales of less than €100 million. More detailed information concerning the companies interviewed can be gleaned from Figure 15.1.

While all participating companies show a marked trend toward greater strategic alignment and comprehensive coordination of the supply chain, only about 15 percent truly differentiate themselves from the competition. These organizational talents provide a high logistics service with an

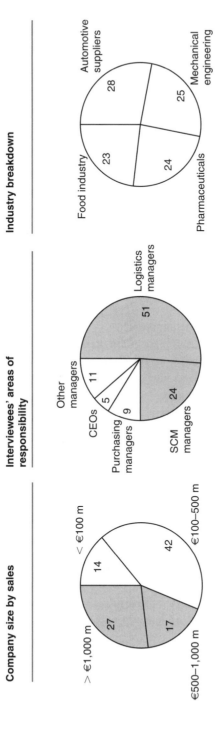

**Figure 15.1** Breakdown of companies interviewed in terms of size, area of responsibility, and industry(%)

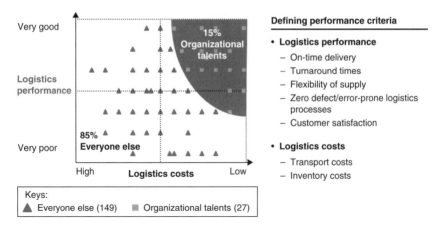

**Figure 15.2**  Organizational talents have outstanding logistics capabilities

optimized cost structure. As well as securing low transport and low inventory costs, they also enjoy on-time deliveries, good turnaround times, supply flexibility, zero-defect processes, and high customer satisfaction. Reducing costs, increasing reliability with supply partners, and reducing lead times are the common goals underpinning the desire for companies to improve their supply chains. Organizational talents reach those goals. The spread between organizational talents and their weaker competitors is shown in Figure 15.2.

Filtering out the information gained from the responses, three best practice principles could be derived from the study results. Successful companies:

- Implement a supply chain organization
- Implement coordination tools
- Coordinate their external supply chains.

## Implement supply chain organization

Organizational talents have one thing in common: their supply chain management is thoroughly embedded within the organization. To accomplish this, companies need their top management to participate actively and support this strategy. This is a key success factor. When top management focuses attentively on supply chain management, a clearly defined supply chain strategy emerges. Frequently, companies set up divisions or functions that are solely responsible for managing the supply chain throughout the entire company. This guarantees that the right people have the necessary authority to make decisions that affect functional entities within the organization.

More than 80 percent of organizational talents have established a supply chain center that is responsible for coordinating purchasing, manufacturing, distribution, and reverse logistics. This helps them achieve the best trade-off between service, cost, and capital employed.

Often they combine several elements:

- Temporary supply chain functions are usually set up to solve certain specific problems or to develop concept improvements. They are organized as a project for its duration and usually resource from different functions across the company. Sometimes, they are the starting point of company-wide supply chain functions.
- Strategic staff functions are typically responsible for supply chain planning and coordination. They consolidate sales forecasts, and production and purchasing plans, and assure the feasibility of internal and external supply chains. Their role is to coordinate the supply chain; they enjoy directive rights over different functions. Often, activities controlling supply chain performance fall within their scope.
- Operative supply chain functions have clearly defined operational tasks such as order processing or collaborative planning with suppliers.

Strategic and operative functions are horizontally and vertically aligned and bundled within a supply chain responsibility. Furthermore, responsibility for the supply chain is frequently assigned according to differentiated supply chains – for example, by product segment or business units.

## Implement coordination tools

Best practice companies deploy coordination tools, which effectively work as the oil lubricating the supply chain to make sure that it operates perfectly. Companies have an array of coordinating tools at their disposal to enhance performance.

Organizational talents clearly formulate their strategic supply chain goals, set clear targets with a careful selected set of key performance indicators (KPIs), set clear targets for these KPIs, and monitor them continuously. Such strategic supply chain goals pertain to individual divisions that are oriented toward gaining improved performance over the entire supply chain. Even better results are obtained when divisional goals are linked to variable compensation. This tool only makes sense when performance-based compensation is the strategy followed throughout the entire company. Coordinating divisional goals is not without its difficulties. Consider planning. Whereas marketing and sales divisions usually want to set ambitious goals in order to motivate sales staff, production generally wants to be able to forecast volumes as accurately as possible so that they can use capacity to the best advantage.

The round table was the most widely used coordinating tool among companies in the survey. Organizational talents not only use round tables more often than their weaker counterparts, they hold such meetings regularly, carefully prepare for them, and follow strict agendas. This helps them gain a comprehensive view on the current situation and objectives, which are ideally based on quantitative KPIs such as budget, delta, and action. Less organized companies tend to use round table discussions to exchange ideas and focus on resolving operational problems as they arise. They are firefighters, responding to problems reactively.

Exceptionally few companies use staff rotation to support supply chain coordination. Managers and other employees still hold reservations, believing that they will lose good staff and start-up time as employees become familiar with their new environment. Small to medium-sized companies, especially those that are owner-managed, are particularly hesitant to use this coordination tool. Companies that deploy staff rotation need to have a clear strategy to minimize start-up time losses. A good starting point for companies is to apply staff rotation on new recruits and trainees where blocking points apply to a lesser degree.

## Coordinate external supply chain

The third key success factor common to organizational talents is simple: they work more intensively on developing a better external supply chain. Indeed, 67 percent of all organizational talents work with their major suppliers to optimize the supply chain. They exchange sales forecasts, on-time-delivery information, delivery flexibility, and general satisfaction levels concerning overall performance on a regular basis. They also define and monitor goals together with their suppliers and reward top performance. The mutual trust that develops as a consequence of this action leads to greater success with both operational and strategic topics. It also enables organizational talents to state optimization targets clearly in their contracts.

Companies that work together with their suppliers to improve their supply chain are more likely to achieve their targets than companies that take a more 'go-it-alone' approach. Interestingly, companies in the automotive supply industry tend to work with suppliers more frequently than do companies in the mechanical engineering industry, which engage suppliers only now and then.

The interaction between a company's employees and the employees of the supplier is decisive for close and mutually beneficial buyer–supplier relationships. As such, the survey revealed that a lack of staff with the right capabilities on both sides was a key blocking point to efficient supplier coordination. As one cannot always send multi-functional teams, employees with a wide overview of both the company's and the supplier's supply chain are needed to bring value.

## How to achieve best practice? Food for thought

So, what are the insights we can glean from the study? Some companies have a better grip than others on their supply chain organizations, and only these companies can fully benefit from the size of this opportunity. Companies wishing to get the upper hand on their supply chain organization would be wise to answer the following set of questions:

1. Does the current organization adequately reflect the importance of supply chain management?
   - Is this also reflected in accountability, especially with respect to hierarchical levels?
   - Can end-to-end supply chain management be embedded without losing critical synergies on a functional level?

2. Are the correct decision-making mechanisms and coordination tools in place?
   - Does your company already have the right mechanisms or tools?
   - Are they being applied correctly and effectively?

3. How should the company organize the external supply chain?
   - How could your company's relationships with suppliers become more effective and efficient?

## Roland Berger's approach to supply chain organization

The operations strategy team at Roland Berger constantly works on improving companies' supply chain management. However, companies that approach us are not primarily concerned with enhancing their supply chain organization. More often than not, they ask for advice because they want to improve service levels, bring cost down or reduce working capital and release cash. The experience shows that, for achieving these goals, it is actually improved supply chain organization that enables these companies to develop supply chains that work more effectively and efficiently.

In our experience, companies need to take three steps before the supply chain organization can truly be optimized:

1. Understand their own internal and external factors
2. Develop and assess organizational options
3. Agree on the target organization before defining steps for transformation.

As step three is usually part of an overall supply chain improvement implementation program, we will focus here on the first and second steps only.

## Step 1: Understanding internal and external factors

The first step is to get a clear understanding of factors affecting your company. It is important to understand right from the start that there is no standard formula or best practice template for supply chain organizations. Although best practice companies share many characteristics, the environment in which each company operates is unique. External factors such as market structure and client expectations are different for each company.

For one of our clients, for example, we found across Europe two market clusters relevant to the design of a supply chain organization:

- A highly mature cluster of Western and Central European countries, where customer requirements were quite similar and competitive logistics services were easily available – for these mature countries, the company decided to centralize supply chain management functions in order to focus on efficiency through cost synergies. At the same time, a central supply chain control function was established to manage a comparable set of key performance criteria, such as raw material inventory levels and production capacity utilization, as well as service levels.
- A set of countries with highly differentiated customer requirements and constantly changing demand situations – as a result, when designing the

supply chain organization the decision was taken to establish supply chain management functions such as material and capacity locally in order to enable maximum flexibility to react to customer requirements.

Each company has its own set of internal requirements too, such as the availability of IT systems, and people skills. Full analysis of such internal and external factors is crucial for the design of a workable supply chain organization.

One client company, for example, was just coming out of a major restructuring phase during which the whole purchasing department was focused only on one objective: reduce purchasing prices. A decision was taken to reshuffle the organization in order to accelerate the transition to a more collaborative approach towards purchasing. This was achieved by allocating the purchasing function, together with the production function, underneath a single global supply chain responsibility, and underpinning this new structure with a reviewed collaboration-oriented KPI and incentive system.

Small steps might need to be taken at first to set the groundwork for cultural change, which might be necessary in order to create a best practice organization.

Typical external factors that might be relevant for determining the requirements of the organizational design are:

- Globalization (market entries, low-cost country sourcing, off-shoring fragments of the supply chain)
- A need for flexibility, arising from M&As
- Deregulation
- High-maintenance partnerships
- Market requirements.

The latter factor comprises a mixed bag of local and global customer requirements, tax regulations, labor laws, and so forth.

Typical internal factors are:

- Culture
- Capabilities
- Systems.

Effective supply chain management requires a company culture that puts the supply chain above functional targets. Such a culture clearly does not evolve overnight and management has to make considerable efforts to achieve systematic development at all levels of the company and in all regions where it operates. A special skill set is required of supply chain managers. They need to display specific capabilities.

The correct system is also critical. Even if an internationally optimized supply chain makes sense, the company might not have the right sort of IT infrastructure in place to enable it to operate. Organization transition has to develop alongside IT capability. Typical internal and external factors that might be relevant for determining the requirements of the organizational design are shown in Figure 15.3.

## Step 2: Develop and assess organizational options

Once a company has analyzed the external and internal factors, the results must be translated into clear design requirements. This creates a checklist, making it easier for companies to assess the organizational options open to them. When defining options for organizations, it is a good idea to perform a gap analysis that shows the cleft between the current organization and how it should look in the future, based on the defined requirements. This creates transparency, and it shows where adjustments in the organization need to be made. With this knowledge, options can be developed.

The description of options should then happen along a framework that allows a relatively quick description of an option. This enables the individual options to be assessed on a high level against the design criteria. Detailing of the organization can then be limited to a few options, or even only one – the preferred option. The relevant dimensions should be considered when outlining the organizational option:

- **Segmentation**  Companies should look at the way the supply chain organization is segmented. Is it spliced according to product, customer, market, order type or speed? The goal is to achieve a strong customer/market orientation end-to-end.
- **Centralization**  Companies should look at the level at which the supply chain organization is centralized or decentralized with respect to regions.
- **Process-orientation**  The organization should ensure an end-to-end process responsibility.
- **Decision making**  Companies should look at the decision-making process and structure. They should consider which entity has what responsibility and autonomy, and what coordination tools are applied.

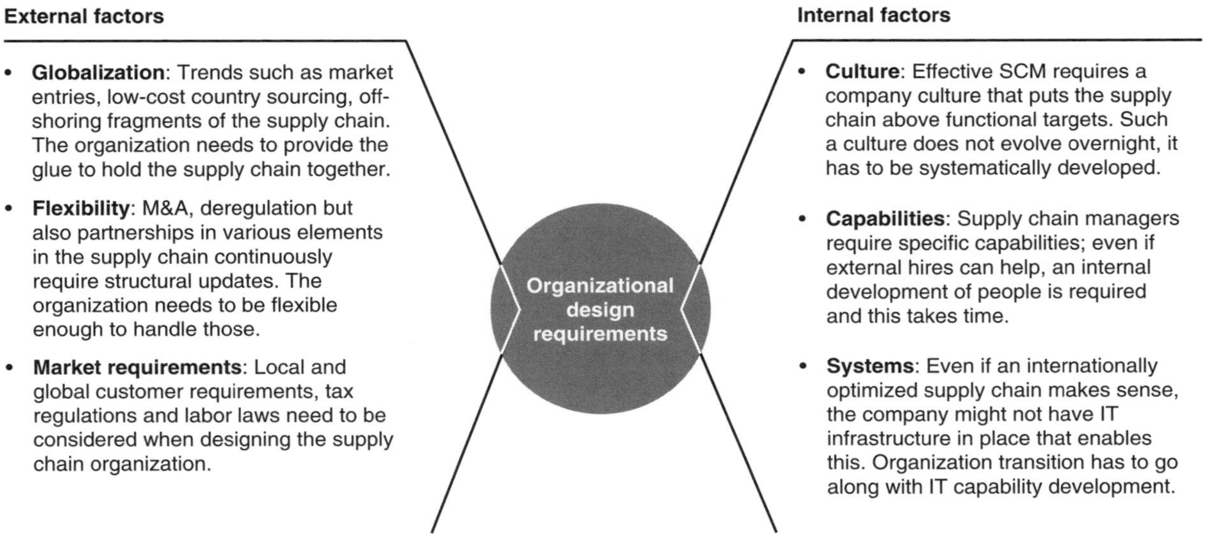

**External factors**

- **Globalization**: Trends such as market entries, low-cost country sourcing, off-shoring fragments of the supply chain. The organization needs to provide the glue to hold the supply chain together.

- **Flexibility**: M&A, deregulation but also partnerships in various elements in the supply chain continuously require structural updates. The organization needs to be flexible enough to handle those.

- **Market requirements**: Local and global customer requirements, tax regulations and labor laws need to be considered when designing the supply chain organization.

**Internal factors**

- **Culture**: Effective SCM requires a company culture that puts the supply chain above functional targets. Such a culture does not evolve overnight, it has to be systematically developed.

- **Capabilities**: Supply chain managers require specific capabilities; even if external hires can help, an internal development of people is required and this takes time.

- **Systems**: Even if an internationally optimized supply chain makes sense, the company might not have IT infrastructure in place that enables this. Organization transition has to go along with IT capability development.

Organizational design requirements

**Figure 15.3**  External and internal factors to be analyzed prior to designing organizations

- **Supplier integration**   Companies also need to investigate the way their internal supply chain organization is linked to the comprehensive supply chain, including suppliers.

Additionally, only functions that strongly impact the supply chain control of differentiated product segments should be grouped into a segment responsibility. Shared service functions – such as warehousing and transportation – should be set up to realize cross-segment synergies.

Companies also benefit from conducting a 'what-if' scenario analysis, which tests how flexible the organization is. Both external and internal factors should be used for measuring the company's flexibility. This helps create a stable supply chain organization and promotes a culture of sustainability.

## Outlook

As the study and feedback from participants demonstrate, supply chain organization is seen as a key success factor for companies across many kinds of industries. Organizational talents are guides, showing how companies can design an effective and efficient supply chain organization. But companies must be aware that there is no single golden way. To define the best option, each company needs to consider its own external and internal factors. Internal factors need special consideration.

Any company working on its supply chain organization needs to understand that supply chain management has more to do with company culture than with company structure. Organizations today still tend to be functionally designed, with responsibility limited to distinct functions. End-to-end responsibility for the entire supply chain is rare. This needs to change. A best-practice organizational structure helps companies thrive, but this requires everyone in the organization to develop an end-to-end mindset. Since supply chain management is probably the most cross-functional of all core business disciplines, this cultural change clearly must start with top management and filter downwards.

## Note

1. Stephan Wagner, Axel Schmidt, Ingo Schröter, Sebastian Durst, Eckhard Lindemann (2006) Roland Berger/WHU Otto-Beisheim School of Management.

## Further reading

Durst, Sebastian M. *et al.* (2006) *Getting to Grips with the Supply Chain. How Organizational Stars Organize their Supply Chains*. Stuttgart: Roland Berger.

# Index